G000242919

Li

La Paz
Potosí
Salta
Tucuman
Santiago
del Estero
Santa Fé
Rosario
Buenos
Aires

São Paulo

V I A

PARAGUAY

Verde
Pilcomayo
Bermejo

Paraguai

Asunción

Foz
do Iguaçu

Cataratas
del Iguazú
(Falls)

Iguaçu

Paraná

B R A Z I L

Paraná

Argentina
San Guillermo
Morteros
Brinkmann
San Francisco

anta Fé

San
Lorenzo

Rosario

U R U G U A Y

Uruguay

Negro

ATLANTIC OCEAN

San Isidro
Lujan
Buenos Aires

Rio de la Plata

Montevideo

300 miles

0

0

500 km

Peter McClure 1991

NO GUNS, BIG SMILE

No Guns, Big Smile:

SOUTH AMERICA BY HORSE

James Greenwood

PELHAM BOOKS

PELHAM BOOKS

Published by the Penguin Group
27 Wrights Lane, London W8 5TZ, England
Penguin Books USA Inc., 375 Hudson Street, New York, New York 10014 USA
Penguin Books Australia Ltd, Ringwood, Victoria, Australia
Penguin Books Canada Ltd, 10 Alcorn Avenue, Suite 300, Toronto, Ontario, Canada M4V 3B2
Penguin Books (NZ) Ltd, 182–190 Wairau Road, Auckland 10, New Zealand

Penguin Books Ltd, Registered Offices: Harmondsworth, Middlesex, England

First published 1992

Typeset in 11/12½ pt Photina
Printed in England by Clays Ltd, St Ives plc

ISBN 0 7207 1947 X

A CIP catalogue record for this book is available from the British Library

The moral right of the author has been asserted.

This book is dedicated to:
Carina,
my parents
and my horses.

ALL ALONG THE WATCHTOWER

'There must be some way out of here,'
    said the joker to the thief.
'There's too much confusion, I can't get no relief.
Businessmen they drink my wine, plowmen dig my earth,
None of them along the line know what any of it is worth.'

'No reason to get excited,' the thief he kindly spoke.
'There are many here among us who feel that life is
    but a joke.
But you and I, we've been through that, and this is
    not our fate.
So let us not talk falsely, the hour is getting late.'

All along the watchtower, princes kept the view
While the women they came and went, barefoot servants too.

Outside in the distance a wildcat did growl,
Two riders were approaching, the wind began to howl.

Written and performed by Bob Dylan,
performed by Jimi Hendrix, U2

CONTENTS

ACKNOWLEDGEMENTS

I would like to thank the peoples of Argentina, Bolivia and Peru, without whom this expedition would have been both impossible and worthless.

In particular, I would like to thank Alex Schulte, the Bowens, the Crespos, my parents, John Beaton, René Plaza, Peter Newey, Gordon Roddick, the Royal Geographical Society, the Foreign Office, Humberto Fernandez, the de Tellas, the Romeros, Andy Pedrazza and Alicia, Barry, Alex and the rest of the Cuzco crowd, Don Humberto Bernal, the Howards, the Zamoras, Cha Stroud, the Hanbury-Tenisons, Marcus Armytage, Jim Lowther, Charlie Gladstone, Johnny Sutcliffe, Rosamund Gladstone, Devina Cannon, The Riding for the Disabled Association, Dan Green, Rupert Edwards, Natasha Beaston, Christopher Portway, John Blashford-Snell, Caroline Lonsdale, the Kennards, Elspeth Milne, Robert Eustace, Mac Head, Alison Payne, Anthony Routhe, Aldo Piaggio, David Caruth and Felipe Benavides.

I am also extremely grateful to Puffa, Barbour, Kodak, North Face, Allen and Caswell, Vernon-Carus, Ethicon, Coopers, Parke-Davis, Hoechst, Vet Drug, Glaxovet, Mustad Horsecare and Pelham Books for their support.

My faith in the human race has been strengthened by the warmth, kindness, generosity and friendship that I have received from many others over the last two years.

Thank you.

Introduction

THE INSPIRATION FOR this journey across South America was the Swiss-born writer and traveller, A. F. Tschiffely.

He was educated in Britain, before becoming a schoolmaster after a brief spell as a professional footballer. He used to supplement his paltry income during the holidays as a prize fighter in the East End of London. When offered the chance to teach at a school outside Buenos Aires, Argentina, he leapt at the opportunity. Again it was the holidays that he seemed to enjoy most as he travelled around Argentina and fell in love with the gaucho life of horses and the pampas.

There is some argument as to why he set off on the journey that was to be his life's major achievement. Some say that it was in protest at North American tariffs against Argentine beef. Some say that he went for the hell of it. At the time many said 'Impossible!' 'Absurd!' and told him he was mad.

In 1925 he saddled up two horses and rode the 9600 miles from Buenos Aires to Washington D.C., arriving after a two-and-a-half-year journey. His subsequent book on his travels known as both *Southern Cross to Pole Star* and *Tschiffely's Ride* was a bestseller.

He died at the age of 58 in London in 1958.

When I was fifteen, my grandfather gave me a copy of Tschiffely's book and I read it from cover to cover one night. I promised myself that one day I would ride across South America as Tschiffely had done.

It took me eight years to finish my schooling and quit my job at a leading London merchant bank.

1

Second Monday

THE SETTING: Interior of mock-Tudor pub, sawdust on the floor, groups of men and women in business clothes clutching umbrellas, briefcases and Burberry raincoats, drinking wine. Linger on a young man about twenty-four years old, six foot plus, 175 pounds, brown curly cropped hair, green eyes, scuffed shoes.

I am standing alone in a City pub, surrounded by the end-of-work talk about deals, mortgages, and business character assessments. For a moment, it all seems very cosy. This has been my last day of work at a merchant bank, where I have, for eighteen months, been described as a 'corporate strategist within the corporate finance department'. Another guy, my age, left the week before amidst much back-slapping and engraved pen-giving. I decide that I have said my goodbyes and that it is time to leave, pen-less. From my immediate colleagues, I received a beautiful knife and a bullwhip, but I was rather hoping for an official pen. 'Oh well, what the hell,' I think and make for the door.

A very senior executive, a man I respect, peels off from his group of cronies and stops me.

Senior Executive: 'Well, you're off then James.'

Me: 'Yeah, I'm off.'

Senior Executive: 'You know that when you walk through that door you are on your own.'

Me: 'Yup.'

Senior Executive: 'And it'll be a lot harder to get back in.'

Me: 'Yup.'

Senior Executive: 'No fancy salary, no mortgage help, no position.'

Me: 'Yeah, I know.'

Senior Executive: 'And you're ready?'

Me: 'I hope so.'

Senior Executive: 'Well, I think you're mad. You have a good job with a good company and you're leaving to bum around on a couple of horses.'

Me: 'Yeah.'

Senior Executive: 'I always thought you would.' (Shakes me by the hand.) 'Good luck.'

I make for the door as he turns back to his cronies, but he stops, turns back and says: 'James, I envy you.'

But he was one of the few. In the weeks before my departure, I had had a few heart-to-heart chats with my immediate colleagues. I had assumed that they would be eating their hearts out at the fact I was going to travel across South America by horse, but I was wrong. For the first time they spoke to me openly, business images dropped, about what they wanted and what they were doing. They also dropped the perennial habit of moaning about 'The Brothers' (as we called the organisation that we worked for) and had expressed themselves as being happy and stimulated with their work to such an extent that the cost of long hours in a stuffy office was negated. It had been a surprise, their content with a situation that I had found restrictive and oppressive.

I walked out of the pub and into a wet London going-home mood. It had rained that afternoon and the streets were damp, the traffic and lights huddled.

I was told by my friends that I had walked out of the office down to London Bridge where I had thrown my briefcase into the Thames. In fact, I walked straight into the nearest Tube and caught trains up to Cumbria and Scotland for my first holiday in fourteen months.

A friend met me with a bottle of champagne at Penrith station. We drove back to his home at Askham, talking about the future, never about the past. I think he was glad someone else had given up his job in the City, having chucked in his six months earlier. We went to the pub and drank Castle Eden, went back to his house and smoked and talked for a while by the fire. I felt wonderfully charged up.

It had been a good job, well-paid, stimulating and interesting but there were political moves afoot within the corporate finance division and I felt, as a pawn, I was going to be moved to another part of the bank: better paid, with a higher profile but very boring as I would have spent five years completing my white collar apprenticeship.

The City had become a strange animal. Clients were charged excessive fees for insubstantial and often shoddy work. The City founded its reputation on being a guardian and supplier of money: banks to the big boys. Obviously, institutions advised on how to raise money but they had, for too long, advised how to use it as well. In fact, although many institutions regarded themselves as advisers, they had little or no knowledge of the industry in which their clients operated. I had many conversations with friends and colleagues, trying to see if we really created any value. Time and time again, I would hear from people who had spent much of their life in the business, that they were not very confident that this was so. Personally, they had become richer but they were not sure if they had actually done anything positive to create wealth in society. If they create only the service of holding clients' hands, I wish they would call themselves what they are: commercial 'pimps' rather than what they see themselves to be, commercial 'godheads'.

So I went up to Scotland to facilitate my conversion from commercial pimp to expedition prostitute. I had a great feeling of freedom but a strong desire to get on with the expedition; a desire to make things happen. The cocoon of my upbringing had been broken. School, Edinburgh University and 'The Brothers' had always ordered me and, I have to admit, I did not try and do any more than they expected. Much of my education had been focused on cutting corners to arrive at the A Level, degree, report and finishing line in one piece with as much juice left in the tank as possible.

The expedition was different. It was an undertaking I had decided on. On Monday, 30th November, 1989, I sat down at a desk that I had constructed entirely from oil drums salvaged from a skip, with a blank piece of paper and started work on the expedition.

First, I sent out a press release to the financial diaries of the folding national newspapers, which resulted in the following in *The Independent*: 'More hope for those trying to escape the confines of the City. James Greenwood has just given up his post as corporate strategist at Lazard Brothers to explore South America. But the poor boy may find the sixteen-month trip even more daunting, for he is travelling 3500 miles by horse.'

It was all rather exciting as I read the piece. The aim had been to solicit sponsorship enquiries but, I think, only my friends and colleagues at the bank read it.

The sponsorship proposal slowly took shape and I devised a logo. The logo was supposed to incorporate the idea of horses, mountains, and South America, but people kept asking why there was a helicopter hovering over the peaks.

Things really got started after I had been to see Robin Hanbury-Tenison on Sunday, 13th November. I had read his book *White Horses Over France*, the account of his and his wife's trip from the

5

Camargue to his home in Cornwall, astride two Camargue horses. His book begins with a quote from Revelations: 'And I saw heaven opened and behold a White Horse'. I loved the wit, perception, descriptions and obvious love for horses. As one of the country's top explorers and the founder of Survival International, he was a man whom I wanted to meet and whose support I needed. Hopefully, he would agree to be a patron, and his belief in my ability would be crucial to the expedition and above all to my own self-confidence. Even so, I felt ever more frightened about meeting him at his home. It had taken me two weeks to pluck up the courage to write to him, and a further two weeks to have the balls to ring him.

We settled into Robin's low-ceilinged study, with a blazing fire and large gin and tonics, to start a conversation that went on into the small hours of Monday morning. Louella, Robin's very beautiful wife, gave us a delicious dinner, and me some very valuable information concerning the care of horses.

After dinner, we settled back into the study and my Pentel tried hard to record Robin's ideas and suggestions.

'You have to show sponsors that you are obsessed – obsessed without being mad.' No problem.

'Take as little kit as possible. Read as much as possible before leaving.'

'Make a big thing of not being North American,' record my notes.

'Don't give up smoking, because if you smoke you will always have a packet of cigarettes and therefore will always have a present' – best excuse I have ever heard.

He gave me names galore, enough to fill an expeditionary *Who's Who*. But he gave me something far more valuable to the expedition and myself. After dinner I knew the time had come to ask him to be patron of the expedition. I was so nervous that my heart was trying to force blood out through my eyes, and my vision and hearing narrowed to a small pinprick. I asked Robin and he said quite simply, 'Yes – delighted'.

The next morning we took Thibert and Tiki, his Camargue horses, out on to Bodmin Moor, past Little Brown Willie, through ruins, into valleys. It was a beautiful day and we talked about our respective schooling, education, horses and expeditions. To me it was a wonderful morning, riding over a truly special landscape talking to a much respected man about ideas and the expedition. It was also my second Monday since leaving the City.

2

Asking for Tips

THE SPONSORSHIP PROPOSAL was finished a few days later and I was trying to get a City printing firm to print it for me. They had expressed excitement about doing a colour brochure, and I was invited along for a final interview in front of the board. Instead a sidekick was sent to say that they could not help, but would I like a diary?

As far as a sponsorship proposal goes, it was a total waste of time, although I was chuffed to bits with what I regarded as a very eloquent piece of writing. I started to send out the proposals in small numbers – in small numbers because the proposals were expensive and time-consuming to produce as colour photographs had to be stuck on by hand.

I started to ring up and meet more people. John Blashford-Snell met me at his Operation Raleigh headquarters quite appropriately called the Powerhouse. An impressive man, with an ill-fitting suit and notes scribbled on his hands, he reminded me of a small Boy Scout, a personality trait common to many expeditioners. Operation Raleigh, the multinational of expeditions, seemed to run in complete chaos. Papers, people running about, charts and more papers were everywhere, particularly on John Blashford-Snell's desk. He gave me a book on setting up expeditions he had written called *Expeditions* and advised me to get some false ID in case I ever ran into trouble.

I also met a man who was interested in financing the trip, in his flat on the A40 going to Oxford. He rolled an incredibly large joint and as we talked became increasingly incoherent until he dried up altogether and crashed out on the sofa, so I left. It was not that he rolled a joint and got stoned during our meeting that annoyed me; it was the fact that he did not offer the joint around.

I spoke to more potential sponsors without success, and wrote in my diary:

7

Sponsorship has become a major industry in its own right over the last ten years. No longer do companies sponsor the Chairman's favourite hobby but now measure the return in column inches, TV seconds and 'awareness generation'. It is into this world of professionals that I have plunged looking and sounding, as a friend said, 'like a small boy asking for a tip'. Everyone I have spoken to seems interested but after a couple of months I have raised zero sponsorship. I wrote a proposal that captured the spirit of the trip, but it said little of what the ride could do for the sponsors. Many people have wanted to be involved but none with cash.

After two months of totally incompetent money-raising, I had £1 in the coffers, which I had received a week or so after leaving work from my girlfriend Carina's flatmate. For me it was a momentous and rather confusing occasion, being given money to do what I wanted.

My second financial patron was Gordon Roddick, financial wizard of The Body Shop. His name came up when I read Christopher Portway's book, *Journey Along the Spine of the Andes*. It recounted how *a* Gordon Roddick had attempted Tschiffely's Ride, riding two criollo horses from Argentina to Bolivia. The Body Shop headquarters gave me the impression that Gordon Roddick, rider and Gordon Roddick, Body Shop founder were one and the same. I looked at the paper for a market valuation of the company and thought: 'Bloody hell, a guy that tried Tschiffely's Ride himself is chairman of a multi-million pound multinational.'

I wrote to Gordon and we arranged to meet in Scotland, where I was going to be for the New Year. We went into the newly-decorated country house and sat in a sumptuous drawing-room, next to a fax machine. This was when fax machines were found more in offices and it seemed very incongruous to have one in a private house in the Highlands. We sat, drank coffee and I heard the whole story.

In 1974 Gordon, at the age of thirty-two, wrote to Christopher Portway asking for advice and help concerning a proposal to recreate Tschiffely's Ride. With the help of the *Observer* and Christopher, who gave him a one-way ticket from London to Buenos Aires, Gordon left his very capable wife, Anita, running the then small natural cosmetics business and went to Buenos Aires. Argentina welcomed Gordon with a military government, deep internal problems and a civil war in the northern provinces of Salta and Tucuman. Settling into a hotel, he started to look for horses through the Criollo Horse Association (Associacion de Criaderos de Caballos Criollos) and was given the name of Gonzalo Torres. Gonzalo part-sold him two horses, and in May Gordon left from outside Rosario, following a modified and significantly harder route due to the problems in Salta and Tucuman. He crossed the Chaco, a major feat in itself. The Chaco is an enormous desert, almost completely devoid of any water and edible vegetation. Temperatures can be extreme and very unpleasant. He crossed Paraguay and was climbing into the Bolivian altiplano (the high plains of the Andes) when he had a disaster. Traversing a steep path with a guide, Gordon rounded a corner with his two horses, one of which spooked, whipped round and charged back down the path. On the corner was a bush, which obscured a drop of thirty metres to rocks below. Gordon's horse ploughed through the bush, plunging down to break its back below. Without two suitable horses, Gordon was forced to return to the UK.

All ended happily however, as Anita, frustrated by Gordon's absence, had decided to open the second of their natural cosmetics shops in Brighton, called The Body Shop. With Anita's ideas and Gordon's financial flair, the rest is history.

Having linked Gordon with Tschiffely's Ride, I thought that my sponsorship problems were solved. However, I was presumptuous, and as Gordon said 'did not present a clearly thought-out deal for The Body Shop'. I received from Gordon, personally, £1000 and, as he had been given fifteen years ago, a one-way ticket from London to Buenos Aires. It was perfect.

I met Christopher Portway, a great character and traveller of some note, at a Sealink promotional piss-up in Islington. 'Get this down you,' were his first words. 'They're free.' He handed me a Guinness.

We sat down to an 'Irish Lunch'. Christopher, elegant in his grey hair and beard, talked incessantly about Gordon, South America, his own expeditions and experiences. The first course was a choice of soup or cold meats and I was slightly surprised to see Christopher put away both, drinking both the white and the red wines laid out on the table. We moved on to the second course: a choice of stew, roast or further cold meats.

'What are you having?' shouted Christopher.

'Er . . . a bit of stew,' I said.

'I'm having all three. Make the most of these freebies,' replied Christopher.

And he did. He placed a plate of stew on top of his starter remains, which was followed by roast and cold meats. The pile of plates rose precariously high but deft handling of knife and fork kept it steady. Wine and beer flowed, pudding and cheese followed, before a talk from the Sealink man. Christopher took all their brochures and talked throughout the speech.

He wanted very much to become part of the trip, acting as an agent in the UK, dealing with the press and sponsors while I was away. But in a way – and looking back, stupidly – I had taken the decision to go off on my own, away from the mainstream, and (a) wanted to be alone and (b) felt that I could only do the trip alone. I felt that once in South America I could not rely on help 7000 miles away, and could rely only on my own native cunning.

At about this time I started to become involved in the film side of expeditions. 'Get a film and your sponsorship problems are over' ran the expedition wisdom. I saw three producers: two of whom were enthusiastic and one of whom showed me the door within ten minutes of arriving. I wasted a great deal of time in 'production costs', 'research programme' and 'film crew' talk. André Singer, of Inca Productions, persuaded Channel 4 to foot half our research costs with enthusiastic noises for the rest of the budget, an incredible £200,000 (the norm for expedition films); but we failed to obtain the rest – luckily, as I realized later.

I created some publicity in the local newspapers, both in London and the Berkshire–Wiltshire region where my parents live. I learned quickly that journalists do not miraculously create stories. You have to go and knock on the door and then camp outside, explaining the merits and excitements of your story before they take any interest.

But I kept saying to myself: 'I haven't done anything yet. How can I explain the expedition when it hasn't happened? If I knew what was going to happen then there would be no point going.'

People would ask: 'Well, what are you going to do then?'

'I don't know, that's why I'm going.' I bullshitted enough to keep the expedition going but that was all. As I learned more about its possibilities I could say more about what I thought might happen.

One of the ways in which I was preparing myself was my diet. Subconsciously, I was cutting down on fancy food, that is to say anything other than potatoes and meat. I had a feeling that they would be my diet in various combinations. As far as exercise went, I was biking about a bit. There was very little riding. I was getting ready in a very different way: changing my life-style, my eating, my time habits, becoming more South American.

Although I was not riding, I was thinking about the horses hard, and wrote to the Edinburgh Veterinary College for advice. Doctor Elspeth Milne was most helpful in supplying a list of products to include in a veterinary pack. I was also lucky enough to meet Robert Eustace at the Bristol University Laminitis Clinic, one of the world's experts in laminitis, a disease that attacks the hoof's internal suspension system. In fact, he is obsessive about it, and has a compassion for animals that I had never met before.

Robert was trying out some plastic horseshoes that he thought might interest me.

'What? Plastic horseshoes did you say?'

'Yes, plastic horseshoes.'

I watched him do some very delicate work on a horse that, obviously, was not worth it. He cut away the hoof to relieve pressure on the tender laminal tissue below, repositioning the paedal bone angle.

'The Americans induce laminitis into 1000 animals at a time to carry out their research. I just do what I can,' he said, pointing at his motley selection of horses. He further criticised the United States for jumping to sweeping conclusions. 'We work a little more methodically here.'

The plastic horseshoes are perhaps the first development in horseshoes for 1000 years. Made by a Swiss company, Mustad, they come in various forms and are fixed to the horse's hoof by glue rather than nails. Robert explained that Mustad had so far spent around twelve million dollars developing the shoe, and that it really was a breakthrough. Why didn't I use the Mustad Easy Glu horseshoe on the ride?

I really wanted Mustad's sponsorship, not only for the money, but also to promote this shoe which was so easily affixed with the minimum of effort and knowledge. Horsepeople could put on the shoe by themselves. I learned from various blacksmiths how to stick them on. You need dry, clean conditions and a little acetone, having prepared and balanced the foot. Shoes were to be provided. The only trouble was that Peter Kreis, the MD of Mustad, would not be drawn on whether he would give me any money up front.

'We'll wait and see until after the trip,' he said. 'We'll pay you when you get back. We'll see what you do.' Exactly, Peter, exactly.

I did see myself as some sort of shining knight charging off into the wilderness carrying the banner of commercial enterprise over which any sponsor would want to have his name splashed. I certainly thought that charities would leap at the opportunity, raising money, promoting their cause. Cafod, a Catholic overseas development charity, was excited for a while but turned it down due to the danger aspect. Greenpeace and Friends of the Earth were both in such chaos that I gave up. The final comment from Greenpeace was: 'Yes, we do have South American groups but none are operational as they are all fighting each other.'

Another friend suggested that I talk to Devina Cannon, press officer of Riding for the Disabled, to see who else might be interested. She was. We met at Euston Station and discussed endless possibilities: setting up a special fund to give disabled riders the chance to ride abroad, mammoth publicity campaigns. It seemed that there might be something really useful to come out of the expedition.

Devina asked me to a lunch for all the RDA bigwigs in Saddler's Hall. Rather timidly, I entered the room full of braying voices and was met by a very friendly and interested barrage of questions. The talk was strongly horse orientated and most people knew the story of Tschiffely. 'A hero', they kept saying. I was introduced to the directors whose reception was somewhat cooler; it later transpired that they too were worried by the 'danger factor'.

Riding for the Disabled is an international organisation, that has been in existence for thirty years. Its aims have always been simple: to give handicapped children and adults the chance to ride horses and ponies. Twenty-five thousand people regularly get out of their wheelchairs, and away from their crutches and use the horse as recreation like any of us. The many local groups, organised and staffed by volunteers, regularly report the improvement of co-ordination, behavioural and social skills over the duration of the riding.

When I was fifteen, I helped my mother at her local RDA group in Newbury. Initially, I was shocked and sickened by the range of handicaps, mental and physical. I was appalled by the idea of twenty-four-hour attention and the loss of freedom that those handicaps entailed. But I was also struck by the change as the children arrived. For some it was an awesomely terrifying challenge, that if met, would produce great grins and eloquent speeches. For some, the smile would appear on arrival and vanish when they were dragged off their mount and escorted back to the minibus. Unfortunately, I was leaving too soon for any organised fund-raising campaign to be mounted in aid of the charity while I was away.

A further area of charity work in which I was interested was drugs. The Institute for the Study of Drug Dependency's major aim is the 'dissemination of knowledge regarding drugs'. I felt sympathetic to the ISDD because it is against the abuse of drugs, rather than the use. They collate, process and push out information. They aim to improve the knowledge of journalists through their library, and they go into schools. With the ride passing through the major coca leaf-producing countries in the world I thought that I might be able to do something for the Institute, which I regard as one of the major tools in the long-term fight against drug addiction and its associated problems. I went to see them.

First of all I met Andy Cardell who said: 'Yes, of course, we need help. We have a project that needs £10,000 and another that needs £45,000.'

'Er ... well,' I said 'Yes ... um, I was thinking more in terms of publicity.'

'Right,' said Andy. 'Let's go and see Jasper.'

Jasper, the director of the ISDD, opened the door of his office to reveal himself as a Gene Wilder look-alike. Wild grey hair flew back from his head like lightning bolts.

We had a very entertaining half-hour; Jasper quite rightly saying that we should hold off all publicity until I got back. He used words like 'narcos' which I later learned was a well-used abbreviation for 'narco-trafficantes'. He came up with the classic line: 'I have to say, I am addicted to drug information.'

This was all very useful but I was still a long way from my target of raising enough money to ride across South America. I was determined to go, but there only seemed to be one way financially that I was going to make it – and that was down. I had some savings. It was not enough, but it would get me going and then I would see.

Then I had a breakthrough. I had been talking to Marcus Armytage, an up-and-coming horse and racing journalist and a great friend. We had ridden together in the Pony Club and in various school teams. Marcus had been writing a few pieces on the trip for the local papers and *Horse and Hound* but he gave me a great helping hand when he said: 'Ring John Beaton.'

I rang John Beaton: 'Yes, hello, my name is James Greenwood. I am organising an expedition through South America, planning to cross the Argentine pampa, the Andes and the Coastal Desert. All this by horse. I was wondering if you might possibly perhaps be vaguely interested in me writing a book.'

'Yes,' he said.

'Yes what?'

'Yes, I am interested. Can you come in next Monday at 3 pm? Good. See you on Monday.' He put the phone down.

'Oh my God,' I thought, 'someone's interested.' I sent John some stuff on the trip and sweated out the weekend before our Monday meeting. All went well until the obvious, crucial, crunch question:

'Have you had any writing experience, James?'

On Wednesday the phone rang. I was not even expecting him to call.

'Yes, we are prepared to offer you an advance for a book on your expedition. I'll send you a letter. Think it over and get in touch. OK?'

'Yes, fine. Thank you, John.'

Yes, fine. Thank you, John? Yes, amazing, I'm dying of excitement, good on you mate, you old bastard. I wandered in a daze around the flat with the chant 'I've been offered a book commission, I've been offered a book commission', going round and round in my head. I had. I had been offered a book commission. If all went well I was going to write a book, one of my aspirations since university. As Gordon Roddick said: 'Tschiffely has given people dreams.'

I was still a long way from being ready, finding myself in London nowhere near horses.

'Have you got the horses yet?' was a question I was continually being asked. I would always give the standard mumble of truth about waiting to get to Argentina and to see horses for myself before deciding. But I was worried that I seemed to be making very little progress at making a start. I wrote to the Associacion de Criaderos de Caballos Criollos, to a vet, and a number of landowners without receiving any reply. I did, however, know the type of horse that I wanted to use.

The criollo, the Argentine criollo, was made famous by Tschiffely himself. Originally of Arab and Barb stock, the criollo was taken over to South America by the Spanish invaders as a war horse. Renowned for their strength, manoeuvrability and ability to travel very large distances without huge quantities of food and water, they were perfect for exploring and taking over the American subcontinent. Mendoza took them to Argentina in 1536. History says that during an Indian uprising criollos were captured, driven south, escaped and ran wild in the Patagonia region.

Patagonia is not really a region but a world in itself: huge expanses of wide open country buffeted by strong winds and starved vegetation. In this world, the criollo toughened up further and adapted more fully to the cold and lack of food and water. At the beginning of the century, they were redomesticated and brought north by Solanet. In 1925 Tschiffely set off, and the horses are now big business. The criollos have their own association, own legends, own shows and as I was to find out, their own price. Meanwhile I rode my bike to the butchers, the tube station and Balham for Spanish lessons, but that was about as close as I got to riding.

I knew some Latin American, having spent a few months over the years in Mexico, Central and South America. I knew enough to make teaching me a real hassle. The first eight-hour-long session was spent dismantling what I had learned and the next seventeen hours learning some basic grammar and key words such as saddle, 'where is the chemist?', 'over there'; and talking. Biking down to Balham in the morning I always looked forward to the lessons. Spanish is an easy language to learn so I was making progress and it was a relief to get away for a while from a telephone that never rang.

3

Departure I

A S MY PLANNED departure date neared, I realised that I was not going to raise any sponsorship cash so I might as well stop wasting time and get ready. At this point a load of equipment sponsors stepped in. Regent supplied some great boots; Barbour a jacket; Puffa a puffa; North Face cheap equipment; and various veterinary suppliers a load of supplies.

Having organised penicillin, antibiotics, anti-inflammatories, bandages and further supplies for the horses, I thought that I had better do something about my own medical care. Jabbed, I went to the Royal Geographical Society Expedition Advisory Council seminar on expedition health. It was attended predominantly by medical students and was rather highbrow for laymen like me. The last lecture of the day was the longest and, according to the speaker, the area of least concern to the explorer – dangerous, slippery, slidey, hairy things.

'Er, excuse me professor,' I asked, at the end of his talk.

'Yes,' he said.

'Er . . . um . . . you didn't say anything about vampire bats.'

'Oh don't worry about vampires. You only find them in serious numbers in South America,' he said and turned back to a serious question.

'Thank you,' I said and left.

A medical friend told me that they really only bite animals, but if I did get bitten to treat myself as if I were a rabid dog. Shoot myself?

In reality, I was unworried by the prospect of pests. In fact, as time got closer to my departure, I was very unworried about everything – except failure. I suffered several private confidence failures, especially as everyone else seemed so confident in my ability. 'Cross South America on a horse? No sweat, mate.'

Gordon Roddick sent me a cheque for a flight to Buenos Aires which I booked for 1st April.

'You're off on 1st April? April Fool's Day?' I was asked by people hiding grins.

'Yes,' I replied, grinning. I did not realise that the date had a second significance until I arrived in Buenos Aires.

Mental preparation had continued throughout the four months since I had left 'The Brothers'. I had generally become rougher, hairier and fatter. Starting with three good meals a day I had worked up to three good meals a day plus snacks. Unaware of my reasons, I had become more animal-like: eating, drinking, sleeping when I felt like it. I was slowly cutting my ties from banking and living in London.

But there was one tie which had grown stronger over the preparation. It was becoming less of a tie and more a part of me: my relationship with my girlfriend Carina. Working social hours, when I wanted to work, had given us more time together and a closer, deeper understanding. And I was worried. It was the one area of my life in which I did not know what to do. There was no choice – I was in love.

'What are you going to do about Carina?' asked one friend in his usual harpoon manner.

'What do you mean "what am I going to do?"' I asked in reply.

'You know, now that you are going off?'

'But I am going with Carina,' I said.

I never asked Carina if she wanted to come and she never asked if she could. She had her own things to get on with in London, being an ambitious and innovative teacher. She could not stop me from wanting to do my trip and I did not want to drag her away from her own work. And also we had our joint expedition – us. But I never realised what a wrench it would be to leave. And I was totally unprepared.

Endsleigh supplied my insurance, the cheapest by half but still costing £800 because I was travelling by horse. My insurance cost more than my air fare; and would cost more than the horses. I bought last minute essentials, completely ignoring Robin Hanbury-Tenison's advice to 'take the barest minimum of kit'. The bill mounted up as karrimat, stove, compass, and waterproofs were added to my Youth Hostel shopping basket. I worked out that if I was to attempt to purify all my drinking water I would need well over 3285 Puritabs, so I left those behind.

I bought and was given books: *Heart of Darkness*, *One Hundred Years of Solitude*, a few John Fowles's, a couple of Paul Theroux's and a book called *Fortune*. And I put aside my last remaining copy of *Tschiffely's Ride* – the rest had been borrowed and lost.

I started to feel very alone. Since leaving the City, I had spent a lot of time alone, preparing the expedition from my flat, but the fear of loneliness became greater as my departure date neared. I knew that I would be leaving the security of my friends and the utter security of Carina. No longer could I pontificate at parties about what I thought would happen; it was about to become a reality.

I said farewell to many of the people who had helped, supported and befriended me at a party at my flat. People turned up and stayed and left and arrived. I looked around at the bloodshot eyes and drunken faces of friends and listened to high-strung, often sharp talk. I was not sad to be leaving. I wanted to go and I wanted them out of my house. I wanted to be left alone with Carina. I wanted to be alone.

I escorted each guest to the door. Goodbyes were of the 'stiff-upper-lip' sort.

'Good luck.'

'Thanks.'

'See you soon.'

'Yeah.'

'All right, bye then,' and another figure would retreat up the steps back into London and their own life. Jim gave me a hug, Anthony a bottle of homeopathic abrasion antiseptic.

Carina and I waded through the wreckage of the party and back to the garden, in which a huge bonfire was still blazing. We lay on the grass and stared at the sky. We didn't speak. I couldn't, I couldn't even think. My mind was clear, the thinking had been done. It was time to go.

Next morning was another beautiful spring day. But it was not beautiful in London; it was hot and ITV were coming in half an hour to interview me and I still had not packed. I bundled kit into bags and a rucksack, thinking about excess baggage. I had so much stuff.

Carina drove us to Sloane Square tube and as we crossed Clapham Common I thought: 'How beautiful. Why haven't I noticed before?'

We parked, and climbed into the tube to Heathrow. We chatted and laughed and exhibited before the returning commuters. Insecure ourselves, we had to reconfirm what I was doing by mocking the security of others. The commuters ignored our prancing or perhaps never noticed.

At Heathrow we met my parents and we all felt very vulnerable surrounded by the speed, confidence and brashness of international travel.

'Thirty-eight kilos,' said the check-in girl, 'eighteen kilos over-weight. If you can transfer one or two items to your hand luggage, I will let you through.'

We bought cashew nuts and my parents left. It was sweet of them to come and I was glad that they had. Carina and I sat at the pot-planted table in the 'High as a Kite' café. Carina gave me a little jewellery bag and I brought out a St Christopher, a silver horseshoe and a gold heart that spun on its axis, like a globe.

'I thought you could always sell them if you get into real trouble,' she said. I knew I would have to be in real trouble to sell these. I tied them to my neck. I could not believe I was leaving Carina. I could not believe we would be separated. And as I passed through the customs I was crying.

Behind I left Carina and a country I was not even sure I liked very much. The mood in the UK was still confident although there was talk of a 'soft landing' for the economy. Carling Black Label were running 'Bet he drinks Carling Black Label', and Perrier had their 'eau' campaign. The Poll Tax occupied two per cent of conversations.

Goodbye UK. Goodbye, James Greenwood, merchant banker. Hello, James Greenwood, sharp-eyed travel writer, and adventurer?

4

Las Malvinas son Argentinas

A S THE AIR France plane came into Buenos Aires, I remembered Paul Theroux's comment that he hated people starting travel books with a description of the view from their aeroplane window. The land around the city stretched for miles.

I turned to my Argentine neighbour and said in English: 'Big plains.'

'Yes, 747, hold 500 passengers.'

Bump. I felt that thrill of arriving in a new country, the excitement of the unknown and the fear of leaving the aeroplane and its tenuous link with the UK. I was also frightened of the Argentine customs, as I was packing a lot of drugs for my non-existent horses, and was unsure of Argentine customs regulations.

They waved me straight through into the arms of Pablo, the chauffeur of a friend of my father's, George Bowen. George had very kindly said that I could stay at his house in San Isidro, a suburb of Buenos Aires, and that I could even use his wife's car while she was away.

'Welcome to Argentina,' said Pablo, backdropped by a small group of demonstrators with signs saying 'Las Malvinas Son Argentinas'.

'Thank you,' I said, pleased with my fluency in Latin American.

I was also expecting to meet Humberto Fernandez, a vet, to whom I had written and spoken on the telephone. No sign of Humberto so Pablo and I went to have a cup of coffee.

Pablo, dressed in tight jeans and a polo shirt from which hung a pair of Ray-bans, told me about his girlfriend and their plans to marry and build a house. He had in fact started but was unable to get the roof tiles needed to continue the work, and was living with his parents.

'How old are you Pablo?' I said, starting to string some long sentences together.

'Thirty,' he replied. My God, thirty and still living with parents. 'Custom,' said Pablo.

The demonstrators were peaceably evicted and there was still no sign of Humberto. He had definitely said he would be there. I started to worry that I was in the wrong place or had given him the wrong times, and hesitantly rang his home and put announcements over the public address system. Still no sign.

Pablo and I stayed for a while but eventually, so wired up on coffee and cigarettes, and finding it difficult to wait in a place of movement, left the airport. We stepped outside and I took a large lungful of South America. Uppermost in the cocktail was the smell of hot engines and fumes. Pungent and poisonous, the smell of burnt-up petrol and alcohol is, for me, South America. And it fills me with excitement, passion and hope every time.

Across the tarmac, George's car was waiting.

'What is it?' I said to Pablo, looking at a 1960s or 1970s Ford; big, tanker-like, functional.

'A Ford Falcon,' said Pablo, easing himself into the pilot's seat.

I was being driven in a Ford Falcon, instrument of terror, used by the Security forces in the 1970s to drive victims to killing grounds, which we were now passing. The road from the airport into Buenos Aires was two-laned and lined by parks in which the weekend Porteños (the residents of Buenos Aires) were playing, and in which corpses were regularly found a long time ago (a long time in Latin American terms).

Pablo drove very fast, overtaking on both sides and flying from one side of the road to the other. He pulled up after a couple of kilometres and said, 'You drive'.

'What?' I said.

'You drive now to try out the car.'

We swapped, and I crunched the car into gear. I pulled straight out into the path of another car which swerved and hooted. 'Well done,' said Pablo, meaning it. We motored along for another twenty minutes, listening to a man ranting on the radio.

'What's he talking about?' I asked.

'The Malvinas. He says the Malvinas are Argentine and the British should return them.'

'And what do you think, Pablo?'

'It was a stupid war – a politician's war.'

'And on whose authority does the man on the radio have the Malvinas as being Argentine?'

Pablo looked at me and smiled. 'God's,' he said. 'The man on the radio is a bishop.'

I wondered what the Archbishop of Canterbury's God was whispering in his ear.

After much weaving and bad driving, we turned off the impressive dual carriageway and into San Isidro. I had seen areas like San Isidro before in Connecticut in the USA but was unprepared for Connecticut in Argentina. As we drove down leafy lanes, I could hear through the trees the cries and splashes of people playing in their swimming pools, and could see the odd lobbed tennis ball.

At George's house, Pablo gave me the keys to the car. I felt that I had passed some sort of test, undoubtedly due to my erratic indicating, and annoying other drivers by keeping to my lane. The Ford Falcon was obviously Pablo's chariot and it felt a great honour that I was being lent the car with Pablo's approval. He also gave me an envelope which contained a couple of brown notes, and a few blue ones.

'Two thousand, two hundred and fifty australes,' said Pablo: 'fifty dollars' worth at forty-five australes to the dollar.'

'Thanks,' I said, really meaning it. I was liquid and I was mobile – always more important than housing, to which I was now introduced.

George was away and his house was being caretaken by his tennis coach, Eduardo, who came swinging out of the house to welcome me. He gave me a mighty handshake which made me glad I was not a tennis ball, and the three of us ferried all my equipment into the spare room. In fact, I had a spare flat all to myself – three bedrooms and a bathroom.

Eduardo was having lunch and I joined him. We spoke in Spanish although Eduardo was very fond of using the two words of English that he knew: 'money' and 'fucking'. He pulled half a cow out of the fridge and asked me if I wanted a steak. Yes, I thought, a steak would be lovely, expecting him to quarter off a piece and cook it with some vegetables. He slapped the whole piece on a skillet part of the cooker and went back to his lunch, the other half of the cow. I realised that the steak was all for me; I reckoned that it was twenty centimetres in diameter and about one and a half pounds of pure, cardiac-arresting red meat. I flipped it over with a fork-lift sized spatula and then on to a half-cow plate. Welcome to Argentina, I thought.

'Welcome to Argentina,' said Eduardo.

I suggested a beer for which Eduardo accused me of being an alcoholic, and we talked about money and fucking for a while before Eduardo swung off for a siesta.

My attention wandered to the newspaper on the table. 'Las Malvinas Son Argentinas' ran the headline.

'Oh no,' I thought. My mind wandered back to the number of times I had told people in the UK that I did not think that the Falklands War would be a problem for the expedition. 'I'll just be a tourist,' I kept saying. The article referred a number of times to 2nd April, the day's date, and then it dawned on me. I had arrived in Argentina on the anniversary of the Argentine invasion of the Falkland Islands. I had arrived on a day that commemorated the start of a huge humiliation of the Argentines at the hands of the British – and I had been welcomed.

5

Caveat Gringo

I SWAM IN THE afternoon and lay in a deck-chair feeling very divorced from the UK, very divorced from the expedition and very divorced from Argentina. Eduardo appeared bleary-eyed from his siesta and explained that he had organised a party that night. He told me that he had told all his friends that he was renting George's house and that it was important that I did not let slip that he was actually the caretaker in George's absence.

We drove down to the Carrefour, an out-of-town, American-style shopping centre, and bought the cheapest wine and a few bottles of beer, about ten in all. I asked Eduardo how many people were coming, and he answered about thirty.

'These ten bottles for thirty people?' I asked in amazement.

'Yes, do you think it's too much?' he asked in surprise.

'No,' I said. 'In Britain five people would drink this before even thinking of going to a party,' which just reconfirmed Eduardo's opinion that the British were all alcoholics. I realised that it was my first piece of 'ambassador for Britain' work.

We arrived back at the house at 8 pm and I went to get changed. Washed and brushed, I found Eduardo watching videos in George's study.

At 11 pm the first guests arrived and I went to answer the door to two girls. I offered my hand to the first. She grabbed it, kissed me on the cheek and flew past to make way for the second girl, who dispensed with my hand and just kissed me, before also rushing off to find Eduardo.

'Wow,' I thought, and went to look at myself in the mirror to see if a few hours in Argentina had made me so irresistible that strange girls kissed me on sight. More guests arrived and kissed each other and me and were handed a glass of wine or beer, which were held, rather than drunk, like some sort of ornament. There was a lot of talk about the exchange rate, and I was asked where I was from and what I was doing in Argentina before the games started, at about 2 am.

It was just like being at an old-fashioned country house party in the UK. We played charades first, then wink murder, and then a drinking game with the intention of embarrassing miscreants rather than getting them drunk. Then there were a few sexual innuendo games, and nobody wanted to play with me. The best game involved two people of the opposite sex, and scraps of paper with the parts of the body written on them. The two players each chose a piece of paper and then had to hold the scraps between the parts of the body described: for example, 'knee' to 'cheek' or 'nose' to 'elbow'. The whole idea, of course, was to get the people entwined as closely as possible. Mouth to mouth produced shrieks of laughter from the audience; crutch to crutch red faces and side-holding; and a double mouth to crutch rolling on the floor.

As no one wanted to play with me I went to bed. A few days later I processed a film to see if my new camera was working OK to find a lot of 'heel' to 'armpit' shots, which must have been taken when I had gone to bed.

In a way, my first day in Argentina was a disappointment. The Carrefour, party games and even people's looks were similar to if not copies of their counterparts in Britain. (Later, I was to find out that there was only one supermarket of the Carrefour's type in Argentina.)

Next morning I contacted Humberto Fernandez on the phone and he came round. About fifty years old and of great size, he talked non-stop about his career (as a vet), his descendancy (German and Irish) and the people he knew (Prince Philip). When I steered him on to the question of finding horses and organising their papers, he said there would be no problem, but I would not be able to go through Peru. Then he left.

'But I have to go through Peru,' I thought. 'If I can't go through Peru, then the expedition is a disaster, now.'

Lunch consisted of chorizo, which can best be described as a fat sausage. Rather than ground-up meat and potatoes used in a British sausage, the Argentines squeeze lumps of fat into a skin. Chorizos can be very dry but if cooked very slowly drip with tasty grease and are delicious. Eduardo cooked the chorizos that day and they were very dry and disgusting, especially as Eduardo insisted that I eat them Argentine-style in a large roll. When I made a move for some beers, two bottles left over from the party, I caught Eduardo's admonishing eye and chewed in silence and pain.

Two sixteen-year-old girls came round in the afternoon to see Eduardo, who had gone out. One had a gorgeous mouth so I rang Carina, the first call of a series that would lead to telephone bills of thousands.

'Hello, James. How are you?' came a tiny voice down the phone. 'I miss you so much. How is it going? Have you got the horses?'

No, I was nowhere near horses. I tried to explain what had happened and how exciting it had been going to the supermarket and watching people playing after-dinner games. As I talked, I realised how stupid it all sounded, raving about a visit to the supermarket, which I could just as easily do in the UK, with Carina, whom I missed unbearably. We hung up and I felt very depressed. Her smell was still with me and as I unpacked my gear I saw her in every piece. Britain seemed so full of opportunities for exploration and expression which I had never taken. What was I doing in Argentina?

The next day was Monday so I was able to start. Pulling out of San Isidro I turned into the Buenos Aires to Tigre freeway and caught the mid-morning traffic lull. I had my shades on, the window open, Marvin Gaye on the speakers, a four-litre engine – and it felt great. I thought I was the coolest dude around, as did every other dude with shades and a car.

My first stop was the Instituto Geographico Militar, where I wanted to buy maps I had been unable to obtain in Stanfords in London. I needed these maps badly and being afraid of being British in an Argentine military organisation, I had invented a cock-and-bull story about being a Frenchman looking to invest in property in Argentina. For this I was wearing a suit and carrying a briefcase.

I walked into an Orwellian concrete mammoth and accosted the guard.

'Yes, hello, good morning. My name is James Boisvert and I represent a French consortium who are . . .'

'What do you want?' said the guard respectfully.

'My name is James Boisvert and . . .'

'Yes,' he said, 'I heard. What do you want, sir?'

'Maps.'

'Right. Through there, turn left.'

I walked through there and turned left into a high ceilinged room, stuffed with maps, smelling of libraries, with a wooden counter as centre stage.

'My name is James Boisvert and . . .'

'What do you require, sir?' said the map man.

'Maps.'

I walked out five minutes later with all the 1:100,000 and 1:250,000 maps I needed. The map man even managed to sell me booklets detailing mineral reserves and locations, and detailed breakdowns of climate, agricultural production, population and planned investment for each province, which I expect are more cock-and-bull than my own investment story.

I drove down to La Boca past a huge sign saying 'Las Malvinas Son Argentinas'. La Boca is the old part of Buenos Aires, now a vaguely bohemian artistic centre. The village of La Boca itself is centred around a pedestrian zone, down which artists set up stalls of their work. I looked at their stuff, caricatures of 1920s and 1930s Buenos Aires street characters, street scenes and animals, none of which I liked. But the street is a work of art in itself. A higgledy-piggledy ramshackle of concrete, brick and wooden boards, the houses have been thrown together and on top of each other. The facade seemed to move and breathe like an animal, especially as each facet of the street had been painted a different colour. The walls are blue, yellow, pink, green; the window frames clash and there is the odd mural here and there. Washing hangs in every available space and a few old women hang like vultures on their balconies surveying the tourists and street merchants below. In the surrounding streets there are numerous junk shops that sell junk, pure and simple: old gramophones, monocles, dirty postcards, ships' bells, and top hats can all be bought under one roof. Surprisingly, in this cacophony of colour and crap, the residents looked surprisingly normal. Even a couple of old hookers who shouted down to me from a balcony were dressed in jeans and t-shirts. I would have expected feather boas and boots.

More beautiful to me than the village, though, was the industrial decay of the port that surrounds it. A jumble of shapes, new machinery, rotting machinery and smells. I am always impressed by the size of industrial wastelands. In La Boca there were whole ships falling apart and miles and miles of unused railway tracks. I snapped a few pictures of sun reflected in waves off water on to rusty walls and decided to go back to San Isidro.

I walked back to the car, turned on the ignition and realised I had no idea where I lived. I rang the house but Maria, the maid, was out. I knew that I lived in San Isidro which was a start, so I asked directions and spent three hours getting back to the area of San Isidro. It had taken me twenty-five minutes to get out on a motorway but I did not even see a motorway on the way back. Eventually I was back at San Isidro and somewhere in those leafy lanes, so charming yesterday, a maze today, was my house. I circled around in the Falcon like a lion relishing the kill. It took another three hours to get back to the house.

My Spanish was improving and I felt pleased with my progress. The lessons in Balham had helped without a doubt, and I was now not only able to speak the words but also to get an idea of the meaning, sometimes different, behind the words spoken to me and conveyed to others.

I received a call that night for George from a friend of his, Willie Chapman. Although George was still away, when he heard my British accent he asked me where I was from and immediately invited me round to a welcome dinner at his 'castle'. It was nearby, but he picked me up and drove very carefully back to his house, set in a beautiful garden behind elaborately secured gates and a high wall. He gave me an indication of the fear that many in South America feel; of a huge divide between rich and poor that can often spark extreme violence. I was surprised, as my impressions of Buenos Aires so far had been of security and stability.

Terry, Willie's friendly wife, welcomed me into the bar: a real bar with stools, beer mats, pint mugs and even a Visa card triangle. Willie and Terry were the first example of members of the Anglo-Argentine community that I met. Willie is a high-ranking member as in semi-retirement he manages the English Club. Once in his house, Willie abandoned me to his wife and, like a true Englishman, allowed her to do all the talking. He fixed me a very powerful gin and tonic and listened with amusement and far-away eyes to our chat about England and how much his wife, who I think had hardly set foot inside the place, missed it. For dinner we had what I described as 'meat slices fried in breadcrumbs'. I learnt in time that they are called milanesas, and are the height of Argentine cuisine. I developed an addiction for them. We talked about multinationals with me doing my 'rapists of the country – growth has to come from within' bit, and Willie saying 'investment from abroad is crucial'.

The following day I was to make a personal pilgrimage and left early from Buenos Aires for the one-and-a-half hour drive to Lujan.

Lujan, for Argentine Catholics, is the centre of their religion and faith. Housed in an extraordinary Gothic basilica that is visible for miles in the open pampa is a statue like a miniscule Barbie doll dressed in a teepee. In a small chapel behind the altar, worshippers sit in reverence and pray to the Virgin of Lujan. The story goes that the idol of the Virgin was being carried by a cart across the pampa. I do not know why it was not in someone's pocket. At the site of present day Lujan, the cart became bogged down and all attempts to shift it failed. This sticking-in-the-mud was taken as a heavenly sign that the bog was where the idol wished to live, and there she stayed.

My Mecca was not the Virgin but the Museum of Transport containing two stuffed horses. To the horror of many purists, Mancha and Gato on their deaths at twenty-four and twenty-five were skinned, stuffed and put on display as the vehicles of the longest ride in history.

I smoothed the Ford Falcon out on to Route 9, changed for Route 8 and followed the signs to Lujan. It was my first time in the pampas and I was frightened by their size. Cows and horses grazed in fields along the side of the road, but the fields were so big and the animals so perspectively small I wondered if I would ever arrive.

At last I saw the Lujan basilica stretching into the sky like two cake icing tubes, injecting prayers up to the Almighty. I reached the outskirts and was in the centre, to my surprise, within seconds. Large Argentine towns are small and Lujan is no exception. A wide avenue, the size of a motorway, led me down towards the plaza and the church, where a man charged me for parking.

'Where is the Museum of Transport?' I asked him.

'The entrance to the Virgin is over to the left,' he said, inserting my five and ten australe notes into a soggy wad.

'No, the Museum of Transport.'

'Museum over there but Virgin here. I guide you.' He reverted to English.

'No thanks,' I said and followed the direction in which he had pointed to the museum. It was shut so I walked around, trying out my new secondhand Nikon on parties of schoolchildren. One of the teachers stared at me as if to say 'Get lost, pervert' so I ordered a coffee in a café. As I was sitting there in the shade, a lorry backed up and into the café and dumped a load of sand in amongst the tables. I watched the owner and assorted brothers shovel it away. I was asked what I was doing in Argentina, explained, and was disbelieved. I produced a sheet of information in Spanish that described the expedition. They asked me to sign it and I felt like a celebrity.

I wandered back to the museum, past a man painting a mural. The museum was open and the girl at the door directed me to Mancha and Gato. Between a Model-T Ford and a seaplane stood a large glass cage, and in it were the skins of Mancha and Gato. The director of the museum came over and I asked him to open the case. I stepped inside and ran my hand down Mancha's scarred neck. Their skins had been used to cover frames that were too large. There were deep gaps where the lips of the cuts did not meet and their bodies bulged, as did their glass eyes, staring forever at the wall. I was disappointed. It was great to see an attempt at keeping alive two of the greatest horses in history but they were so obviously dead – just two stuffed animals.

The director suggested that I take some pictures and snapped his fingers for minions to lower blinds and raise lights as I wanted. I photographed the two hides from every angle and inspected Tschiffely's kit. He had a simple anglicised Western saddle and a pack saddle overlaid by heavy leather wallets, like a fold-up suit carrier. For saddle padding he had used folded blankets. But I was not sure that this was really his kit, having heard that he kept his saddles, hats and equipment in his house in Chelsea until his death. In 1974 Gordon Roddick had been to see Tschiffely's wife, who had continued to live there after his death in 1958. She had shown Gordon what he described as 'her shrine to Tschiffely', a study filled with his diaries, books and possessions. Inexplicably, the couple never had children and, after his wife's death, members of related families descended on the house, squabbled over and looted 'the shrine', dispersing it in all directions.

As I left the museum, the director asked for a tip which I gave him and, surprisingly, he gave me a receipt. In the gift shop I bought a Falkland Island Invasion commemorative ashtray for Dan Green, my first patron.

My first brush with the police was on the way back to Buenos Aires, and the only time I suffered at their hands. At the edge of the town, there were three lorries pulled over to the side, a police car, two policemen amongst the lorries and two policemen flagging me down. They said they had seen that my back brake light was faulty. That was tricky as I had been driving towards them. They asked for registration, insurance and my driving licence which I handed over. The new pink UK driving licence has 'Permiso de conduccion' written all over it, and it was this that I showed.

'No, your licence?' said the policeman, in a friendly way.

'Yes, this is my licence,' I said.

'No, your licence to drive'.

'Yes, this is my driving licence. Look. "Permiso de conduccion",' I stabbed at the slip of pink paper, focus of all interest.

'No, no. I need your driving licence like this.' He pulled a credit card, bearing his photograph, from his pocket. I went into my dumb tourist routine.

'I have just arrived . . . Told by authorities. This is OK . . . Applied for a new one . . . Papers in the post . . . Not much money . . . Just a student . . . Wonderful, marvellous country, etc, etc . . .'

'Well, you can't drive,' interrupted policeman number two, just as I thought I was melting the heart of the first policeman.

'Can't drive?'

'No, you must wait here. Do you have any friends here in Argentina?'

Another opening I thought. 'Yes, the British Ambassador.'

'Well, can he come out and collect the car?' countered policeman two.

'Um, I'm not sure if he will be free right now.' I smiled wondering if I had overstepped the mark. They smiled but they were not letting me go.

'You must stay here until someone can collect the car.'

'Shit,' I thought. 'It's miles to Buenos Aires. Oh well, time for a bribe.'

'Excuse me,' I said to two smiling faces, 'would it be OK if I like paid the fine – I don't need the receipt – now? I have only 500 australes. Will that be enough to cover the ticket, the fine?'

'Yes.' I handed over a 1000 austral note and received 500 back. Shook their hands. And left.

I was rather pleased with myself initially and then furious about the incident, especially when I discovered that I had paid about twenty times too much. My 500 australes was equivalent to five working days in a police job.

Later that day I was having a bath when the doorbell went. Padding to the door, and opening it I saw a huge man in a terrible rage. We shook hands, presumed who the other was and George came in. George had returned to Argentina a day earlier than his office had expected and Pablo accordingly had failed to meet him at the airport. As George had taken a taxi, I failed to see what the problem was. In time I learned that things can go so wrong in South America that unless everything goes totally smoothly, immense anxiety is created by even tiny hitches. I got George a glass of water and he went off to unpack and organise being home.

Before I left the UK, I had contacted the breeder from whom Gordon Roddick had bought his horses, Gonzalo Torres. Gonzalo had telegrammed that I was welcome to come and see him. Humberto Fernandez, the vet, had introduced me to Alex Schulte a young, nearly-qualified vet, who agreed to come with me to look at horses.

Alex and I left at 5.30 am and headed north for Rosario. It took us four and a half hours over good roads to reach the village of Torres, a neat quadrangle of six blocks of houses round a plaza, and an old rail station. We drove down the hill and branched off into the pampa for a few kilometres. Eucalyptus trees led down to a verandahed house facing a great stone square tower.

Standing in front of his house to greet us was Gonzalo Torres, dressed to kill. He was wearing a light blue cotton shirt, baggy trousers tucked into pigskin boots, and tucked into the back of his thick leather cummerbund was a large knife. He had a straw hat on his head. As I stepped from the car, dirty and bedraggled with my shirt hanging out, I learnt there and then that I had broken a code of Argentine life, to look as smart as possible all the time. Gonzalo ignored my looks, welcomed us to his house with the greeting 'this house is yours' and took us into the kitchen through a clacking mosquito door.

Obviously unable to constrain himself, he took Alex and me straight through the kitchen to his personal hall of fame. Down the sides of a passage were mounted, in chronological order, pictures of horses and the prizes that they had won. In each picture was a horse mounted by a man wearing the kit Gonzalo had on. Horse and man stood side on to the camera staring at a point always unseen. Gonzalo pointed out the winners over the years: his father's horses and his own.

At last he came to a picture distinct from the others, of a Chilean horse performing in a competition called the media luna. The horse was coming to a halt from a full gallop. Its back was at an angle of fifty degrees to the sawdust floor and its front legs were off the ground. Its hindquarters and hind legs were ground into a spray of dust, as man and horse strained to stop but locked into the turn that would control the turn of a bullock.

I had seen the media luna before in Chile at a local rodeo. Two mounted men aim to drive a bullock around the outside of a bullring-type area. Within two painted lines in the whitewashed wall, they must time their arrival and drive the animal back in the opposite direction to complete a similar manoeuvre on the opposite side of the ring. It sounds dead easy and, to the uninitiated observer, is boring. I was bored at the time but in that picture on Gonzalo's wall I saw the grace of man, horse and quarry in a sport that does not kill but is directed at skill. For an Argentine it was strange to have a Chilean picture on his wall.

The Argentines have a similar competition to the Chileans' directed at skill in manipulating cattle; another competition of co-ordinated skills; and the longest races in the world – the carreras. It was because of their fame through Tschiffely and their reputation for endurance that I was looking for criollos.

'The carrera,' said Gonzalo, 'lasts for fourteen days and is run over 700 kilometres. The horses average fifty kilometres a day but some days will do forty and make the rest up along the way. They travel mostly at the trot and are allowed to eat only natural pasture. They must carry at least 100 kilos of weight. A vet checks their condition at each stage.' I was looking for horses that could cover on average seventeen kilometres a day, living off the best hay and grain that dollars could buy. It seemed that the criollo would be suitable.

Out we went to look at some of Gonzalo's criollos. They were standing, lined up in a wooden barn tied to rings. My heart dropped to my Regent boots: the criollos were tiny, or appeared so as I was more used to steeplechasers. Squat, rounded and about fourteen hands, they showed the whites of their eyes as they turned to watch us approaching.

Gonzalo's peon hitched up the girth of a mare and led her out.

'My God, I can't ride 4000 miles on that,' I thought.

'Do you want to buy her?' said Gonzalo.

'Er, yes please, but I am not looking for a mare.'

'Jump up then,' said Gonzalo, ignoring my remark.

'More like step over,' I thought as I swung into the saddle.

I knew that I was being watched by Gonzalo and Alex to see if I could ride, to see if I knew anything about horses or was just another bullshitter. I walked off on the mare with my legs scraping along the ground. She did not walk as I knew a horse to walk but half walked half joggled like a professional human walking racer. I pulled on my right rein to turn to the right. She went off to the left. I pulled harder. She veered to the left and stopped.

'Like a cowboy,' shouted Gonzalo, 'like a cowboy. One hand. Use one hand.'

'Of course,' I thought, 'like a cowboy.' I switched reins to one hand and by drawing them across her neck to the right, the mare executed a perfect right turn. I rode her about the outbuildings and returned to Gonzalo and Alex.

'What do you think?' said Gonzalo.

'Like riding an uncomfortable donkey,' I thought, replying, 'Great'.

'Try the other,' said Gonzalo, sensing my disappointment. I tried the other. The problem was not one horse against the other. It was the whole race of criollos that bothered me. They were small and uncomfortable. There was no way I could cross the Andes on a Shetland pony. I was horrorstruck: I had come 7000 miles to ride two horses across the Andes and I hated the only breed suitable. Gonzalo suggested some more and the peon, also called Torres, ('My father you know,' said Gonzalo shrugging his shoulders and giving me a leery grin) was saddling as fast as he could. They got worse and worse, until the first one I had ridden seemed like a dream.

'This is hopeless,' I thought, and Gonzalo suggested we look around. I was so disappointed I could not speak and left Gonzalo and Alex to chat alone.

We walked out into one of the corrals holding about twenty horses and Gonzalo showed me an equine lesbian. She had a face like a man. We walked down a line of boxes and from the end box I saw a head appear. It looked at us, looked around with interest and went back into its box. As if doing a doubletake its head reappeared and watched us walk towards it.

'Careful, James,' said Gonzalo as I looked into the horse's box. 'He's pretty mean.'

What I saw was a 15.2 ball of strength and muscle with an intelligent and interested head, which tried to bite me. A horse with spirit, I thought.

'What is this horse?' I asked Gonzalo.

'Fogonacio [machine gun fire]. He's from Chile. Young but strong. I'm preparing him for the show at Palermo.'

'So he's for sale.'

'Yes, he's for sale. They all are, except the first two mares you rode. But you don't want him. You can ride him after lunch.'

I looked in at the box and he looked great. Seriously good. His legs as far as I could see were clean, he was fat but well formed and he had a look and feel about him that was keen and alive. The horse had even crossed the Andes already.

We sat at a long table upon which light from a central skylight dropped. In the room there was an abundance of lace cloth, high quality bric-a-brac and a chandelier. Around the table were Gonzalo, Mrs Torres, Torres junior, his daughter, daughter-in-law, cousin, brother and assorted friends. I was sitting next to a stunning girl with short-cropped blonde hair and a deep man's voice. All the men were wearing traditional gaucho gear: big cotton shirts, the baggy trousers called bombachas, wide belts and boots. Knives and spurs had been left outside. We ate a sort of bean stew called gizo, and if John Wayne had walked in, he would have fitted right in as long as his Spanish had been up to it. We drank wine, red, followed by a sweet heady white. I was asked numerous questions about the trip and how I intended to make it, questions about the UK, and then Mrs Torres cornered me:

'Are you married?' she said.

'No.'

'But you have a girlfriend?'

'Yes.'

'And you left her behind?'

'Well, I didn't actually leave her behind.'

'But where is she?'

'In England, in London.'

'So not with you?'

'No.'

She looked at me with incomprehension. I tried to explain.

'She's a teacher and she has a job.'

'She's working while you ride?'

'Yes.'

'I don't understand.'

Gonzalo interrupted.

'James, you know that you are eating meat of horse [carne de caballo]?'

I looked at my stew with horror and the little cubes of meat amongst the beans.

'Horse meat?' I said in disgust, and everyone around the table laughed.

'"Carne de caballo" is dried beef. We call it carne de caballo because in the past, and even now, gauchos may spend many days in the pampa. They carry dried meat as food and place it between their saddle and horse blankets. The sweat from their horse keeps the meat supple and moist.'

'Yum, yum,' I thought. 'Biltong marinated in horse sweat.'

'It's delicious,' I said. 'I mean it.' I did.

Gonzalo smiled and slapped me on the back. 'Welcome to Argentina. Time for a siesta.' He showed me to a spare room and I lay fully clothed on the valley-shaped bed. I dreamt of black stallions and blonde girls with masculine voices, of Carina, of heat and dust, of Argentina, of men in kit, of mountains.

I woke after an hour and went outside. Gonzalo was sitting on a bench with Alex and looked as if he was taking a toke on a bong. He was inhaling from a gourd through a thin silver tube. 'Maté,' I thought. He filled the open-topped gourd with what looked like tea-leaves, and hot water from a plastic thermos and handed it to me.

'Maté,' he said.

'I've never tried it,' I said, worried that it would give me an enormous hit and I would fall over or something. 'What does it feel like?'

'Feel like? What do you mean?'

'Well, you know. Will I feel . . .' and made a circling movement around my temples with my index finger. More incomprehension.

'It's like tea,' said Alex interrupting in English, 'like strong tea. Suck on the tube.'

My mouth was filled with a hot, acrid, dry flavour and my tongue recoiled against the hot stream of warm liquid.

'Delicious,' I said to Gonzalo, handing him the gourd. He filled it again from the thermos, handed it to Alex, did one for himself and then it was my turn again. We kept passing it around and once I was included in the party we talked. I felt after a few sucks as if I had drunk a lot of strong coffee, slightly nerved up and feverish, but with a clear mind washed of the wine and the siesta.

'So you want to try the stallion?' said Gonzalo.

He was saddled up and brought out. He looked even bigger out of his box and very strong. The peon was obviously a little more wary of him than the others and was told to accompany me on another horse. I walked Fogonacio about a bit and then took him out on to the pampa. The difference between him and the horses I had ridden before lunch was immediately apparent. He wanted to go. He was keen, fast, comfortable and powerful. I cantered him back.

We went back inside the house and ate a particularly uninspired dish that Mrs Torres told me was a national speciality – fried batter. I wanted Fogonacio badly and found it hard to join in the conversation. I felt Gonzalo's hand on my shoulder.

'Shall we talk?' he said, and we went outside, Gonzalo slipping on a frog. He asked me about the others and said he knew I wanted to buy Fogonacio.

'How much do you want?' I said, hoping that it would be a one thousand dollar question.

'I can get $10,000 at Palermo, so my bottom price is $8000,' and that was that. There was no way I could spend eighty per cent of my funds on one horse.

Fogonacio was sold at auction a few months later for $5000.

I had another disaster with the next horse I tried to buy. A few days after the Fogonacio affair I drove into Buenos Aires to go to the offices of the Associacion de Criaderos de Caballos Criollos. I was met by the fat and pompous director of the association, Señor Giordano who obviously thought I was wasting his time. He grudgingly gave me the date of a criollo show and auction in a few days and the name and number of a breeder, a Señor Pini.

At the weekend, I went to the show of around eighty horses in a suburb of Buenos Aires close to San Isidro. The first day was taken up by qualifying competitions and the second with the finals and an auction of the competitors. I drove to the show and entered a typical rural horse show scene. Men were standing around in groups talking, animals were enclosed in corrals and padding about in the background; and a muffled PA system announced competitions and results. Giordano, already drunk, was rushing from group to group ingratiating himself with the breeders.

There was a series of competitions for each age and sex group: stallions, mares and geldings. The first, and to me the most boring, was the showing. Horses were walked and cantered around a grass ring enclosed by white posts and railings, judged, buffed up by the peons, and re-shown for the final line-up. The next two competitions were far more interesting. First was the rienda which Giordano described through wine-laden breath as 'dressage'. British dressage aficionados would be appalled by Argentine criollo dressage. Horses were galloped and stopped at a certain spot. They were whirled around 180 degrees, 90 degrees, jumped straight into a canter, stopped, whirled around. The impression was of dust and horses straining, but the effect was graceful. Horses were showing their ability to move rapidly amongst cattle, often within a corral. There was one movement when the riders dismounted, leaving the reins hanging to the grass. They walked around the horse at a distance of twenty metres and then remounted. A perfect execution was when the horse remained still, showing that it would not gallop off if left alone in the pampa while its owner dealt with a problem. It made me laugh that often the horse trotted off leaving a floundering gaucho in its wake.

The third competition was like an upmarket bending race. Four drums were placed in a line, leading into a square marked by a drum at each corner. Horse and rider had to wind through the drums to reach the square, circle the drums at each corner and return to their starting place, bending through the initial line of drums. It sounds pretty simple but as the competition was against the clock, fluidity, co-ordination and balance won the races. At each turn the riders waved their ribenques (large whips) in the air and slapped them down their horse's neck or quarters. The whips made a loud slap but caused no pain due to their thickness.

There was one horse that I particularly liked – No. 38. I had seen him when I was walking through the corrals checking out the horses. I had noticed him because he was the only one that was looking at his surroundings with interest. He had looked at me with pricked ears, caught my eye and his gaze had gone on. I looked him up in the book. A six-year-old gelding called Devil Cross – perfect. I checked his legs and back over. They were fine. Standing, he looked fat – chunky like a tug. But he could move. In the gymkhana race, he whirled and pirouetted around the drums, smashing every other rider's time. He was perfect: good condition, good age and obviously very agile. I went home excited at the prospect of buying him the next day. I presumed that I had effective economic fire power, being a dollar carrier.

Nerved up and with Alex in attendance, we went back to the show the next day. We watched the finals of the dressage and the gymkhana, and Alex agreed that Devil Cross was a good horse. I was introduced to the head of the criollo fraternity. He had met Tschiffely personally, and told me a story about Tschiffely's horses recognising him a few years after the trip: Tschiffely had brought English oats to give them.

His eyes settled on my jodhpur boots.

'He walked a lot, you know,' he said.

'Yeah, I know. I've got some better boots.'

'Hmph.' He walked off. The interview was over.

The criollo people did not do much to help me that afternoon. Word had leaked out that I was interested in the horse. I had worked out that the horse was expected to sell for about $250, and I had $1000 to spend. I wanted the horse badly and I was prepared to spend four times its price to get it. Of course, I did not tell anyone this, but I had been seen looking at and trying the horse. The sale began. The prices were steady although the first horse sold cheaply and the second horse expensively. The poker game had started and the first guy got a bargain, the second got screwed. The auctioneer came to No. 38's section – geldings between six and ten years – and the prices were as I expected.

'No sweat,' I thought. 'I'll pay $300, $400, $700, double, triple or whatever, up to $1000.'

The horse came into the ring doing a flashy turn and looking great.

'What am I bid?' said the auctioneer. '$200?'

No response. '$150.' No response. '$100.'

I raised my programme thinking, 'Bugger this. Let's start. Let's get it over and done with.'

'$100 I have.'
A bid came from across the ring.
'$150,' said the man on the podium.
I raised my hand.
'$200.'
All nerves, all energy, all senses were outward, towards threat.
'$250,' bid the guy across the ring.
'$300?' I raised my hand.
What happened then was a nightmare. A guy standing behind me in the crowd stepped into the bidding. All three bidders cranked it up to $500.
'No sweat, double,' I thought.
The first bidder against me dropped out, and the unseen man behind me bid against every move I made. At $750 (treble) I knew what was going on.
'I'm being bid up,' I said, turning to Alex.
The crowd were by now well cranked up. I had been bid up to three times the market price.
But the guy did not stop. I bid against him until $1000 and stopped. He petered out at $1050.
'Fuck,' I said to Alex. In moments of stress language becomes well distilled. 'I was fucking set up. Fuck.' We saw the auctioneer talk to the buyer. Alex pointed him out to me. As I walked past, they smiled.
I smiled back. 'Fuck you,' I thought. I was speechless with rage.
After a few days when I had cooled down I tried to buy the horse privately. There was a deflation in the Argentine currency and I had more money, so I offered. But they wanted still more; they wanted to make a killing. But I did not feel like shedding as much as a toenail more to the horse dealer Alex and I had christened 'The Shark'.
Apart from experience and a scrap of education, one good thing that came out of this was the Crespo family. Guillermo Crespo was the owner of the horse and obviously not involved in any way with the horse dealer's and auctioneer's scam. After the auction, I found him and his son, Martin, and asked if they had any more horses for sale. They said they would think about it, look around and give me a call.
Martin rang the next day. Yes, they did have a horse. Could I come out next week to take a look? Sure, I said.
I spent the week smarting from the humiliation of the auction and became very angry that I was not making any progress. I had been in Argentina for ten days and had seen two horses. I decided to go and see Señor Pini, the breeder whose name I had been given by Giordano.

Señor Pini's office was in a smart business district, and sat behind a huge double door leading to the street. I was buzzed through the door and climbed an impressive marble staircase guided by wooden handrails. At the top was a secretary who showed me into the big man's office. He was sitting behind a large desk, reading a newspaper. His office was stunning. Wooden panelling lined the walls and the ceiling was high and corniced. Sñr Pini had positioned his desk so that he sat dead centre of one of the panels. In each panel was a circle motif. The impression given was of Sñr Pini sitting at his desk with a circle surrounding his head as if he was wearing a halo. I doubt whether he was entitled to wear it. We talked about horses and he asked about my trip and how I was intending to proceed logistically. After a while I got the feeling that I was being interviewed rather than me interviewing him. Obviously, Giordano at the Associacion had become sick of me and passed me on to Pini. Pini was checking me out, and if I failed my interview the word would be put around and it would be extra hard to buy the horses.

So I steeled up. I sat up straight in my chair, paid attention to the questions, answered them directly and generally tried to persuade Pini that I was a pretty tough, macho sort of bloke – fist clenching, shoulder lifting, mean staring. It went well. I was pleased and relieved to have seen the trap in time and saved my neck in the interview. I had obviously passed, as Pini said that he had a horse I could see and would put the word around. He walked me out of his office.

We shook hands, and said goodbye. I turned to leave and fell straight down the stairs. End of macho image. (How's he going to cross the Andes if he can't negotiate the stairs?) I did the best I could. Although in great agony (marble leaves no room for doubt) I smiled at Pini above, said I was fine, got up with difficulty and hobbled (as little as possible) into the street.

I had screwed it again. I went to see his horse, which he must have switched as it was totally unsuitable; and the breeders were never forthcoming.

With the disappointment of the auction still burning deep, Alex and I set off to see a full brother of Devil Cross, and I tried to dampen any hope of the horse being what I wanted. We arrived at Martin Crespo's shop, and walked into a horseman's and bondage freak's Aladdin's cave: saddles, bridles, whips, spurs, girths, lassos, hobbles. There was everything there for mounting and controlling a horse. I wandered around in fascination feeling the textures and smelling the leather. We followed Martin in his beaten-up Dodge from the shop to his farm, twenty-five kilometres from Rosario. We pounded down a dirt track for a few kilometres before entering the outer gate of the estancia. A sign read 'La Baguala': Wild Mare.

We turned into the final yard, and there tied under a tree was the oddest-looking horse I have ever seen. He was fat, and out of condition but well-formed and strong.

'What is he called?'

'Cruz Diablo el Chapeton,' said Martin.

'I thought that the other one at the show was called Cruz Diablo?'

'He was. All our horses are. Cruz Diablo is the stud name.'

'Oh. So what does el Chapeton mean?'

'The Outsider, Stranger.'

I liked it. The other reason for el Chapeton's strange appearance was his colour. Excluding the stuffed Mancha in the museum, he was the first manchado that I had seen. Manchado in the flesh is a brown that turns to orange, overlaid and bordered by white, with black flicked from the divine paint brush and splotched around. He had a wall eye and something extraordinary had been done to his feet, cutting them away around the bottom. He certainly was not as beautiful as Devil Cross but I liked his look. He rolled his eyes, showed their surrounding whites and generally looked pretty keen and wild. A peon saddled him up and we took him out into a neighbouring field.

He may not have been much to look at but to ride he was incredible. He was a small horse, about fifteen hands at the withers but when I got on him he felt huge. He reminded me of the Tardis: pretty small to look at, but functionally huge. He walked and trotted and cantered with real economy but real force. Alex trotted him up and down, patted him, felt his legs, looked at his eyes, sniffed his breath and pronounced him fit.

We all went into the house, a single storey sitting in a small garden. It consisted of one room centred around a huge fire, a kitchen that was being extended, a study and a number of bedrooms. Around the walls were whips, spurs and sets of bridles, headcollars and hobbles. All were festooned with pure silver, and the workmanship was to an impossible perfection.

Guillermo was a tall thin man, whose background was in many ways different to the other top breeders of criollos. His farm was small, and he therefore worked in the province of Entre Rios, a five-hour drive from Rosario. He was steadily building up the farm with an emphasis on horses of which he had about forty.

We sat around a large table and talked about Tschiffely's Ride. He brought out articles and pictures of his own horses including el Chapeton. We drank maté and I felt very at home. At last it came to the time to discuss business. I said I wanted to buy the horse. Guillermo said he wanted to sell it to me. We agreed on a price and I included two more factors in the deal.

'I want to get a discount at Martin's shop.'

Giullermo looked at Martin and got the nod.

'And I want to keep el Chapeton here, bring the second horse here when I have bought it, live here for a month and train the horses. I have a tent and could live in the garden.'

'The horse is yours,' said Guillermo. I had bought my first horse.

We went outside to look him over again. Alex took some blood for analysis, and I took some templates of his feet. I could fax them back to Mustad in Switzerland to be sized up against the plastic horseshoes, which they would then send out.

We drove back to Buenos Aires and San Isidro and the local video shop, where I pulled *Missing*. Its portrayal of violence, deceit and strength of will in South America was excellent and rather disturbing. I had felt that fear from the Dirty War in the 1970s still remained in Buenos Aires. When I asked delicately, Alex said yes it had changed the fabric of Argentina and there was a legacy of fear and mistrust. About 9000 people had disappeared in Tucuman, Salta and Buenos Aires, predominantly in a war between the military government forces and left wing 'subversives'. There was open fighting in the hills around Tucuman, but, on the whole, the war was one of torture, harassment and murder. *Missing*, although set in Chile, dramatised much of what happened in Argentina during the early 1970s. I think the film freaked out Alex more, as he had told me that he had done his military service during this period, and had spent fifteen days fighting his own people.

The next week continued to be rather depressing. I had bought a horse, but was no closer to buying the second and found it very hard to get out of bed in the morning and make an effort to keep the expedition going. Humberto Fernandez suggested that Alex and I go to the central cattle market in Buenos Aires at Las Llenas. We set off at six in the morning to arrive at the twenty-five hectare site in good time.

Fifteen to twenty thousand head of cattle were auctioned off each day for export and for the domestic market. During the early morning, dealers inspected the cattle, and at around 8 am the auctions started.

The place reminded me of the Stock Exchange, a place I visited as a child. There were cattle in their pens (the trading floor), steam rising, bells ringing and then the auction began. Traders on walkways above shouted prices and waved papers until the desired price was reached (about twenty-five US cents per kilo that day) and they started on the next lot. We spoke to the two men who controlled all the horses, used in the market to herd cattle from one pen to another. Peons arrived in the morning and hired a horse by the day, like taxi drivers. The horses were beautiful specimens, well cared for and powerful. However, the two owners did not want to sell so we left empty-handed.

There was a novel system of parking in the overcrowded multi-storey car park. The first line of cars, as usual, were parked perpendicular to the back wall. Bridget's car was one of these and I was furious to find that a line of cars had parked across our front. But Alex knew the score, and went down the line until he found a space into which he could push a car, like the beginning of a square puzzle. Into each newly created space he pushed the next car until he was able to clear the car in front of ours. They had all been left with their hand-brakes off for this express purpose.

We drove back to George and Bridget's house in San Isidro and demolished half a pig each for breakfast. I was rapidly becoming used to the vast quantities of meat consumed at each sitting. And not just meat but livers, heart, entrails, balls and kidneys too. I was even getting used to the foul black tobacco cigarettes that Alex would start on first thing in the morning. I was sticking to Camel myself (about twenty cents a packet).

After breakfast that day, I drove up to Rosario to pay the Crespos for el Chapeton. The agreed price had been 50,000 australes. The austral was continuing to plummet and I felt that I should pay the Crespos as soon as possible. However, only six days later, the 50,000 australes I had in my pocket were worth only sixty per cent in dollar terms.

The possibilities for speculation in South America were enormous. There were times when the government artificially held the exchange rate down by dumping dollar reserves. Many accumulated dollars, knowing through inside information that controls would be lifted when the reserves ran out. They could treble their money overnight. The ones without capital, the middle and lower classes, however, were not protected and food prices, many related to oil and international trade, could treble.

I handed the cash over to Martin and drove out to La Baguala. The

43

saddle I had bought the week before fitted well, and I took el Chapeton out for an hour or so covering, I reckoned, 5.8 kilometres per hour. The saddle was also pretty comfortable on my arse, being a seventy-year-old cavalry saddle, copied from a German model. Rather like a modern day dressage saddle, it had a high back and high pommel to encourage the rider to sit deep into the seat. It also had lots of knobs on to which gear could be tied.

The other purpose of my trip to Rosario was to visit Roberto Luraschi, just a few miles down the road from La Baguala. He ran a local auction for bovine breeding stock and also bred criollos. Martin and I went together to a very different type of market from that in Las Llenas. It was a bitterly cold afternoon, and bombachaed figures huddled round a small sand ring or the stall that dispensed mouth-size shots of coffee or maté. Luraschi was riding a nice grey and pointed us towards the horses he was interested in selling. Martin and I wandered in their direction, and came round a corner head on to a bull being driven at speed to the auction ring. Martin did the correct thing and leapt lightly on to the surrounding rails, but I was rooted to the spot by the sight of this piggy-eyed, horned monster. It kept coming, more fearful of the men behind on horses goading it with sticks than me. Something, an instinct, launched me on to the offensive and I started towards it yelling and with my arms held aloft. We both stopped and I had time to jump over the railings. The gauchos roared with laughter and I heard someone say: 'This bloody gringo. He thinks he can cross the Andes by horse and now he's trying to be a bloody matador.'

I found Martin and we laughed and laughed. I felt very quivery – what a bloody stupid thing to do.

There were three horses huddled up against the cold: what I was now calling a 'pure' criollo, small and squat; a Chilean larger-all-round model; and a real neurotic. They were all miserable, Luraschi was miserable, and we all agreed, 'Fuck it. Let's look at them tomorrow.'

It was not solely because of the cold that I wanted to delay, but also the fact that Alex was free the next day. I increasingly relied on his excellent judgement of horses, and also as a mediator between my European personality and way of doing things and the Argentines. I knew I was becoming more Argentine each day but there was room for Alex's diplomacy. I rang him up that night and told him I had seen a good possibility, the long Chilean, but that it had a splint.

I rode all three the next day and liked them all. The 'pure' criollo was a good horse but small, and the neurotic needed a lot of time to turn into a decent horse. The Chilean, called Viento Norte, I liked the most. He gave me that Tardis feeling but he had two problems: one area of old saddle damage that had taken off all the hair and left a scar the size of a ten pence bit, and the splint.

'The sore is fine: dry and cleared up,' said Alex. 'But the splint – I just don't know.' I respected Alex enormously for saying so, and realised at that moment that if Argentina does not get to him before he gets to the horses he will become an excellent vet.

'Would you mind if I called Humberto in?' I asked him.

'No, I'd be pleased.'

So we had not yet arrived. I still had one horse to buy, and a week to wait before Humberto could see Viento Norte. We took blood for the anaemia test which he passed that week. One vet inspection and I would have my horses.

Alex, Humberto and I met in San Isidro at 6 am and drove at 160 kilometres per hour the whole way to Rosario. Humberto had super-charged his Renault, and was driving like a maniac. We were a little late for Roberto Luraschi, who was waiting for us at the auction ring. He told us to go on ahead and check the horse over. We did. A peon saddled him up and rode him around so Humberto could check his wind, which in horse-speak means 'respiration system'. He felt Viento Norte's legs, did some strange jabbing things with his fingers and pronounced the horse fit.

I now had to buy him. I made the critical error in my dealings with Roberto of starting in dollars rather than australes, but we concluded at a price and at last I was mobile – horse mobile.

We drank some maté together, arranged transporting the horse to La Baguala and Alex, Humberto and I left to celebrate at Perisini's.

Perisini was an Italian immigrant who ran a boliche at the turn off to La Baguala. A boliche is basically a general store, pub and restaurant hybrid. I had gone in the week before to have lunch, and had been met by what appeared to be Salvador Dali, residing behind the counter. But this long grey-haired, long grey-faced, moustached figure was Perisini. He cooked me a superb steak with chips and I drank beer and coffee, all for sixty US cents. Between bouts of cutting up a cow using a sawmill device that sounded like a dentist's drill, he told me about his problems. He had a son who wanted to be a ballet dancer, who had trained in Buenos Aires but needed to spend time in Europe. Perisini ran a typical middle-class Argentine business and, as a result, had been stuffed by inflation. As he said, he was going to have to sell a lot of steak, chips, beer and coffee lunches to make sufficient profit to buy a $2000 air ticket. Most of his customers were like the gaucho who had come in during my lunch. He had hitched his horse outside and was nursing a small singani, described to me as weak gin.

I loved Perisini's place. You could buy everything from beer to brooms, lunch, supper, get things sent on the bus or just go in and have a coke and a chat with Perisini. We usually talked about the economy, politics and football, three of Argentina's national pastimes. As Perisini said: 'The problem of Argentine football is we have eleven men on the pitch rather than a team. Argentina's political problems are because we have thirty-six million republics in Argentina.' He put in a nutshell one of the features of Argentina that I was beginning to love. Each member of the 36 million population regards himself as an individual, a whole encapsulated unit without fusion to others (except his family), to class or to country.

The other thing about Perisini's was his daughter.

Alex, Humberto and I walked in and ordered lunch, the menu being a choice between rump or sirloin steak. Humberto told us stories about his time in the UK as a cavalry officer. He remembered Prince Philip, the pubs and the women – not necessarily in that order. He gave me two Argentine sayings:

'The hair of a woman has more strength than a team of oxen.' (This was the 'family' version.)

'With a head, you can either think or wear a hat.'

That night was my first at La Baguala. The arrangement made with Guillermo was that I should sleep in my tent in the garden – there was a hole-in-the-ground loo next to one of the tack rooms – and during the week I could use the shower of Peti, the peon. Someone had whitewashed the loo walls and cleaned up the hole, and I was shown Peti's shower. My tent I pointed away from the house looking over the fields, stretching west. I bunged a whole heap of kit into it and watched the sun go down. A ground mist formed, and the horses and cattle that stretched away to the distance seemed almost transparent.

I felt very happy. The Crespo family had made me very welcome and I had a perfect and very beautiful training ground for the horses and myself. I knew that the horses needed work, feeding up, and practice to get the saddlery fitting perfectly. And, as for myself, I needed to ride but also I knew I was not ready to go. Chains of fear, unease and insecurity were dissolving but I still had to find that strength to break free.

The Crespo family comprised Guillermo and his wife Margaritta; Martin, the son, and their daughter, also called Margaritta, aged about twenty-six and twenty-five respectively. Margaritta's boyfriend, Marcus, was Martin's business partner in the saddlery shop and more importantly, I felt, his pair in 'la corrida' which they promised they would demonstrate the next day, Sunday, 30th April.

Twenty-nine days to find two horses in Argentina, famed for its quality and quantity. I never believed it would take so long. I had been aiming to be ready and leaving Buenos Aires by the 23rd of April, Tschiffely's departure date in 1925. However, I was pleased with the horses. As Carlos, Martin's uncle said: 'I know these two horses,' (he had been given el Chapeton by Guillermo, but gave him back for the trip) 'and they can take you to the end of the world.'

They all knew all the criollos in the area and Viento Norte, I felt, caused a certain amount of mirth amongst the criollo freaks.

'James, do you know the North Wind?' said Guillermo. He didn't wait for my reply. 'In Argentina, the north wind is also called "The Madman's Wind" as you will find out.'

'Yeah,' interrupted someone else. 'A madman riding the Madman's Wind.'

'But I thought all criollos were mad!' It seemed to be the right thing to have said because they looked at me, paused and laughed even louder. But I knew there was something about Viento Norte still.

Sunday started a routine that was with me whenever I stayed at La Baguala. We would start with a maté in the morning although Margaritta, Guillermo's wife, refused to believe that I wanted maté instead of bread, cheese, dulce de leche (sweetened condensed milk) and café con leche. It was the bane of my life, when the family were staying at La Baguala, that I could never join in the morning maté sessions with Martin and Guillermo. That was all they had for breakfast, and it was all I needed. They would sit at a table by the fire talking while I waded through mountains of bread and coffee under the maternal stares of Margaritta and their maid, Betty.

In the morning during the weekends, everyone would muck around with their own horses. Guillermo would tend to the farm on his favourites, Martin would lunge and bring on new horses and I would take el Chapeton and, when he arrived, Viento Norte, out for rides. That morning I took el Chapeton down to the main road, five kilometres away, to see what he thought of the odd passing vehicle.

The Crespos mended all their saddlery themselves, and before lunch was allotted to sewing and cleaning. Throughout the whole trip I never bothered to clean my saddlery much, just sewing it up and strengthening the weak parts. Cleaning tack reminded me of Pony Club and all that equine officiousness and fussiness that I wanted to leave behind. The only thing I checked obsessively was the padding I used between the horses' backs and the saddle. Against all conventional criollo wisdom I was using foam rubber rather than traditional saddle blankets. This was partly on Robin Hanbury-Tenison's advice; partly because all conventional criollos apart from the Crespos seemed to give their horses sore backs; and mainly because I was paranoid in keeping this all-important surface clean of dirt and irritating seeds and burrs.

Lunch every day was an asado. Asado both means barbecue and refers to a cut of meat. Ribs of beef are cut crossways by a saw, so the end result is a strip about 25 cms long and 6 cms wide, of squares of rib held together by meat and fat. It sounds disgusting but cooked over a fire, rib side first it is delicious. Fat drips through the meat that a toothless octogenarian would have no problems with. The meat I tasted in Rosario and Santa Fe was the best I tasted anywhere in Argentina, and certainly any place outside Argentina.

Lunch was followed swiftly by a siesta. Guillermo would disappear for an hour and a half exactly, before returning to get the post-siesta maté up and running. He always took this time to talk to me and explain Argentina, its people, landscape, wildlife, visitors, history and culture. Sometimes I took a siesta, but usually I smoked something that a Porteño friend had given me, and read.

The afternoon was free time. As the finals of the corrida in Palermo were approaching, Guillermo, Martin and Marcus would practise. Sometimes I would take the horses out again, sometimes help with the corrida.

At dusk there was another maté session. Stories and talk before those who were going left. The only way the Crespos diverged from the typical criollo life of horses, maté and asado was in the evening when we would watch videos and the television. But the television is now very much part of the South American's life, although the Argentine diet of soap, games and local news bored me to death before I became addicted to one of the quiz/game shows.

During the week, there was no telly and only Peti around, and although I kept the basic routine I behaved in a much more versatile, flexible and animal manner. I would sleep, eat and ride when I wanted. I knew that this ability to adapt, both inherent and trained, would help me when the trip started.

On Sundays, the Crespos always practised for the corrida, one of the main tests of the criollo horse. The corrida is rather like playing tennis against an automatic machine that spits balls out of a tube. But in this case, the balls being spat out are cows out of a forty-metre-long tunnel, which is made of two high wooden walls about one metre apart. Cattle are herded into the main corral behind the tunnel. A gate is opened between the corral and the tunnel and the cattle, seeing light, make a dash for freedom. To get them more rattled and going faster, a thick telegraph pole runs along the ground the length of the tunnel to the opening.

A corrida team consists of two men on horses. They wait by the opening gate on either side of the tunnel. As the cow runs down the tunnel, the horsemen look over the wall and keep level with it. As it breaks from the end, they drive their horses' shoulders into the cow's sides, just behind its shoulders. The cow should then be clamped, and although moving forward unable to escape. The horsemen attempt to keep the cow going forward in a dead straight line within a six metre boundary for forty metres.

I stayed a month at La Baguala; probably one of the best in my life. During the weekends I often reverse commuted to Buenos Aires, went and watched films, saw friends, explored Buenos Aires, and tried to organise papers and various administrative matters. I was not too worried about papers as the Argentine mission to the UK had told me that export papers were needed only for mules, as they had military significance. I thought that this must be some historical legacy, but Humberto told me that there was a 2000 mule school in Buenos Aires, and that they were still used as pack animals for patrolling Argentina's huge and often inaccessible border. I picked up some semi-bogus sanitation certificates as a last resort for the border, but hoped I could get better ones nearer the time.

Otherwise I just enjoyed being in Buenos Aires – the frontier and papers all seemed so far away. George and Bridget continued to make me feel very at home, never hassled by what I was up to. I could borrow a car when I needed and loved to talk to them both. George had nearly gone into UK politics, and I always thought that it was a shame that he and politics had passed each other by. A conservative in the British sense, he believed that the solution for Argentina would be a free market system.

Bridget provided me with one delicious meal after another, and kept everyone ticking along. She found Argentina and Buenos Aires hard, but had taken the initiative to start a job and become involved.

Viento Norte was moved from Roberto Luraschi's place to La

Baguala and I started taking him and el Chapeton out together, training him for some inexplicable reason to follow upsides, with his head level at my knee, rather than tagging along behind.

Living at La Baguala was the part that I loved. In the morning I would often ride down to Perisini's, hitch the horses outside and go in for a coke. It was good training for the horses to stand and wait outside public places, but I also enjoyed talking with Perisini and hoping for a glimpse of his daughter whom he jealously guarded. I wanted to ask her out, but there was an equally strong force holding me back. 'You've got a beautiful girl whom you love very much. What more do you want?' I said to myself. I wanted Carina and no one else, but my machismo would fight back. 'No. Take the Perisini girl out. Take what you can.'

Peti and Guillermo taught me tricks and how to look after the horses. Guillermo taught me how to accustom the horse to being staked by a long rope at night. A long broad strip of leather was tied to the base of a tree or fence post, and the other end to the horse's headcollar. They would pull away and wrap the leather around their legs. The leather was so thick that it was inflexible and the horses could easily disentangle themselves, a trick they would need when their rope was longer and thinner.

Peti taught me how to stake them at night when there was no tree or fence about, using a bone or stirrup. One end of a rope was tied to the headcollar and the other tied to a bone (and there were always plenty of bones in Argentina). The bone was buried in a small hole about 15 cm deep. The horse can only exert a force on the bone on a horizontal plane and therefore against the side of the hole. The bone acts like an anchor, but can be easily removed by pulling it straight up.

Martin's shop in Rosario supplied most of my saddlery and it slowly started to mount up:

2 mattress/saddle blankets	1 pair of stirrup leathers
2 ponchos	2 headcollars
2 coronas (thick leather saddle-cloths)	1 leading rein
	1 bridle
2 girths	1 bit
2 saddles	2 overgirths
1 lasso	2 hobbles
4 pieces of foam rubber	and various spares.
1 pair of stirrups	

A factory in Buenos Aires, Casimiri Gomez, made a saddle to my specifications (nothing special – just a saddle with most of the leather cut away to reduce weight) and threw in a few odds and ends, for US$400.

The owner of the factory was a lively man of fifty plus. Alex had come with me, and we were ushered into his office, where he sat with an assistant. We exchanged cigarettes and greetings and he took us through the catalogues of saddlery in stock. The assistant was despatched to collect a saddle and we grouped around it. The owner only paused to take drags on his cigarette, but he dragged too deeply and started to cough, doubling up over the saddle. At last he was able to stand straight but a lurking cough took him by surprise and he hacked loudly. Something flew from his mouth and landed on the saddle.

His teeth.

We all stared at them for a second. They started to slide towards the floor but their host lunged for them, caught them, fumbled, but made the catch and popped them in his mouth. And without a comment, shrug, show of expression or smile, carried on with his spiel. For the half-hour more that Alex and I were in his office, we made every effort not to catch each other's eye.

The horses started to get into shape and I felt myself becoming more remote from the people around me. I put off my departure until after the national elections, and until after Palermo, the international criollo horse fair. I think I would have found more excuses if I could.

May moved on and I spent more time at La Baguala. I rode, read and ate, strengthening myself and the horses mentally and physically. In the evening I would often walk around the farm, trying to spot a viscacha, a sort of underground squirrel. They are like magpies, loving anything bright and have great strength and courage to steal what they can in the night. My knife had once been carried about fifty metres, and I could not understand how I had dropped it until Guillermo explained.

As time progressed, I found myself at the end of my walk staring out over the perimeter fence of La Baguala. There was little to look at. The area around Rosario is flat, with very few trees. I no longer felt agrophobia, but very close to the land around me. It is a friendly land; everything grows. There is water, warmth, and the winds are light. I would look over the fence and stare out into the horizon beyond. I realised, at last, that my body was telling me something. It was telling me that I was ready to go.

6

Departure II

GEORGE AND BRIDGET, Alex, Pablo the chauffeur and the Crespos came to see us off from the Sociedad Rural agricultural showground.

There had been major rioting in Rosario during the week before Sunday, 4th June, the day I found myself saddling up two horses to ride a long way. Inflation had reached all time rampant levels, running at about 1000 per cent monthly. Many people were unable to afford basic supplies. Many shopkeepers, unable to keep pace with price rises, shut their shops and speculated. 'Why sell a bottle of beer today for fifty australes when tomorrow it's worth sixty?' said Perisini, my retail consultant. 'Anyway, what is the value of a bottle of beer?' His moustache had drooped steadily with each inflationary rise.

The crowds had therefore taken to the streets and looted every supermarket, every foodstore. They had smashed shop windows, torn down shutters and poured in to grab anything at hand. Alex and I happened to be in town that day, as we had taken the horses in to the centre to get them shod. The blacksmith was one of the very best I have ever seen. But unfortunately he had a belly that, for some medical reason, had lost all muscle strength and therefore hung to his knees.

His forge was located at the edge of a shanty town. This was actually shrewd business practice as the horse is the poor man's form of transport in Argentina. Obviously, in the remoter and larger estancias the horse is an invaluable tool for getting around and mustering, although I heard talk of motor bikes, as in Australia, coming in to replace the horse. In other more built-up areas, the horse is used as a lorry unit, for pulling a cart and as a way of getting about. However, a bicycle is faster, needs less maintenance and does not eat. So someone who gets a bit of cash together will trade in his horse and get a bicycle (note, more expensive), to travel to and from work. The shanty town dwellers, being amongst the poorest, are still reliant on the horse, hence the blacksmith's shop at its edge. The looters during that week at the end of May came from the shanty towns, although there were reports of people stepping from cars and helping themselves. Anyone with a car in South America is rich. In Argentina, the rich drive, the poor pedal and the very poor ride.

We unloaded the horses from a truck and took them into the blacksmith shop, as a young man, about twenty-five, rushed past clutching a crate of whisky. The horses were very unused to the blacksmith, so we put the twitch on el Chapeton first, and the bellyless farrier stepped in to do some very nifty hoof balancing and preparation. A gang of four ran past, struggling with a sack of flour. Everyone in the shop was very keyed up, which did not help the poor horses. We could hear shots, and the whole town seemed to be in complete turmoil. A man ran past with half a cow on his shoulders and ducked into one of the shanty town alleys. He was really moving, and we saw why a second later, as two armed and helmeted policemen came round the corner after him. They stopped, looked around, could not see the half-cow man, so fired at another group clutching a sack about 150 yards off.

'Fucking hell,' I said to Alex. 'What the fuck is going on? Let's get these fucking fuckers [I meant the horses] the fuck out of here.'

I think all the guns and shooting had helped me slip into army vernacular. We loaded the horses up as soon as possible, paid the blacksmith who had done a good job under fire and who was rapidly closing his shop, and legged it; through barricades, chanting mobs, armed police and soldiers, the twenty-five kilometres back to La Baguala, where peace reigned as ever.

We watched the news later that night. All the shops had been looted, there was a death or two, and due to jail crowding, a lot of people were locked up in the stadium of the Sociedad Rural from where I was leaving.

As I saddled up the horses, we could see and hear the prisoners inside makeshift jails underneath the seats of the stadium. It felt very strange being watched, especially by the Crespo experts. It was a routine that I would get very used to: brush the horses down, pick out their feet, foam, blankets, leather, saddle, sheepskin and overgirth, or overgirth and saddlebags (for the pack-saddle).

At last, I was ready. Five months of preparation and I was ready. I turned and gave George a very stiff-upper-lip handshake, which broke into an Argentine hug. Hugs all round, tears from Guillermo and I got up on el Chapeton. We rode out past the prisoners, some of whom were being led out of their cells to have a pee. Later, Alex said that it must have felt weird embarking on such freedom, riding past the prisoners. In fact, at the time, I felt great empathy with them as I was now tied to my horses like Conrad's sailors in *Heart of Darkness*, whose 'home is always with them – the ship: and so is their country – the sea.'

I posed to George's camera, waved grandly at the party of eight and left. And got about 100 metres before Viento Norte's pack-saddle slipped under his belly.

The followers had gone to get their cars, and in order to right the saddle I turned into the Sociedad Rural, off the road and out of sight. The followers came round the corner and flashed past our hiding place with obvious disbelief all over their faces at our disappearance. I waved at them madly but they did not see us, until we reappeared.

They chugged along behind as we skittered through the relatively deserted streets. Viento Norte was terrified of bicycles; and pavements, to el Chapeton, were totally alien. I presumed later that having been brought up in the flat pampa he had never had to step up and step down something. At the age of eight he just could not understand the whole process. I was supposed to be climbing the Andes on this horse.

George, Bridget, Pablo and Alex soon turned away back to Buenos Aires. Martin and his uncle Carlos were following me to the ring road. Security in Rosario was still very tight and I was stopped at a military road-block by two soldiers in full battle gear.

'Where are you going?' asked one, obviously thinking I was a local, transporting something about. I was wearing local gear: boots, bombachas, a jacket and a hat.

'To the Pacific,' I replied, as I knew he was not listening. As he had me there I posed no threat, so he could check other cars, people in the area.

It slowly sank in. 'What?' he said looking at me for the first time.

'The Pacific. I am going to Peru.'

I could see his thoughts written all over his face, loud and clear – 'NUTTER!' – but he said OK and waved me on.

The ring road was a forty-minute ride down open roads. It was pretty tense as the horses had never been in a town in their lives. Martin helped me re-tie the pack-saddle, and gave me back some gear which had slipped off completely unnoticed. He gave me some advice about the ring road: how I would have to pass seven bridges to reach my turn-off and that we would have to walk over two of the bridges as they crossed rivers, rather than roads below. The ring road

(TOP) Inadvertently arriving in Argentina on the anniversary of the Falkland Islands/Malvinas Invasion, I could not have been more warmly welcomed.

(ABOVE) The stuffed bodies of Tschiffely's horses, Mancha and Gato, in the Museum of Transport in Lujan.

(ABOVE) The
monthly interest
payable on a bank
deposit – inflation
was said to be
running at over one
million per cent per
annum for a few days.

(RIGHT) Viento
Norte, 15 hands
high, aged 5.

(BELOW) El Chapeton
at La Baguala with
Alex Schulte and
Martin Crespo in the
background.

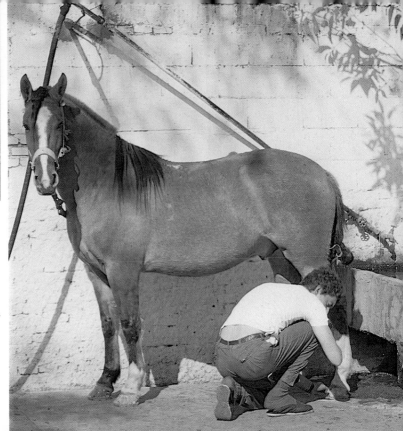

(LEFT) The inside of Martin Crespo's shop.

(BOTTOM) Guillermo Crespo demonstrating the corrida.

(BELOW) Outside the police station in which we stayed. Viento Norte is carrying the packsaddle containing 35 kilos of superfluous junk.

Changing a Mustad Easy Glu shoe – the first development in horseshoes for 1000 years.

A team of mules bringing in the sugar harvest in Tucuman.

Sausages – it is normal to eat a kilo of meat in a sitting.

Carina, my girlfriend, came to visit me for a month in Argentina.

(OPPOSITE) The Iguazu Falls.

(TOP) Andy Pedrassa, Pablo and George Bowen in the Terminal Café.

(ABOVE) Having crossed the stream that marks the border between Argentina and Bolivia, we were followed into Villazon by four 'hoods'. (*George Bowen*)

(TOP) A street stall in Potosi selling coca leaves, fuses and sticks of dynamite.

(ABOVE) The Puente del Diablo on the road between Potosi and Oruro.

was a well-constructed dual carriageway, one of the best in Argentina; I suppose the closest thing that the Argentines have to London's M25, so the traffic travels at speed.

We shook hands, and Martin and Carlos watched us set off up the central reservation before they turned back to La Baguala.

I wondered what they would have for lunch at La Baguala and realised it would be asado. I thought about the traffic that Bridget, George and Alex would have on the way back to Buenos Aires, and realised that with Pablo driving there would be very little. I looked at the pack-saddle and thought it looked very ugly, very ungainly and that I hated it. I felt very alone and very absurd: sitting up like a beacon with two horses in the middle of the central reservation, looking like a fool in my gaucho fancy dress, receiving incredulous stares from the occasional car of Sunday drivers.

7

Argentina, Argentina

SUNDAY HAD SEEMED a good day to leave and I was right. There was little traffic on the by-pass and we were able to cross the bridges without problems, the horses peering over the edge in complete disbelief. We were helped by the riots and a curfew, and I think many people that day stayed at home. But then there is rarely much traffic in Argentina anyway.

A man in a Ford Sierra, which is a very smart car in Argentina, went past. He stopped ahead at a place that bordered the dual carriageway, so that we would come up to him. He was large and nervous, and accompanied by a couple of side-kicks. We shook hands and I got off to straighten the pack-saddle, a long laborious business as I had to take off the saddle-bags, undo the girths, inch them up and rebuckle the saddle-bags.

'Your lasso's on the wrong side,' he said.

'What?'

'Your lasso's on the wrong side. It should be on the left so that when you are getting off there's no chance of your right leg catching it.'

'Right,' I said, storing another piece, in this case, of useless information, and carried on with the pack-saddle.

'Aren't you going to change it round?' he asked.

'Well,' I said as I looked up at him and knew I would have to. 'All right.' So I tied it on the left side of my saddle.

He talked rapidly at length, chasing me around Viento Norte as I fixed his saddle. At last I was ready, and waited as he desperately scribbled an address further up the road on a piece of paper. I think he pissed me off at the time because in a purist rush, now I had started, I did not want to talk to men in Sierras. I wanted to be out in the open, riding like a gaucho, living off cows and singing haunting ballads – to be my pre-imagined self.

We padded along the side of another shanty town, well organised with electricity and water in the houses, marked streets, people playing football. 'Be careful of the shanty towns,' someone had said before I left. 'They'll rob everything you have.'

I felt rather frightened until the football players stopped and shouted questions.

'Where are you going?'

'What are you doing?'

'Good luck.'

An array of out-of-town shops marked the turn-off: a car dealership, a camping shop, and a garden centre. We turned off under the dual carriageway, meeting a large lorry which freaked out el Chapeton, and I clubbed him on the side of the head with my map case to calm him down. We came out from under the bridge to face a few houses, and then nothing. I was sure we were on the wrong road, as it was single lane and very badly maintained. I could not believe that it was the main road north and turned back to ask.

'Where are you going?' asked a shopkeeper.

'North.'

'Yes, that's the one.'

A dirt track bordered the road and I pushed el Chapeton along, walking. There was no way that we could trot as the pack-saddle would have been off in seconds. I was also worried about rubbing their backs. The largest training ride I had done to date had been all of ten kilometres and it had been a disaster. I had checked the saddle after five and continued on. When I got back to La Baguala and had taken the saddle off el Chapeton, I saw to my horror a patch of hair 5 cm in diameter rubbed off behind. Ten kilometres and I had given him a sore. In fact it was negligible, as it had taken off the hair alone and the skin was pink and healthy. However, it made me think: it made me paranoid. A near disaster after ten kilometres, and on my first day I was aiming at twenty-five.

I was hoping to arrive at Marcelo Borras's farm outside the village of Borras. In my money pouch tucked into my shirt, I carried a letter of introduction from Guillermo. It took us four hours to reach Borras.

I was very bored. I sat and we rode. I looked around at the flat surrounding pampa, at the grasses at the ditch along the side of the road. I felt elated that we had started, an incredible energy that I could only dissipate through my head and sitting on el Chapeton. I worried about our reception from Marcelo Borras, I worried about the pack-saddle. Five months of preparation culminating in riding alone along a dirt track beside an untravelled main road. I thought about putting on my Walkman but was afraid of upsetting the equilibrium of moving forward.

We reached Borras, by-passed by the main road, and I stopped at its boliche to ask for Estancia Borras. The owners were new and knew nothing of Borras. They suggested I go back to an estancia that had polo ponies, so I had a coke. We had a chat and they were not at all impressed that they were serving me my first drink on the trip. We exchanged Camel and Parliament cigarettes before they remembered that Estancia Borras was about one kilometre north of the village itself.

The drive to the house was an impressive line of eucalyptus trees and I could see a group of people watching our progress from the verandah of the big house. Señor Borras was away, so I handed my letter of introduction to the man who introduced himself as Coco. He read it, looked at me, read the paper again. He was obviously very suspicious. I groaned inwardly, as I had imagined my first night to be without problems. He asked me a few questions and decided I was kosher. I was led off to a shed and watched while I unsaddled the horses. He watered them and put them out in a well-grassed paddock before searching for hay and grain. In the shed was a bed and a lurid picture of Christ holding a heart. The floor was dirt so I put down a plastic poncho to protect my saddlery and another on the bed to protect myself at night.

I asked Coco if there were eggs or anything that I could buy. He told me to come up to the big house when I was ready. I organised my kit and then sat, smoking a Camel in the doorway watching the horses eat and allowing the sun to wash over me. I felt absolutely knackered. Twenty-five kilometres and I was exhausted. Twenty-five kilometres and only 5975 to go. I did not dwell on the future, just allowed myself to feel pleased for myself and the horses, having successfully completed the first day.

Coco showed me round the outside of the house, a great colonial monstrosity with heavy church doors and an arched verandah. We sat at a long table talking about my trip and dairy farming, and watched on the news a litany of price rises, heavily featured on national news programmes at the time. 'Sugar, the kilo: up 100 australes, ten per cent. Maté, the kilo: up 150 australes, fifteen per cent. Beef, the kilo: up 200 australes, twenty per cent. Bread, up ten per cent,' as the camera panned along supermarket shelves. Gripping stuff for national news but as addictive as football.

I slept a wine-induced sleep all night, my plastic poncho protecting me from the mattress, alive with bugs. I dreamt that my stove was on fire, but George was putting it out using the flapping of a bird's wings. The bird was a silver badge that Martin's grandmother had given me, representing the Holy Spirit. She assured me that it would look after us. It was beautifully designed. I had pinned it to my jacket to strengthen the talismans that Carina had given me, the St Christopher, the little silver horseshoe, and the heart which hung around my neck.

It took me a long time to get out of bed, saddle the horses and leave. There was yet another maté to be drunk with Coco, and I felt as stiff as starch. The horses did not want to leave, standing disconsolately while I brushed them down and picked out their feet.

At midday we were away, aiming for a short afternoon to the next village, only twelve kilometres away. The pack kept slipping round Viento Norte's fat tummy, and the land continued to be flat, fertile and full of cattle-stocked fields. The weather closed in and it started to drizzle lightly. The wind was strong, and as there was no sign of the police who were expecting me at the comisaría (the police station), I ate a meal in the service station at the edge of town – milanesas.

The small and bouncy jefe (chief) of the police station tracked me down as I slid the last chip down my gullet. He and his men had been looking out for us all day, expecting me to have arrived the day before. God only knows how they and their battered blue and white jeep failed to find us, as there is only one road we could have travelled.

The horses were put into a tiny corral next to the railroad station, and I went off to do some shopping for the night. As they were looking after me so well it was obvious that I was expected to provide food and drink, so I bought asado, bread, maté and wine for ourselves and some barley grain for the horses, at this point their favourite thing in life. I made the mistake of buying a large carafe of wine. Wine in Argentina comes in a standard bottle, and then a cross between a bottle and an oil drum which holds a lot of litres.

Someone had lit the asado fire in the main room of the three-roomed police station. A tarpaulin had been slung over the front of the jeep's garage and a bed placed in the middle: my room for the night. The main room had a large table, a sink, and a table for the radio which constantly sounded like a man clearing his throat. The fire was raised up to waist height to facilitate cooking. We ate the delicious meat and passed round the wine until everyone was well away. The jefe decided that he needed more cigarettes and sped off in the jeep to the next village, ours having run out of cigarettes. We talked about horses and one of the sergeants showed me some fine leather working he did on the job in slack periods, which seemed to be every time he was working. We drifted on to gun talk and they all brought out their revolvers and pistols to wave and show around. Then we all sang, before one after another five police heads sank into anaesthetized sleep and I went to bed; only to be woken by the jefe to finish off the wine and share a late night cigarette or two.

I felt as rough as hell the next morning as the sun sneaked around the tarpaulin, across the garage front and into my head. The weather in early June was perfect for riding – cool crisp nights and warmish days. The morning was best of all, as the cold from the night hung around. It was like cool, damp and light Scottish weather, and perfect for me. The problem was getting up and ready in time to make the most of it.

The drunkards from the night before all looked remarkably fresh and laughed at me as I staggered through to warm myself up by the fire. Sitting on the embers was a blackened kettle and from this the maté gourds were regularly replenished.

Pablo, the one with the .38, handed me a maté and I took a grateful suck. Into my mouth and nostrils and head streamed a line of molten sugar.

'Yuck!' I exclaimed, shaking my head and snorting maté in disgust.

'Problem?' asked Pablo.

'Yeah, the sugar. It's full of sugar.'

'Yes, that's the custom.'

'Not the matés I have been drinking.'

'But you have been living with criollos who maintain old traditions of drinking maté amargo [bitter].' He took the maté gourd back, put in a pinch of the maté herb, a teaspoon of sugar and filled it with water.

'That much sugar!' I burst out. 'You put that much sugar in?'

Pablo turned to me with an expression of you-talk-too-much-in-the-morning amigo, obviously not finding me as amusing as he had the night before when he had sworn undying friendship across all the seas, all lands.

'Yes,' he said curtly, syphoning a teaspoon of sugar into his mouth.

He refilled the maté gourd with sugar and handed it over. I tentatively put the bombilla to my mouth and sucked as Pablo said quickly:

'In Argentina, we have one of the worst problems of diabetes in the world. We drink so much sugar.'

'Thanks, Pablo,' I said, and went to look for the horses.

It was sweet how generous the horses had become with their affections, only two days out from their own territory. When he saw me (or more likely the bucket of grain) el Chapeton knickered and came over to talk to me. Viento Norte was more reserved, and still very frightened of human beings.

At La Baguala I had thought that he and I were becoming pretty pally. One way of checking and usually forming a closer bond is to blow very gently up a horse's nose, à la Barbara Woodhouse. I do not know why but they blow back, and seem to enjoy it. Viento Norte was tied up to one of the hitching rails among the Crespo horses. I stroked his nose, positioned my mouth by his nostril and then very gently blew. All hell broke loose, as did the hitching rail, as Viento Norte pulled back from me in complete horror. He was pulling and pulling, digging in his heels, desperate to get away. The hitching rail came off its posts and there were horses galloping about in every direction, totally freaked out by Viento Norte's fear. I used nose-blowing very warily after that.

My body, arms, legs and hands felt very sluggish as I prepared the horses and saddled them up. It took me an hour and a half to make sure that everything was on properly with no fear of sore backs. My pack-saddle filled me with particular hatred as I'd not needed to unpack anything, staying as we were with hospitable people who provided everything. At last, all was ready and I had signed one of my sheets for the jefe. He instructed one of his men to guide us to a short cut and off we went: the jeep with lights flashing and siren wailing – until someone leant out of their window and complained – preceded el Chapeton carrying me, and Viento Norte bringing up the rear carrying the pack-saddle.

I was riding el Chapeton exclusively at this time as he was in far better condition than Viento Norte. I weighed myself and my saddle and reckoned that total weight for the ridden horse would be 100 kilograms, which was perfect. The pack-saddle weighed nine kilos and I had, unbelievably, thirty-two kilos of kit. I started with everything: tent, sleeping bag (the superbly and aptly named 'Tangerine Dream' from North Face), cooker, books, shoeing equipment, medical kit, veterinary kit, spare Easy Glu horseshoes and a lot of other totally superfluous equipment. Still it was an improvement, as I had checked thirty-eight kilos out of Heathrow.

Viento Norte needed to build up so I thought the pack-saddle, being lighter, would be less hard work than my hulking self. Many maintain that even a light pack is harder work than a man as it wobbles around, destroying balance and equilibrium, whereas a rider always subconsciously alters his or her position to ease stress and balance. Of course, everyone argues and there is never any final agreement.

We came to the track that led off on the short cut. Juan and Pablo stepped down from the jeep and we shook hands.

'One thing, James,' said Juan, 'you should have your lasso on the right-hand side of your horse so you can grab it with your right hand.'

'Right,' I said, doing nothing.

'Do you want me to change it for you?'

'Well, someone said I should have it on the left because . . .'

Too late. He was changing it over.

We had a magical day, riding twenty kilometres to Salto Grande, a large village, where I stayed with the sister of the chief policeman. He was the biggest man I had seen in Argentina and the biggest I would see for the rest of the trip. As a caricature for a South American general or police officer he was perfect, dressed in an immaculate uniform festooned in braid, colours and medals like a Christmas tree and he never took his dark glasses off, even at night. He was very welcoming, suggesting that I put the horses in the corrals of the local feria, or cattle market. There was a bit of grass and we supplemented this with hay and grain.

His sister lived in a very smart bungalow with plenty of modern appliances, including a deliciously hot shower. I was able to take my clothes off and wash for the first time in three days. As temperatures reached 30 degrees centigrade during the day I must have stunk, and I was certainly dirty judging by the alluvial plains that formed at my feet. We had a dinner of milanesas and the old man of the house, the chief's father, gave me a whip he had made. Like a jockey's whip it was thin, well-balanced and beautifully made with interweaving leather bands covering the outside. The flap was inscribed in leather with a heart.

The local 'padre' came around after supper and, although professing to be full of food, put away the remaining milanesas, about two kilos of meat, followed by a series of diabetes-inducing matés. He played with Maria's son after his food, in what seemed to me a very unhealthy fondling manner. Still, as he was knocking ninety, they were probably the best kicks he would get.

The family were religious, and in my immaculate room I found a superb piece of religious kitsch. A plastic, 15 cm high statue of the Virgin of Lujan stood before a scenic backdrop of Lujan. From behind her trailed a flex leading to a switch. Flicking the switch, a light underneath her skirt lit up. Beneath the rosy glow of the Virgin, I dreamed of whips, hearts and Carina.

We headed off for Lazo Fuerte the following morning, well refreshed and laden with food, presents and tear- (not my own) stained cheeks. People throughout the trip cried copiously at times when we left. In or around Lazo Fuerte lived another driver whom I had met on the road. Also called Guillermo, he ran a large dairy concern and had asked us to stay the night. The going was hard as the track along the road had petered out and we were forced to plough through the rough vegetation at the side of the road. There was very little traffic, mainly dairy tankers, but they drove at great speed, and the horses were still unaccustomed to traffic. There was a strip of ground between the road and the railroad tracks along which we travelled. It was obviously intended for the future time when the government has enough money to turn the road, the major road north, into a dual carriageway. The grass on this track was knee-high and hard on the horses, or had been cleared and was under cultivation, giving soft, boggy going.

I found out a couple of days later that on the other side of the railroad was a road specifically for horse traffic. In many parts of Argentina the verge has been cleared and levelled to produce a horse and carriage lane off the tarmac and lorry path. On this lane there was little horse traffic, but the surrounding landowners were still obliged to care for it.

Guillermo met us at the entrance to Lazo Fuerte and we put the horses out in a thirty hectare field of knee-high green barley, the equestrian equivalent of being ducked into a swimming pool full of caviar, and rather daunting. The horses hung around the outside of the field, nibbling at the scrabbly bits round the wire fence. My home for the night was again an outside shed, this time full of gardening equipment.

Guillermo took me on a tour of the very impressive estate. Five dairies had been bought up and were supplying a local co-operative which was producing cheeses and dulce de leche. The central estancia house had been renovated and was surrounded by eucalyptus trees. A pale yellow colour, it had its own chapel, some lovely criollo horses in the garden and was unlived in. The proprietor lived in Rosario or Buenos Aires and came out for the weekends. Guillermo was in essence the estate manager, having recently qualified as an agricultural engineer. He was also a certificated artificial inseminator. Young and ambitious, he had introduced the latest technology to Lazo Fuerte: computers that related feed to milk quantities and fat percentages, and machinery to distribute milk straight from the tank to the tanker.

At La Baguala I often rode down to Perisini's with a man driving a horse and cart with a churn of milk on the back. At Perisini's he would wait for the tanker to arrive. The tanker driver would hoist the churn on to a platform where he would take a sample for analysis. Then he would tip the milk into the belly of his lorry and give the churn back. The cart man would trundle home to fill up for the next day.

Guillermo's tanker drivers sucked the milk straight from holding tanks without any human contact. In fact, this milk never touched human hands, going straight from the udder to the mouth. Automatic milking machines passed milk to cooling and pasteurising tanks, from where it went to the tanker to the factory to the carton to the guzzler. Guillermo gave me a barrage of figures, including the fact he had 1000 cows producing ten to twenty litres of milk per day, which totalled 15,000 litres daily (about three tankers full).

We went back to Guillermo's house, also stuck in the middle of nowhere. For a twenty-five-year-old he seemed to live a very lonely bachelor existence. During the week, he just worked, sleeping in the house which contained only a bed, a fridge and a shower, although for Argentina it was big. At the weekend, he went into Rosario for a night to meet friends and his girlfriend. But as he said, it was a great opportunity and he was hoping to get to Canada to study dairy farming – so it was worth the isolation. He gave me a cup of coffee, the only victuals in the house. I watched it cooling as I listened to his lonely babble. He stopped.

'Is there anything wrong with the coffee?' he asked, looking slightly hurt at my disregard of his culinary skills.

'No, nothing,' I said, at last able to get a word in. 'I was just wondering if you have a drop of milk.'

'Milk?' he said in amazement. 'I don't drink milk.'

'15,000 litres daily and not a drop in the house?!' We laughed until it hurt. I think I was becoming a little lonely too.

In the evening we bounced back over the internal network of dirt estancia roads in Guillermo's Ford pick-up and drove to the local town. We ate asado, but at least it was asado with a difference. In a ubiquitous Argentine country café, fronted as ever by Coca Cola or Sprite symbols and called La Estancia or something equally inspirational, we sat at a table and waited. Unlike most cafés, it lacked the scrap of paper called a menu or even anything written up on the wall. We waited. A man bustled up and asked what we wanted to drink and went off. We waited. We were talking hard about milk fat content or something, but I was hungry so it seemed as if we were waiting a long time. Our beers came. And then a waiter bustled over, bearing a huge plate of various meats: pork, beef and chicken, sausages, entrails, heart, liver, kidney. He showed it to Guillermo, who pointed to what he wanted. Then it was my turn.

Guillermo watched my plate until politely saying, 'He'll come back, James. Don't worry. He'll come back and you can order some more.' I cooled off. We were given a basket of chips and chewed our way through our plates of meat. As soon as we finished, the waiter would rush over with his tray hot from the asado and we would start again. There was one price for as much as you could eat. I thought it was an excellent system, as did my stomach. I was beginning to find meat addictive. I had grown accustomed to the size of portions, and would eat a pound of full red meat and still feel the desire for more afterwards.

The café was an all-male affair and very silent apart from the television which in *Nineteen Eighty-Four*-style intoned: 'Sugar, the kilo: 250 australes, up fifteen per cent. Maté, the kilo: five million australes . . . etc.' A new word was creeping into the news: *hambre* (hunger). The camera lingered on a pile of tomatoes and its price card which had been crossed out and rewritten several times.

Our first rest stop, after a further three days' ride, was the estancia of el Albion. A friend of George's had come to a farewell party thrown for me by George and Bridget. It had been a very lively affair thrown by Europeans, for Europeans and Argentines. We drank huge quantities of wine and champagne (Moet Chandon at $2 a bottle); there were speeches, present-giving and much bear-hugging. A very Anglo Argentine had suggested that I stay at his estancia, el Albion, where Johnny Sylvester would look after me.

The driveway to el Albion stretched for three kilometres off the main road. Two hundred-foot eucalyptus trees, bordering the drive, created a soft green tunnel leading down to the house. I came around the corner to find a man chipping golf balls with a pitching wedge. We looked at each other in mutual amazement – him at me on my two criollos, and me at him playing golf in his garden.

'Me llamo James Greenwood. Un amigo dijo que possiblemente puedo . . .'

'Hello,' the golfer cut in with a crisp British accent, 'I'm Johnny Sylvester. What can I do for you?'

I asked if I could stay and was treated with marvellous Anglo reserve. Of course I could stay and, very quietly with minimal fuss, was given the best field for my horses and a spare room in the guest house. We watched videos of cricket and golf in the evening when Johnny's wife and children returned.

The following day he showed me around the estancia which was fascinating. It was a company owned by a number of families, and run with factory efficiency. Cereal and beef cattle rotation ensured that maximum output was extracted without damaging soil content. The spectacular line of eucalyptus trees that I had so admired on the way into el Albion was in Johnny's mind a 'pest'. The shadow they cast over the adjoining fields meant less rapid growth of alfalfa and cereals and he would have 'ripped them out' if he could.

He had many interesting stories that interspersed the lectures on farming. At one point he said: 'Listen hard to what I am saying. Perhaps you will learn and communicate to others.' At that point, all facts lodged in my memory were erased and in my desperation to remember, very little stuck in my mind. Although very British sounding, Johnny had spent little time in the UK, only enough to be educated at Cirencester. I do remember, vividly, how he told me of spending time working in Hampshire for a man who had been castrated in the Second World War by the Japanese. Reeling in disgust and horror, and clutching my own balls as a safeguard, I was able to ask the crucial question: 'Did he have a squeaky voice?'

'No. As his chords had been lengthened during puberty, he already had a broken voice when they were removed,' he told me.

I spent part of the afternoon maintaining the Easy Glu shoes which were bearing up well. They are glued to the hoof by a series of ten plastic fingers that come up around the outside of the hoof wall. Every once in a while the bond between the Easy Glu shoe and the hoof wall breaks and, although the shoe is secured perfectly by the other nine, it was best to stick any loose fingers (or 'tabs') back. The job is fiddly and boring as the tab and the hoof wall have to be sanded smooth and washed with acetone before re-gluing.

We went out to dinner that night in the local town, passing the cemetery on the way in. Johnny wanted to show me the plaque on the main gate which read:

> We were what you are
> You will be what we are now

Over chicken and plenty of wine, Johnny told me another story about his life, a story that many people know, as it was the foundation of Graham Greene's *The Honorary Consul*.

Johnny's father was an Honorary Consul, living and working in Rosario for the SWIFT meat processing and packaging multinational. They lived in the town itself, and one morning Johnny was upstairs listening subconsciously to his father leaving for work. He heard his father start the car, open the gates that led to the street, and drive the car out to re-close the gates. He could hear the car engine running but was surprised that it was taking his father so long to shut the gates and drive off.

He looked out of the window on to a chilling scene. The gates were open, as was the door of his father's car. But there was no sign of his father. He knew at once what had happened and drove his father's car straight to the police station to report the kidnap.

Terrorists had abducted his father and demands were soon made. The guerrillas wanted publicity, better conditions at the SWIFT factory and free meat to be distributed to the poor.

Johnny organised the publicity, inviting television crews and journalists round to the house to interview his mother. He demanded that the camera crews all plug into the mains for their power, and the interviews commenced. Johnny himself sat by the mains switch as unofficial censor. As he said, 'If they looked as if they were going to ask my mother anything untoward – flick. They lost their power.'

SWIFT met the demands of improved conditions and free meat and Johnny's father was released, to be received as a national hero in the UK and fêted with an OBE and at a Buckingham Palace Garden Party.

The rest and our pampering from the Sylvester family did us a lot of good. I was wearing clean clothes for the first time as we left el Albion. The land was flat, green brown and the trail stretched northwest, never wavering in its straightness. Dairy cattle and crops crowded our dirt track.

We arrived in Casas, our first day out from el Albion, and went straight to the police station. I tied the horses to a tree outside and went in to talk to the comisarío. There was a boarding house in town, and he fixed me up with a chaperone, Juan. Juan was obviously the police station dogsbody, brewing maté, doing a spot of cleaning and running errands. He was a wealthy man, judging by his house which he took me to, but I think he worked in the police station because he liked the gossip and the occasional crimes.

'How occasional are they, Juan?' I asked.

'Oh, we don't have much crime here. The odd case of rustling but that's about it. What are you doing tonight? There is a fiesta.'

'Going to the fiesta. What's it for?'

He fished in his memory. 'I don't know. I'll see you at 7 pm back here.'

He had a most impressive collection of key rings. 'Two hundred and forty-eight,' his wife told me. Coca Cola, Disneyland, 'I [heart] New York'; they had the lot. I remembered I still had my Rover key ring knocking about, and handed it over.

'It's from a British car,' I said proudly.

At the guesthouse I was treated like a guest. The lady of the house started my shower and put some bedside reading in my room: a pamphlet entitled 'God saves'.

The fiesta was in one of the boliches and was starting when I arrived. I ordered a wine for Juan and a whisky for myself, a brand called 'Breeder's Choice'.

'Whisky?' said Juan.

'Yes. The British love whisky.'

We sat at a long table, thirty men in all. The village elders, deaf old men, sat at one end and everyone ranked themselves accordingly down the table. I was put about third from the bottom.

The proprietor of the boliche had barbecued a whole pig and huge slabs of wet, white meat were brought in to be consumed with wine, bread, salad and a hot green sauce.

'What's the fiesta for?' I asked my neighbour.

'We are celebrating the Malvinas being Argentine.'

'Oh.'

'Where are you from?'

'France,' I said calmly.

'Hey, Juan,' shouted my neighbour to Juan who ranked about sergeant on the table and was half-way up. 'You are clever bringing a Frenchman. The French and the British have always fought.'

'Yes,' shouted Juan back down the table. 'But my French friend drives a British car and drinks whisky like a Britannico.' He waved at me, smiled and slowly closed one eye in a meaningful wink.

'What did you think of the Malvinas war, Francés?' asked someone else.

I paused. 'I thought it was a politicians' war, stupid, a waste.'

'Down with the politicians, eh, Francés?' he said, raising his glass.

We downed one to the downing of politicians.

I was subjected to a barrage of questions. It was rather like sitting in an echo chamber. One of my neighbours would ask a question, say, 'How many horses do you have?' I would say 'Two' and then would hear, 'He has two horses,' 'Two horses,' 'He's got two horses' as the message was passed up the table to the chiefs. There was obviously one seriously deaf old Field Marshal at the end as I would hear 'Two horses, he's got two horses,' bellowed very loudly at the end of the chain.

Often there would be a return as I could hear, 'Where's he going?' gathering in strength like an incoming wave as the question was passed down the table. I would say 'Cañada tomorrow' (a sneaky drop shot), and off it would go, sometimes beating the opposition as they had forgotten their top-spin question by the time the return arrived.

At about one set all, everyone got down to drinking and knocking-up with their neighbours and I was left in peace for a while. Slightly drunk, I felt wonderful: surrounded by the babble of a foreign language, stuffed full of food and having successfully negotiated a tricky moment.

'French,' I thought. 'I'm French now.' I had started saying to Argentines that I was Scottish as (a) it was true, and (b) I thought it would take some of the sting out of possible conflict. This seemed a good idea until someone reminded me that several Scottish regiments had fought in the Falklands War with a ferocity that had poured terror into the heart of many an Argentine conscript.

People in Britain had asked me about being in Argentina so soon (if seven years is soon) after the 1982 war. I had replied naïvely that I thought there would be no problem. I was always treated with great hospitality, generosity and even respect when I said I was British. In my naïvety I had guessed rightly that Argentine spirit would have overcome a national fiasco, leaving little bitterness behind.

We left Juan and his cronies to travel on towards the Harveys at Las Limpias, about 180 kilometres into the trip. Another Anglo-Argentine family, they were the end of the road in terms of contacts. I had breezed along from Rosario to Las Limpias on a wave of confidence and the backs of many supporters. I knew that the Harveys would look after me, but once I left Las Limpias I would be on my own.

The horses were going well, and the saddles were fitting without problems, although I had cinched up Viento Norte's girth too tightly. Like a tight sock round an ankle, it had carved a groove in the fat of his belly.

Michael Harvey, a large man in his early thirties, met us at a certain eucalyptus tree. We had arrived early, so I had taken off all the tack and bags, staked the horses and was asleep in the sun when he arrived. He stepped down from his ropy pick-up and came towards me with his hand extended.

'James Greenwood, I presume.'

'Yeah. Pleased to meet you.'

It was an absurd scene: two men talking English meet by a eucalyptus tree in the wide, wide pampa. We loaded the gear into the pick-up, and he gave me directions to the estancia house.

I climbed on Viento Norte, riding bareback, and we cantered slowly after Michael's disappearing pick-up, me holding el Chapeton's lead rope in my hand. It was great to canter for the first time, mainly having walked from the start of the trip to conserve energy. I felt like one of those open-top car drivers, who waits all winter for the first sign of sun to lower the top and lord it over the other suckers who are less flash than he is. All went well, cantering comfortably, until el Chapeton saw a bogey and stopped suddenly. Unfortunately, I was holding his rope too tightly and Viento Norte was continuing forwards. The dirt track had not received rain for months and had been baked hard. I landed with a crash and my hip attempted to bury itself in the dirt. The track was bordered by a wire fence each side and so as I was separating the horses, they stopped and waited. If they had been together they would have gone, but luckily they stood watching each other, and me lying on the ground.

It really hurt. I had knocked the wind out of my lungs and was shocked. That instant of a blow, of pain, hits your very soul. You are cruising along, fine, alive, and an accident happens. It hurts, but worse, for a split second, you see how distinctly mortal you are.

Somehow, in the fall, I ripped my bombachas and the inside part of both legs fell away as I stood up. My boxers were also torn and I rapidly inspected myself for serious damage. Fine – phew. The horses looked very sheepish as I caught them up, and they walked cautiously after me as I led them down the road.

We still had a few kilometres to go before arriving at Las Limpias and I limped along. My bombachas were getting more and more in the way of my legs and eventually I took them off and walked almost naked down the road. I was very embarrassed when I arrived at the estancia, as unexpectedly a very beautiful woman came out of the house to welcome me – Iris Harvey, Michael's wife. I turned puce and clamped the remains of the bombachas to my groin as we said hello.

Although smelly, roughly-shaven and semi-naked I was made to feel at home. We put the horses into a field and went into the modern two-bedroomed house set among eucalyptus trees. Michael's parents lived down the road in the big house. We had a delicious dinner of pumpkins, potatoes and pork, a great change from standard fare, and watched *The Wild Geese* on the video. It seemed strange that in many houses the video had come before the telephone: Michael was connected to local people by a CB radio.

We talked about Wimbledon and I told them how I had watched Becker playing on television in the last town, before turning off to Las Limpias. I had been early and was trying to waste time before our meeting by the eucalyptus tree. I had gone to the offices of Entel, the national telephone company, to ring Carina but had been unable to get through, so rode back to a bar I had seen. With the horses tied outside in the plaza, I drank beer and ate toasted ham and cheese sandwiches, while watching the television. When I returned outside I found a crowd formed around the horses, and I was asked the usual barrage of questions:

'Where do you come from?'

'Where are you going to?'

'What nationality?'

'What are the horses called? How old?'

As I got up on to the horses and wheeled them away, the crowd of about fifty people started clapping and cheering. I waved royally and left.

My visa was coming to the end of its three month limit and I had been told I would have to leave the country and come back again to receive another three months. Michael said that he could keep the horses for a few days so I decided to head for Uruguay, to the east.

It was awful and I hated Montevideo. Travelling in from the airport, the place seemed to be alight as fires and smoke clouded the road. I was centred in the downtown area (not a good representation of any city, like saying Times Square or Piccadilly are representative of New York and London). It was full of money exchange houses, cinemas and video arcades. I wandered around feeling like a participant in a battle between the Uruguayans and the tourists, who seemed to hunt in pairs on a buddy-buddy system. I knew no one and no one wanted to know me, so I watched one film after another – four in one afternoon.

I took the ferry instead of the plane back to Buenos Aires and at customs they told me I had to renew my visa in an office 200 yards up from the port. I could have done so immediately without leaving the country. I could not believe my stupidity and gullibility in believing the official who had said I had to leave the country. I had totally wasted three days.

As I hitch-hiked back towards Santa Fe, picked up by (according to other sources) the main Argentine nuclear-materials buyer, I realised how much I liked the flat-lands of Santa Fe, the friendliness of the people, and travelling by horse. I was glad to be back but wrote, in confusion, in my diary the next day: 'I am worried about this book, not sure that I can really relate what happened, what I heard, saw and felt. Sometimes I feel bitter about where I am and what I am doing. I envy people with their normal lives. Living with the Harveys has made me jealous of their easy happy home life. Why could I not stay at home, work, settle, marry and have children? What else do I want?'

We spent a further rest day at Las Limpias and I re-glued the Easy Glu horseshoes. I was worried that they needed so much maintenance; time that when travelling I could not afford, although el Chapeton's feet were improving daily. I played with Michael's daughter, Jennifer, and talked to Iris when he was out working. Iris had lovely hazel-green eyes that with her soft mushy Argentine accent drove straight into me. I envied Michael, although like many of the Anglo-Argentines I met, he allowed himself to be bossed around by his wife in a rather un-Latin way.

We left the following day at about ten o'clock setting off into dense mist. A lone bull rumbled out and we passed each other warily on the damp dirt track. A flag-poled building materialised and I presumed it was a local comisaría, although I was surprised to see seven or eight horses parked outside. It was, in fact, the local school. I could hear the children calling out their times tables led by their master, as their horses waited patiently outside to take them home for lunch.

We seemed to lose our way and wandered around in the fog. In fact, we did not really blunder as there was a comprehensive network of dirt roads that ran parallel and at right-angles to each other. Bordered by wire fences they took you in any direction you wanted to go.

The horses slept that night in the scrap yard of a man called Juan Carlos. I had difficulty finding somewhere for them, and as the light failed I was getting pretty desperate. Juan Carlos came up in his truck and started asking questions: 'Where are you going?' 'Where have you come from?' etc.

I was tired and rude to him, but he ignored this and offered the yard, full of the carcases of dead vehicles. In my fifty cents a night hotel, I worried about 'the boys' cutting themselves in the yard. I need not have worried as the next day I found el Chapeton plucking grass from the engine of an old Ford-T and Viento Norte inside the shell of a Leyland bus.

Worry became a feature of my life for a few days: speed, the possibility of saddle sores, my equipment, the slog, and traffic all circled in my head incessantly. On the one hand, I was doing what I had set out to do and was loving the physical process of riding along flat, easy, open land on two beautiful horses in twenty-five degrees sunshine. On the other hand, I felt cut off from the parameters and measuring sticks that in a way had started the whole process; the normal-ness of everyday life, the unexciting lifestyle of a nine to five job, the claustrophobia of London and of my own country. And in an Anglo-Saxon way, I felt guilty that I was no longer part of these. I had wanted to 'do something', an aim that was woolly and vague and that now I was doing it, seemed to have taken me lower – to being a bum on a pointless mission. I missed Carina without reservation. I could only go on.

We stopped in the village of Km 501, a village 501 kilometres by rail from Buenos Aires. It straddled the track and appeared uninhabited on my arrival. I tied up the horses and poked around the house at the entrance to the village. Deserted. But as I went back to the horses I saw the grass move on the other side of the track and spied three peeping faces that ran off when I shouted hello.

We crossed over the tracks and I found Ignacio, a sad man with intensely blue eyes. He asked me in for a maté and told me his story. His family had once owned all the land in the area but through mismanagement, living well and the economy he had been forced to sell the land to 'a middle-class family of graspers'. He still owned the old house and lived, breeding a few pigs, in relative poverty. He said that the 'graspers' would be able to help us.

I rode along to their house and did my spiel.

'Yes, hello. My name is James Greenwood and, recreating the journey of Tschiffely, I am riding two horses . . .'

'What do you want?' said a fat man of twenty-five or so.

'Well, I need help for the night and Ignacio said you would be able to help me. I need a corral, some pasture for my horses and, of course, I can pay.'

'Can't help you,' he said, turning his back. 'Go back to Ignacio.'

'Well he said you owned all the land here.'

Grudgingly, he turned back and said: 'We do. Go back to Ignacio.'

'No room in the inn here,' I thought, and turned back to ask Ignacio's advice.

'You can stay here,' he said, obviously upset at the landowner's response, indicating a patch of grass for the horses around the outside loo. We cornered off the loo and the horses, and he showed me where I could doss down for the night.

There followed an incident which was comic yet sad. Ignacio's son brought out an incredibly ancient Ford to drive me 200 yards to the third house in the village, lived in by a friend of Ignacio's. Ignacio, for some reason, walked carrying two heavy buckets of pigswill. I protested that I could walk, and Ignacio should come in the car with his buckets. Embarrassed for some reason, he said, 'No. No. Go in the car,' and walked off. I felt like some absurd dignitary as I was driven for thirty seconds down the bumpy track.

Ignacio's friend was even poorer than Ignacio but had killed a chicken in my honour, and I was treated like a lord by these nut-brown, weather-beaten-faced people who had very little. The chicken was tasteless, having been boiled, and we sat eating around a small table lit by a kerosene hurricane lamp that the fair-skinned. wife continually had to pump. We had little to talk about and every time the conversation died, the party would pipe up: 'James, eat. Take more. Eat, eat,' and another bone would be piled on my plate. We drank the beers that I had bought, and drove home. Ignacio drove and his son walked.

Leaving Ignacio was sad; he was such a sad man, sinking lower every day, living out his life with the crumbling remainder of his estancia, and breeding pigs. He seemed to have no purpose, he was going nowhere, a position to me that seemed an anathema, horrific and frightening.

A strong north wind was blowing and for the first time I understood why it was called the Madman's Wind. The day as usual was hot, a dry heat that was normally comfortable, more so when cooled by winds from the south, east and west. The north wind only exacerbated the heat. The harder it blew, the hotter the horses and I became. We were riding into its fetid breath and my body seemed unable to cope with both the wind and the rising temperature. The horses became edgy and I felt very frustrated, full of excess energy. I was riding Viento Norte, who was weaving from side to side, snorting and shielding his head from the wind, which picked up particles of dust and hurled them into our eyes. El Chapeton was tied on the back of my saddle or so I thought, until I looked around to check him and was astonished to see a blank space where he should have been. Back down the track I saw a distant speck and cantered back to catch him. He stood there looking gormless as we rode up to him, and allowed me to bend down and scoop up his lead rope. I tied it on tightly so that it would not slip away again and we retraced the last kilometre. I looked around again and there he was, looking up at me questioningly as if to say, 'I'm still here, aren't I?' He was, but his pack-saddle had slipped.

Another small wooded track led off ours, so I pulled in to shelter from the wind and to readjust the saddle. I jumped down from Viento Norte and went back to el Chapeton without untying him from Viento Norte's saddle. They both grazed and I worked on el Chapeton's pack-saddle – until Viento Norte spooked. I saw immediately what would happen and lunged for Viento Norte's bridle. I was too late as he was already picking up speed, and I only managed to grab a stirrup. I tried to reach forward but he was breaking into a canter. My legs were going like crazy but I was being dragged by the stirrup. My pace became larger and larger. The canter became a gallop, and I was covering twenty yards with each stride until eventually I fell to the ground. El Chapeton, still attached to Viento Norte, just steamed over me from behind.

I picked myself up to see the sight that depresses a horseman most: a departing horse arse. These departing arses were not only my transport but also carried my money, passport, papers, tent, sleeping bag, stove, medical kit, plastic horseshoes – and my very *raison d'être*. As I followed them I thought, 'I am supposed to be riding horses through South America but here I am running'. Further thoughts of death, mutilation and having to return to London crossed my mind. They became more acute when I started to find my kit in the long grass of the disused track – my sleeping bag, twenty yards later my tent, fifty yards on my sunglasses and calling cards. By now I was very frightened as I thought that the pack-saddle would have slipped under el Chapeton's belly, which would have terrified him beyond equine comprehension, and he would gallop and gallop until I found him lying on the ground wrapped in girths, traces, Viento Norte and broken legs.

I came out of the avenue of trees to a crossroad and stopped.

'Oh no, now where?' I wailed, half-crying out loud.

A flash of movement in the distance caught my eye. I went straight on. Another kilometre or so, another crossroads. By this stage I was sweating like the Iguazu Falls and puffing like the Iron Rooster. I was also on the verge of tears, the nightmares of horses' broken legs having become worse.

At this crossroads there was no sign of life at all. I could make out the eucalyptus trees exclamation marking the location of farms, a few cows, but no horses and no kit. I looked at the packed-down dirt road surface and could see scuffle marks where the horses had obviously stopped for a few seconds. I got down on my hands and knees to decipher them more clearly. They led off to the right so I checked the other two directions to see if they all had similar marks. No, they had turned right at this junction and, as far as I could see, were still together.

Off I went, each time checking the prints at crossroads, crosschecking and following them. It took a further five kilometres and another hour and a half to catch up with the horses who were tied to some rails in a farmer's yard. El Chapeton was still attached to Viento Norte's saddle, the pack-saddle had remained upright (which was encouraging) and they both seemed fine. As I was checking them over, a strange selection of giants came out of the house. They were big, really big; obviously a father and his three sons.

The father wore traditional bombachas and shirt, as did one of the sons. Another was dressed as a cowboy with full regalia, and the other looked like a 'house' freak, being extremely colourful. They told me they were all dairy farmers, and while tidying up before lunch had seen the horses coming down the lane towards their house. They had stopped and caught them and were now eating their lunch.

'Would you like some?' they asked.

'No thanks,' I said, 'but I would love a cold drink of something.'

A half-litre glass of water was brought out and I quaffed three-quarters of it before I realised it was in fact wine. It was too late to do anything about it but finish it off. I handed the glass back to the Village People clones, thanked them profusely for their hospitality and speed in catching the horses, and set off. I was so pissed that I laughed for most of the two hours into San Francisco.

San Francisco is a large provincial town, about 300 kilometres from Rosario, within the province of Córdoba which stretches away to the west of Argentina and towards the Andes. We rudely interrupted a football game by walking across and laying turds on the pitch, and rode down the main drag to the amusement of what seemed to be most of the 70,000 inhabitants, when we met Señor Peroni who stepped down from his Ford jeep in full 'criollo' gear. We greeted each other and he asked me where I was going, who I knew there, and if I would like him to fix us up.

'Yes, of course.'

'Well follow me.'

So I followed his jeep to the Sociedad Rural where he rapidly organised a corral and feed. He dropped me off at a hotel. I had a luxurious bath before taking a cab to the Post Office to call Carina. In mildly clean clothes I felt almost normal again and it was good, oh so good, to talk to Carina.

Sñr Peroni had invited me around for dinner that night and we ate a pig between us, cooked by his very fat and very beautiful wife. She was so fat and so kind that I wanted to be hugged by her. Her son, aged fifteen, still spent much of his time sitting on her lap. She cooked and smiled and loved Sñr Peroni, who told me the following joke:

An Englishman walks into a boliche and orders a beer in Spanish. A gaucho in the bar leans over and says in Spanish. 'How long have you been in Argentina, Señor?'

Englishman (speaking Spanish): 'About a month.'

Argentine: 'And what are you doing here?'

Englishman: 'Well, I am looking for land to buy in order to settle down.'

Argentine: 'You speak good Spanish for one so recently arrived. What is your secret?'

Englishman (pleased to be complimented) turns round with a smile and says: 'The secret is committing 100 words to memory. I have them stored here (tapping his head) in my arse.'

We watched a Kung Fu video, to me one of the lowest forms of entertainment: a minimal storyline takes the viewer from one session of gratuitous whirling-round-and-kicking-out-with-both-feet sequence to another. I said that I was going to bed but the boyfriend of one of Peroni's daughters insisted that we all go out for the night. We ended up drinking beer in expensive cafés. Sergio, the boyfriend, had piggy eyes and a goatee beard and from a six-inch range shouted as slowly and as loudly as he could into my face. His conversation eventually wore me down, and when I could stand the constant questions no more I left. My diary that night records such gems as: 'Tomorrow is a blank canvas', and 'Tear down the comfort and barricades of the upper-middle classes'.

We had our first proper rest in San Francisco. The horses ate hay and grain supplied by Sñr Peroni and I wandered about the centre buying basic supplies and eating and drinking expensive coffees and ham and cheese toasted sandwiches in the smart café that bordered the square.

I re-shod the horses with the help of the Sociedal Rural blacksmith, and decided that it would be more interesting if I changed Viento Norte over to steel shoes, keeping el Chapeton in the Easy Glus. This, I thought, would allow comparisons to be made in terms of shoe endurance and foot care. El Chapeton played up a great deal, bucking and bouncing around the shoeing area, with whoever was holding his feet being whipped around like a fly on the end of a fishing rod. We put on a twitch, had someone hold his head and took it in turns to hold up the foot to be balanced for the Easy Glu application. I saw for the first time the extraordinary strength that he had for such a small horse. When he got really bored with the proceedings he would break free and toss us about as if we were made of paper.

Blacksmiths in Argentina vary greatly in their knowledge and skill, as they do in the UK, although the disparities there are greater. There is no system comparable to that in Britain where all farriers must undergo a lengthy training and apprenticeship period. The good farriers are, however, very good and operate with a team of low-paid accomplices. The system enables them to work freely and easily. In Britain a farrier works alone, and therefore is required to lift the foot, maintain its height and its steadiness, while working to balance it and fix the shoe. It is a back-breaking job. In Argentina, the farrier will sometimes have four helpers: one to hold the foot, one to hold the horse's head, one to tend the fire and one, like a nurse in an operating theatre, to hand over the tools when demanded.

San Francisco struck me as a pretty boring place – wealthy, middle-class and conservative – falling between the cultural centres of Córdoba and Rosario. The centre, the shops, the streets were bland in look and output. It was a pretty rapid diagnosis since I only spent two days in the town, but I was certainly ready to leave. My one sadness in leaving was saying goodbye to the Peroni family who had invited me round for every meal. We talked about Britain, Argentina, 'The War', music, politics and had a particularly heated argument the final night about homosexuality and drug abuse. Señor Peroni's argument was that homosexuals and drug abusers were bad, malicious and vicious sectors of society that should be wiped out through hard-line punishment policies. I was taking the liberal approach.

Hungover, the both of us, he escorted me on his horse from the Sociedad Rural to the exit from San Francisco. He scribbled some names of friends who lived further along my route, we drank some matés, and said goodbye. The weather had clouded over and drizzled, creating a watery Ready-Brek skin around myself and the horses. We passed a one horse town, miles from anywhere, paddling around the plaza, and a cemetery; and stopped in Luxardo for lunch. Grudgingly, from a huge store, totally out of proportion to the size of the village, I was sold cheese, salami, bread and Coca Cola.

I sat on the step making slabby sandwiches until the horses, restless from our halt in San Francisco, became entangled with each other, the ropes and the tree. I walked across the road and untangled them, returning to find that my lunch had been eaten by a couple of dogs. It was replaced for free by the owner of the dogs, the shop-owner, far less grudgingly than when I had bought it.

Twenty kilometres on we came to and stopped at Freyre, where the horses ate hay in the feria. I returned with my kit to the one and only hotel, and having gone to bed at 4 am the night before, crashed into a deep sleep. I was awoken by rustling in the room, and for a second I thought I had died and gone to heaven. Staring down at me were rows and rows of cherubic faces dressed in white. As I opened my eyes, they all smiled at me. I shut my eyes and opened them again. The faces were still there.

My brain push-started into life and on closer inspection I realised that the angels were schoolchildren. They had heard that a gringo had ridden into town on two horses and had come into my room for a closer inspection. I shut my eyes again and then with a mighty heave, I leaped off the bed with my arms open wide, yelling at the top of my voice. Whoosh, the door slammed and they were gone. I leaned out into the passage and called them back, saying I was only kidding.

They trooped back into my room and the barrage of questions started:

'What are you called?'

'Where are you from?'

'How old are you?'

I was waiting for one question in particular always, asked by children, and, yes, wait, here it came:

'Do you have a girlfriend?' Giggles and red faces all around.

Eventually they got bored and most left, but two girls of about eight or nine stayed behind.

'Yes?' I said as they looked around and out of the door to see that all their friends had gone.

'Well, yes,' said the slightly older. 'Do you have anything from your country? Like a postcard or something? We want a reminder of your visit.'

I felt flattered and fished out one of my hand-outs and gave it to them. They gave it back. 'Oh no,' I thought, mortified. 'That's all I've got.'

'Will you sign it?' they said, to my relief and soothed ego.

I flourished the pen, did some extra underlining, added a few superfluous dots to my signature and handed the sheet back.

'Brilliant,' said one to the other. 'We should be able to sell this for a fortune. Say, 400 australes.'

'No,' said the other. (They seemed to have forgotten my existence in the room.) 'I've got a better idea. We'll photocopy this for ten australes a time and sell copies for twenty australes. Ten australes profit for each copy and *then* we'll sell the original.'

She remembered me. 'Señor, you won't give one of those to anyone else, will you?' she said in a threatening voice.

'I might,' I said. 'Depends on how much they offer,' and laughed.

They were not at all amused and left scowling.

I had a pretty dull political evening in the house of the local vet, a very kind man called Dr Susa. We had an asado in the garden, which took a long time to cook and a great deal of argument. The problems of Argentina were apparent to all: reliance on primary products, backward infrastructure, poor services (especially telephone), rocketing inflation and capital flight. There is, of course, also the problem of massive overseas debt.

Politics and the state of the economy were taken extremely seriously when I was in Argentina. For the upper classes, it involved big business and highly profitable gambling on inside information. For the middle classes, these subjects were almost a sport and I spent many hours listening to discussions on interest rates and dollar fluctuations.

'Hear the dollar's up to 440.'

'Yeah, I sold at 310 but I think it's going down so I'm buying back in.'

'Depends on export figures this month.'

'Yeah, but prices are low,' etc . . .

I did not expect to find the sort of conversation I was used to from the City in London conducted in bars in the centre of the Argentine pampas.

A man who didn't really fall into any class, being a middle-class polo player, looked after me in the town of Brinkmann. He was Israel Lissi, retired ex-cavalry officer, working in Brinkmann as a sort of up-market managerial squire in the feria. I was introduced to him by another vet friend of Sñr Peroni. He was dressed immaculately in the gear of a gaucho: bombachas, boots, spurs and coin-studded belt. A major difference between Israel and a gaucho was the fact that every stitch was perfect, every crease sharp and there was not a speck of dust to be seen. He gave off that slightly vacant, sharp, useless look of a cavalry officer. He was also head of the *Agruppadacion Gauchos Jorge Cafrine*, a club aiming to preserve the criollo life of horses, guitars and the pampa in the memory of the folksinger Jorge Cafrine, who died in the 1970s when a truck hit his horse. Israel told me in a hushed voice that it was a political killing but did not explain further.

We put up the horses outside the casatario, the club house of the gaucho group, and went inside to have a few matés. Israel had a kid of fifteen as a sidekick who was despatched to collect meat, wine and bread for an asado. Israel explained the odd tower, under which the horses were grazing. He said that in days gone by, similar towers had been built from scarce timber, in which to mount guards on a constant lookout for marauding Indians and 'banditos'. Ensconsed in the candle-lit room, furnished with period antiques, pictures of Jorge Cafrine and placards bearing messages such as 'Never lend your horse, your wife or your guitar', it all seemed faintly ridiculous for grown men still to be playing Cowboys and Indians.

The vet in Brinkmann, Dr Lunghi, was employed predominantly by the main employer of the area, La Piedmontesa meat factory. Founded by Italians, emigrating from the area of Piemonte, it dealt with the slaughter of 100 pigs daily, producing salamis, frankfurters, hams and other assorted products. Initially, the factory struck me as being very archaic. We entered the first room after the killing room and I was surprised to see that the factory was still lit by gas lamps that shot out a stream of fire. Seeing my amazement, Lunghi explained that the lamps were actually hair burners used to remove hair from the pig carcases. The rest of the factory seemed very modern using the latest North American technology such as chainsaws on mobile platforms. One machine I liked particularly was a frankfurter gun. Frankfurters were made in one huge long skin. The machine sucked up this enormous sausage, cut and crimped individual frankfurters and spat them out into a waiting paddling pool at the rate of five per second.

I was introduced to the directors, given a plate of products to eat and a package to take away. They also gave me a coloured brochure of their products. Against well lit photographs of hams and salamis were descriptions in Spanish, German and English. I recorded a few in my diary word for word:

Large Sausage: Among standard cold-meat it's one of the best know because it's manufactured with selected meat and using the most advance technology during elaboration so as latest machinery. A regulated and adjusted coction makes possible a terminal product whose organoleptic characteristics are unmistakeable. If we put to afore-mentioned the ways of displaying we'll surely succeed in the most exigent market.

Fantasy: A 'white called' cold meat made of beef and pork meat, with bacon fat and retches: it's put into a veal rectilium which gives it a particular displaying. For tasty to palate.

Cooked Chine, Foreleg and Ham: These are authentic products because they're exclusively made of each pork pice without any special addition except that necessary for achieving sweet-smeeling and inimitable flavour. Manufactured from selected raw stuff they go through a coction process.

Piedmontese Salami in Pork Fat: Manufactured according to the best home-made methods and inimitable Italian tradition, Piedmontese salami has an exceptional quality in every one of its componentes, with a sweet fragrance which turns it into a worthy product. Stuffed into a natural casing, enwrapped in cellophane paper and vacuum-packed, the slight-liness and perfect fastening of slices spear-head among similar salami offered by carnivalship.

I loved the idea of 'carnivalship' and laughed so much in the hotel where I had a chance to read it that the hotel proprietor came to see if I was suffering.

A few kilometres further on, we spent a couple of days in Morteros, a large provincial town with a number of industries including the Sancor factory – the largest factory producing dried milk in South America. I suppose if we had been in the USA there would have been a sign saying something like 'Welcome to Morteros – home of dried milk', but as we cantered along the verge that bent off the main road towards the Sociedad Rural, there was nothing.

The Sociedad Rural had agreed to put up me and the horses, and had invited along a local camera crew to give themselves a bit of publicity.

'And why are you staying at the Sociedal Rural?' I was asked.

'Well, um . . .'

'Is it because you see the Sociedad Rural as the centre of the agricultural district?'

'Er yes . . . I suppose so.'

'Is it because you support the conducting and the dissemination of research to the local farmers?'

'Yes and because . . .'

'Is it because you see agriculture as the backbone of Argentina's economy?'

'Yes.'

'Thank you, Mr Greenwood.'

82

The interview was over and I went off to organise myself and the horses. The concierge, whose name as far as I could make out was Nicola, showed me where I could sleep and we pondered on a place for the horses. In the end we elected to put them in the showing ring and I blocked off all the entrances with my girths. In the barn was a bar and I decided to sleep on that. The prices for wine, whisky and soft drinks were still chalked up on a blackboard, below which I slept.

My mentor during our stay in Morteros was another vet called Gustavo Monzi. He organised for me to be shown around the milk factory. Processing 600,000 litres of milk per day, it required only six men to work on each shift. Gustavo also took me into Morteros, which I had seen the night before when I gave a talk to the English class of a very frustrated teacher. She was obviously bright and intelligent, but her husband was having an affair with one of the girls who worked in his stationery store. She seemed to regard me as some kind of guiding intellectual and cultural light as I came from outside Argentina and particularly from outside her community.

Morteros reminded me of my boarding school where everyone had their own space or cell and knew each other's business intimately. There was a pecking order into which people categorised themselves; and basic tolerance of each other's presence. Many revelled in the comfort, security and friendliness of the community. But every once in a while there was a 'wildcard' like Martha, the teacher, who should have left and gone away to Buenos Aires, but who had stayed, stuck kicking the walls, making herself and others unhappy. If she had been male she would have had more opportunities for self-expression, but she had chosen to ignore and fight off most South American women's route to self-expression: the home, family and community – and influence within these.

I spent most of my time with Gustavo, his family and the horses, who became a major attraction. Often I would come back to the Sociedad Rural to find that parents had brought down their children to look at the horses as an outing. Gustavo's family was close-knit and very welcoming. One superb meal after another was produced and we talked and talked. His sons had been brought up to talk, to be seen and heard, and were eloquent and inquisitive. As if I were one of his sons, Gustavo would explain Argentine history to me. How Peron had used the dollars and gold, acquired from selling meat to both sides during the Second World War, to finance a boom time for the Argentine people. He had undertaken massive infrastructure works, improvement of working class conditions; had bought out foreign investments such as the loss-making rail industry; and had spent huge sums which had gradually whittled away the accumulated wealth by the time of the coup against him.

'The wealth had gone,' said Gustavo, 'but worse happened, because for ten years under Peron the Argentine people became used to having their daily bread provided. Many are still fighting for the belief that the state should pay. We are still fighting to recreate an ethic of work.'

It was a view that I had heard from many. Argentines do not like working. Any Argentine will tell you this, referring to his neighbours rather than to himself. From my impressions I would disagree. When Argentines work, which is often, they work with a concentration and determination that is impressive. The problem, which they are trying to iron out, is that they work alone, sometimes against each other's aims and without any collective spirit.

I enjoyed talking to Gustavo. Being treated as a surrogate son, I enjoyed escaping from the expedition and being wrapped in a cosy family atmosphere. Families always treated me well and were perfect models of domestic bliss, as I am sure tensions and friction that beset every family were buried on my account.

The horses were well and enjoyed their stay in Morteros, denuding the show ring of most of its vegetation and talking to their visitors. El Chapeton was particularly interested in the people and would nose around their pockets, their possessions and their children. Ever so gently, he would check them out and the chance that they were carrying edibles. Viento Norte was still afraid of humans and would stand back at a respectable distance.

Although we had been doing about thirty to thirty-five kilometres daily they were in excellent condition and I decided that we would speed things up.

All went well, until during a fifty kilometre day, the pack-saddle rubbled a two centimetre circle of hair off el Chapeton's back. I was staying with another family of vets in San Guillermo, the Tassos, and Raquel Tasso gave me some cream to put on. I decided to give it a day's rest but was not worried as the patch was so small and only the hair was lost. Juan Andreas Tasso took me show jumping and I was surprised to find myself scared by the jumps.

I realised that I was actually generally afraid at the time. During the expedition planning I had answered questions about the risks of the trip as if they were an abstract idea. Now they were real, and I was afraid of failing, of failing the people who had helped me and afraid of returning to London with no job, no money and no book.

Juan Andreas was a strong talker and very proud of his community. He showed me everything from the vintage Chevrolet to the most expensive car for sale in San Guillermo; the bus station to the local hairdresser who won awards in national competitions. As we wandered around the town, I could hear speakers at full volume in the plaza. It was an omnipresent feeling as the disembodied voice rang across the roofs. Juan Andreas explained that it was the local media, a microphone rigged up to some speakers. It played music, messages, news and advertising to the local people and there was no way that it could be switched off. It struck me as Big Brotherish but it was the sound rather than the content that was uncomfortable.

It was pouring with rain when we left San Guillermo and we slid out of town. The dirt tracks became very treacherous, as the rain softened the top layer of looser grit into a slimy mud that lubricated the harder, compacted bed to the road. The pack-saddle slipped on el Chapeton and I could not be bothered to get off Viento Norte and fix it in the rain. The ground was worse under my own feet than the horses'. When I did stop, the saddle had rubbed off more of el Chapton's hair and I sought refuge in a village where I put the horses in the fields of a dairy farmer. As I trudged back to the hotel in the village, I cursed my stupidity in rubbing off more of el Chapeton's hair and wondered what I should do.

The hotel was magnificent for a village of its size, and for Argentina generally. It was new and contained ten rooms. Most villages in Sante Fe and Córdoba had closed their hotels as roads improved and travellers could pass straight through. I was still the only guest at the hotel and used enough hot water for the ten non-existent guests.

'When in doubt, eat', would be a good motto for many Argentinians. Eating is a national pastime. Thirty minutes' wait before seeing someone in the centre of town? No problem – go and eat a meal. Meet a friend by chance, what to do? Go and eat a meal. I was in serious doubt about el Chapeton's back so I went and ate empanadas (small pasties), roast chicken and peaches with dulce de leche, washed down with beer, followed by whisky – and I had my solution.

We were going to travel light. It had been bugging me from the very start of the trip that it took an hour to an hour and a half to saddle in the morning. The pack-saddle took up seventy-five per cent of that time and I had yet to use the tent, sleeping bag, cooker and other assorted gear. I always looked for a village or estancia in which to spend the night, for food for the horses, food for myself, better security and companions.

The next morning, I dumped the pack-saddle and saddle bags. I felt an uplifting of spirits similar to that physical floating when you take off a heavy rucksack. We set off late and covered a few kilometres before the sun set, and without the pack-saddle were able to canter, trot and joggle.

My bed I had under the saddle – two pieces of thin foam rubber and a poncho – and on top I carried myself, the clothes I was wearing, basic veterinary and medical kits, spare Easy Glus and a file. On my body I wore a knife, a money belt with cash, traveller's cheques, papers and my Walkman. The horses had two headcollars, a leading rope and a hobble between them.

A few days later we were in the flat-lands and salt-lands near to the border between the provinces of Santa Fe and Santiago del Estero. I was in a particularly happy mood as I thought there were going to be less mosquitoes. The day before, our first in the salt-lands, had been nightmarish. A dry dusty path led forward over bridges, and was surrounded by red and green patches of water. The water and its measly vegetation stretched away on both sides as far as the eye could see. There was no relief – no relief in the terrain, no shade, no water. We had stayed with the peon of the whisky-drinking toothless owner of much of this land. The peon, Carlos, had laid on chicken, beef and pork for dinner and we drank all night, playing cards and dice for sums of a few australes. In the morning we played tabas, a game that involved throwing a knuckle bone, for more cash and I left, feeling very guilty, having been fed until I was bursting and won all their money.

The mosquitoes started almost immediately and were vile. They arrived in clouds and swarmed all over me and the horses. They bit through the thin cotton bombachas I was wearing and would cover any bare patch of skin within a few seconds. And I mean *Cover*: two or three per square centimetre. Of course, my mosquito repellant and a rather smart mosquito net that my mother had given me when I left, were sitting in my pack-saddle. I waved my arms around and flapped at my face with my hands, both of which were totally ineffective. In the end I put my jersey on and pulled the head opening half over my head so I could look out through the slit, over which I put my sunglasses. It was hot and muggy and I could see very little through my sunglasses, but there was only one road and we were on it. After an hour or so, I took my glasses off as there seemed less mosquito activity and surfaced like a periscoping submarine to have a look around. The scenery was still the same relentless marsh in every direction, although now I could see ducks, flamingoes and smaller birds. I also saw, with disbelieving horror, that my map and compass which I had wedged beneath the pommel of my saddle had worked loose and dropped off. There was no alternative but to head back into the mosquitoes. We found the map way back, got back to the mosquito-free oasis and continued into more of the little buggers.

We came at last to Argentina, Argentina. Argentina, Argentina evoked all my desires to be a movie star. Great name (like *Paris, Texas*) great location (like *The Good, the Bad and the Ugly*) and like all good French films, nothing happening. Argentina, Argentina, as approached, looks like a bunch of sheds. As we rode into the village we passed a broken-down garage with broken-down vintage pumps. The village was set around a dusty white square reflecting intense light. An Argentine flag flew over a small tin hut, with the egg-shaped sign of the police. The shutters were down and there was no sign of life.

As I threw my poncho over my shoulder, I lit a cheroot, squinting into the mid-afternoon sun. My horses pawed restlessly at the ground. There was gonna be a fight.

In fact, I popped a chewy sweet into my mouth, my poncho was plastic and rolled up on the back of my saddle and the only man wearing a gun was the policeman, Luis, who gave me a cell for the night and cooked up a barbecue.

Argentina, Argentina was poor and Luis was one of the poorest of all, living in a single room shack supporting his wife and a three-month-old baby on a policeman's salary. Of the eight families in the village, seven were paid salaries by the government. As far as I could see they all served each other: there was a policeman, postman, tax inspector, nurse, fireman and two others.

The nights were suddenly much colder and Luis, myself and his family huddled in the single room. His wife and baby were wrapped in layers and layers of clothes which made their movements exaggeratedly slow. The asado was burnt, had cost Luis a fortune and was virtually inedible. I was given the best bits. The whole evening was pitiful. Luis talked about learning English and every time he remembered some from school – 'My name is Luis', 'Door', 'Chair' – he would look across at his wife and beam with pleasure as if to say: 'You see! I speak English and we can move out of here and become rich and powerful.' I felt even more pitiful as I watched Luis's wife carefully pour some milk (a rare commodity) into a bowl, light the gas stove and boil it. It was a beautiful sight as against the cold outside and their miserable house she prepared food for her child. I was horror-struck when she mixed the milk with coffee and handed it to me. I did not want it at all.

Luis had three more years in Argentina before he moved to a larger local town. Three years, with nothing to do and earning at the most US $30 a month.

'Go to the cities. Get out,' I wanted to say, but he knew the shanty towns and the unemployment that ring Buenos Aires better than I did. He was free. He had his family, he was supporting them, he earned money, he had a community. It all seemed OK the next morning, when the sun had swallowed the cold.

I fell off the horses about fifteen kilometres out of Argentina. We came around a bend and Viento Norte, whom I was riding, spooked and whipped round. I hung in mid-air out to the side of the saddle for what seemed like ages before sliding down Viento Norte's left side. I hit the ground with a thud, still holding the reins. Viento Norte set off and I held on, which was my mistake. He panicked and I was dragged along, ploughing up a cloud of dust amongst his hind feet. I let go, and must have blacked out for a second, as the horses had gone fifty metres when I looked up. El Chapeton was still attached and they were travelling fast. By the time I had picked myself up they had disappeared.

I ran after them. My vision was tunnel-like. I felt hot liquid splashing down my neck. I stopped, put my hand to my neck, looked: red. Blood was pumping down the left side of my head.

I ran on and felt faint. I sat down. Got up, ran on, felt faint. I had left my hat behind.

'Do I go and get it?' I could not think. 'It's hot. The horses are going on. Perhaps the hat will scare them into stopping. But they'll run back the way they've come from. How far is my hat?'

I went back, got my hat and started again. As before, I was following the hoofprints.

They had come to a closed gate we had opened earlier and had veered right. They were heading into the open, away from the main track. It was so open in fact that it seemed secure. The sky met the land and in that very narrow strip I would feel safe and catch the horses. It seemed welcoming.

I walked and ran about for about four hours before I saw a house and a moving blob. The horses had been stopped by a closed gate and were picking at coarse grass beside the track. They seemed fine and I led them towards the house, miraculously in the middle of nowhere. I felt very tired. I pulled off the saddle and put the horses in a corral. I walked round to check there was no opening. I walked back to the house, which seemed deserted, and crashed out on the verandah.

I was woken by a foot and a man holding a shotgun.

'What are you doing here?' he said. He was not pointing the gun at me, but he was not out hunting rabbits either.

I jumped to my feet and grabbing my cigarettes, rushed towards him.

'Please, have a cigarette.' All I could remember was Robin Hanbury-Tenison saying, 'Always have cigarettes to offer as a present.'

It worked, because he relaxed marginally, and I explained what had happened. He helped me put the horses into another corral and I watched him, his wife and three daughters unload the trap that they had arrived in. He said I could sleep in the house. I could see that he did not want me to and refused. All I wanted to do was sleep, and the night seemed a long way off.

It was one of the longest of my life. I slept for a while and woke at about 10 pm, frozen. It was a clear night and there was a strong wind blowing. I was very cold. I put on a jersey and was wearing cotton bombachas, a T-shirt, a shirt, a jersey and a jacket. I was still very cold. I walked around a bit and slept for a while in the foetal position between the foam pads and a poncho. I repeated this angle a few times before, at 2 am, I could stand it no more. I walked around the house knocking on doors and windows. I could hear snoring, which stopped. I knocked louder but no one came. I am sure if I had wanted to, said I was sick, they would have let me in. I was in the middle of nowhere covered in blood. I left them in peace.

The next morning I was given a cup of coffee. I changed a horse-shoe, washed some of the blood off and rode to the next town. The wind blew very hard into our faces.

We arrived and went to the police station. They told me the mercury had fallen to -12°C the night before and gave me some food which I ate like an animal. A nurse cut away the hair from my scalp and put iodine on a pretty superficial cut. I wanted to fall asleep on the couch and have her stroke my body.

I had to organise the horses. One of the policemen took me to his house and showed me where I could sleep – on a bed piled high with blankets in a little snug bothy. I was almost in tears. But I had to organise the horses. Fetching food and water seemed to take forever. And when I had at last finished, and was sitting on the bed I could not get my boots off. I slept for sixteen hours – clothed and booted.

8

Down Below the Borderline

W E ARRIVED IN Santiago del Estero, the capital of the province of Santiago del Estero two weeks later. It was seven weeks since I had left Rosario; I had covered 1000 kilometres and was about half-way through the Argentine leg of my journey. We crossed over from La Banda, a neighbouring town, into the city, rode through a dump and on to the Club Hippico, the show-jumping club.

I had been worried on the way that in arriving without warning the club would turn us away. But we were greeted by the head groom who gave me a huge corral for the horses with some shade, a trough and plenty of hay and grain. I put my stuff in one of the storage sheds and within five minutes of arriving was on my way to the city centre to find a hotel.

Santiago seemed a metropolis, as I walked through the outskirts into the plaza. The plaza amazed me as every single side street was festooned with neon signs that leant precariously out over the traffic. They advertised hotels, cafés, ice cream parlours, chemists, all the things I had not seen and had become unaccustomed to in the 'camp' (Anglo-Argentine for countryside). People stared at me as I crossed the plaza in the direction of the best hotel in town. When I got up to my room, with a balcony overlooking the plaza (£2 a night), and looked at myself in the mirror I could see why: matted hair, two days' growth of beard, torn clothes and boots. I could see why the hotel reception made no comment when I walked in and still less when I walked out to collect my stuff. Later that evening, when I was dressed like an Argentine in clean cotton shirt and jeans, I was almost forced to present my passport to prove that I was the tramp who had checked in earlier.

Santiago is one of my favourite towns in South America, in fact anywhere. It lies at the heart of Argentina but is the capital of the poorest province. The monte (scrubland) is low, stunted, ugly and totally unproductive and has grown back over areas of immense deforestation. The timber was ripped out by the British to build the railroads, and for export. Efforts have been made to clear it totally but the conversion to agricultural land is expensive and there are cheaper areas to exploit. The town has, therefore, a very new feel as if it is a frontier town, but it contains all the trappings of civilisation.

I felt like a child let loose in a sweet shop. I did not know where to begin. Go to the cinema? Go shopping? Eat an Italian meal, a Chinese meal, an Argentine meal? Read the newspapers? I rang Carina first and was so excited about arriving that we had a very distant conversation. Selfishly, I felt good and made no effort to find out how she was getting on alone in London. I assumed that she would be buoyed up and aware of my emotions and new knowledge; as excited as I was.

I had intended to spend four days in Santiago del Estero but four became five, which became six, which became the day after tomorrow and 'at the weekend'. We spent ten days there in all. I made myself sick: having phoned Carina I decided that I would eat Italian, then a Chinese, then an asado followed by ice cream, coffee and chocolate. I digested what I could in the cinema and started again. The following day I spent in bed, groaning, or sitting on the loo.

The horses pigged out too, and otherwise slept under the trees, explored the corral and watched the traffic go by. I changed their shoes with the help of another excellent blacksmith, who was fascinated by the Easy Glu shoes.

I made some friends who looked after me and we would meet and drink coffee in the plaza. They gave me dinner, invited me to parties and otherwise left me to get on with the organising of the trip. I wrote a few letters to keep sponsors and people back in the UK informed, generated some local publicity, sent my kit on to Tucuman and checked out Santiago.

We went to a party on the Saturday night of my week there. We first met in a bar and drank beer and smoked cigarettes before going off to a nightclub. I was just getting into the swing of things, when a couple of friends, Raoul and Simon, called me over and said that they had a surprise for me. We went out and drove off in Simon's car. I sat in the back rather bemused as we drove out of Santiago across the bridge to La Banda and into a smartish residential area. I leant forward and asked what we were doing.

'You'll see,' was all I got in reply. They huddled in front, conferring at each corner, pointing at ill-lit street signs before driving off to another corner and conferring again. Once they asked directions from a passer-by but I failed to hear what they said, unconcerned anyway after a few beers and some dancing. We drove off again and swept into a drive of a modern residential house bathed in pink light.

The pink came from a red bulb that hung over the door and I should have realised then where we were, but as I said, I was not totally sober. Inside, there were girls in mini-skirts and young hoods in their best clothes. Suddenly, a bell inside my head rang very loudly.

Raoul and Simon had brought me to a brothel. I could not believe it. There had been a lot of banter about me being alone in the pampas. I considered making a dash for it but instead took a chair at one of the three wooden tables. At the others, kids of eighteen to twenty were sitting around drinking, smoking and watching the girls walk past. They were well dressed and twirled their car keys in their hands in good middle-class style.

I had heard a certain amount from friends about the Argentine male's introduction to sex. At the age of fifteen or sixteen many go for their first visit to a brothel and continue doing so right through adolescence, marriage and until the oat bags are empty. Many Argentine towns have red-light districts, usually in residential areas on the edge of town. The type of neighbourhood determines the class of clientele.

The girls were very beautiful: dark skinned, dark haired and dark eyed, dressed in fluorescent short skirts that reflected the pink lighting. They looked young as well, probably in their teens, although their make-up and the lighting made it hard to tell.

Raoul and Simon came in with a girl in tow. I had forgotten I was not there as an observer.

'It's all arranged,' said one of them.

'What?' I said.

'It's arranged,' he said and went off to order a beer.

I looked at the girl. She looked at me and said, 'Shall we go up?'

I could have chickened out then but allowed myself to be led off, out from the reception room and down a narrow corridor to an open room, again swimming in red light. There was a bowl of water in the corner, two clean towels, a bed turned back, an electric fire adding to the light and pointing at the bed, and a heavy smell of scent.

We stood at the end of the bed looking at each other. She was young, about nineteen or twenty, with an oval face which disappeared as she pulled her dress over her head. I can remember much of what happened, but looking back I cannot remember her physically in any way.

She told me to take my clothes off and she laughed when she saw my money-pouch around my neck. She laughed louder when I pulled out one of two token condoms it had been carrying.

'We don't use those,' she said.

I gave her a lecture about AIDS which she ignored.

'We don't have SIDA [AIDS] here,' she said.

'How do you know? It's men like me, gringos, that carry SIDA. You should be careful.'

'We don't get gringos here,' she said.

We stood facing each other again in the warmth of the fire.

'It's all paid for by your friends,' she said, 'and you can have what you want.'

She made no attempt to give the impression that she was receiving any satisfaction. She asked for a present and I gave her my other condom. She laughed – a genuine and happy laugh.

'Keep it for the next gringo,' I said.

'Gringos don't come here,' she said again.

I asked her for a kiss and she pecked me on the side of the face. I asked her name – Lola.

The next moment I was being driven back to Santiago del Estero. I ignored their nudge-nudge-wink-wink-say-no-more questions by talking without a break about AIDS until we got back. They dropped me at my hotel, and before they drove off I asked them how much they had paid.

'300 australes. About half a dollar.'

I had fantasies for the remainder of my stay in Santiago about going back and taking her away with me. I wanted to go back. I wanted to see her again, but I left and she is now just a memory of bowls of water, an electric fire and red lights.

Someone told me a joke about Santiago. A Santiageño (an inhabitant of the province of Santiago) goatherd is sitting under a tree, dozing, thinking and watching the river. A man in a large, smart car pulls up in a cloud of dust and, leaning out of his window, says: 'Why don't you get off your arse and breed more goats?'

SANTIAGEÑO: 'Why, Señor?'

MAN IN CAR: 'So you can buy more land and breed more goats.'

SANTIAGEÑO: 'Why? What's the point Señor?'

MAN IN CAR: 'So you can build a big meatworks to butcher your goats.'

SANTIAGEÑO: 'Why? What's the point Señor?'

MAN IN CAR: 'So you can buy shops all over the world to sell your meat.'

SANTIAGEÑO: 'Why? What's the point Señor?'

MAN IN CAR: 'So you can become a rich man and sit in the sun, dozing, thinking and watching the river.'

I was sad to be leaving the province of Santiago del Estero, the ethnic mix of Italians and Arabs, the tumbledown adobe huts, the heat, and the pace of life.

At one stage we had been swamped by mud and stopped outside a two-roomed shed to shelter. I went in to be greeted by an old mother, her son, a granddaughter and an odd-job man. There was, as ever, a pile of coals in the middle of the floor to heat water for maté and to heat the adobe house. We sat and drank maté in the draught of open doors and I shared out some of my chocolate. The mother said she had ten children, nine of whom were working in Buenos Aires. I asked what they grew at the farm.

'Cattle?'

'Dead.'

'Goats?'

'Dead.'

'Chickens?'

'Dead.'

'Pigs?'

'Dead.'

I left quietly before someone came along and asked the question: 'Long distance horse rider?'

There was an immediate change crossing the border from Santiago to Tucuman. The farms improved, the houses were better built and sprouted television aerials, and the people were more active. We were entering what some bright municipal spark had labelled 'The Garden of Argentina'. The tracks were good, although worse than Santiago where much of the local traffic was by horse and cart.

The break between villages had become greater and we saw only a few scraggy horses and the first cacti, doing their best to impersonate men on horses. With a great deal of caution I put the saddle on el Chapeton for the first time since I had rubbed off the hair behind his saddle area. I was to learn later that I had been ridiculously cautious. The hair had regrown long before and was ready for the saddle. I was, as someone said, 'sentimental and absurdly pathetically wet' with regard to my horses' feeding and health programmes. Still, it was said by someone who did not have to rely on his horses. Their fitness, fatness and strength would greatly contribute to our safety.

I was extremely attached to the horses but to a depth where I was able to consider them only as machines, as living motorbikes. They had to be oiled, fuelled and maintained. Their emotional condition, of course, was hugely important and I treated them in many ways as humans, attributing to them human emotions, moods and personalities, but I did not want their love any more than I would from a motorbike. I wanted them to travel the distance with minimum fuss. I would often spend hours searching the best food, corral and water for them. Too exhausted for my own whims I would eat anything available and sleep in squalor. In any case, they were building a far closer bond to each other than they were to me.

If they had been human they would not have been close friends in everyday life, but in the business of crossing South America they were excellent partners. Often at different ends of the personality spectrum, they complemented each other perfectly. El Chapeton was loud, overt and highly strung, while Viento Norte was very nervous at first but developed an awareness and perception that came from within. He was also more intelligent than el Chapeton, and learning fast. El Chapeton, for example, had mastered pavements but could not cope with ditches, as the concept of 'taking off' was completely alien to him. He would string himself up beneath and bouncing on his toes would approach the ditch. I would drive him on and he would either make a leap of super-equine proportions, or dance on the edge, held by my legs until he attempted to whip round. Viento Norte learnt that the easiest way to cross was to slide down the bank, step across the ditch and step up to the other side.

El Chapeton bullied Viento Norte constantly, hovering over a pile of feed before driving Viento Norte to his own pile and then returning to the first.

I loved watching Viento Norte come out of his frightened shell, building physically and mentally into superb shape. I also loved watching el Chapeton realise that bluster, although useful on the pampa, rounding up cattle with his horse mates, served no purpose when alone and vulnerable. He learned to temper his bluff and in a way became far more dependent on me than Viento Norte ever did. He would knicker when I turned up at their corral or came out of a boliche to untie them from the post outside. He and Viento Norte were inseparable, and as their overseer I was inseparable from them.

I saw an example of their adaptability on our last night in the state of Santiago. We had ridden for forty kilometres before coming to two almacenes (general stores), which used to serve the old main road on which we were travelling. Both said they could not help, which left the only other family in the village, headed up by Pedro Rosa Heredia and his wife. They were sitting, bagging up charcoal to sell on the streets of the town of Santiago. Many people in this area have small cooking ovens built of clay. Stacks of monte scrubwood are loaded into the clay ovens and burnt to produce charcoal, which ends up on town-dwellers' asados.

A rather blackened Pedro rose to greet us as we rode into the dusty yard of a few scratching chickens. The only place he had for the horses was a pig run made of stakes and bound saplings. The horses had to enter a corridor that closed in on their sides and the entrance to the run itself was just under wither-height. As they came to the end of the corridor, both horses saw the danger of the cross bar and lowering their bodies, ducked underneath. It was an impressive display of dexterity.

I bought feed from the almacene for the horses, some maize and hay, and was rather astounded to realise that the horses' feed was costing more than the average man in Argentina earned in a day. Everyone had warned against giving maize to the horses, saying that it was only palatable after being soaked in water for twenty-four hours. Of course, this was an impossibility so I started them with the odd kilo which seemed to do no damage, and built up from there. Maize, if the horses do not contract colic, is an excellent feed as it has a higher energy content than all other grains.

Pedro's kid took me to see an extraordinary sight. We walked for an hour or so before coming over a hill to look down on a large pool in the river. About twenty men looked as if they were walking on water. They stood on triangular rafts from which they fished with lines. There were bonfires on the beach, to cook the fresh fish, that lit the scene, backdropped by a red sky. Smoke drifted across the fishermen and the duck that shared the water.

The sun went down and then a phenomenon occurred that I had never experienced before coming to Argentina. The sun disappeared from sight and for ten minutes there was a general darkening of the landscape. As my eyes adjusted I could not believe that it was getting lighter. But it was. Although the sun had gone, and it was dark, five minutes later the light seemed to increase in strength. It gave great clarity of vision before fading again. I presumed that rays from the sun were reflected from cloud cover, or even the atmosphere, at an oblique angle.

The fish was very cheap and I wanted to buy some but Pedro had insisted that we cook one of his chickens. A chicken was selling for 3000 australes in Santiago (about sixty bags of charcoal, which his wife could hope to sell in four days) and I was very embarrassed. It was very tough as we all had to chase it around for fifteen minutes before we caught it, but delicious cooked up with oil, tomatoes and spices. We drank my beer and moaned about the economy around a fire.

Many of Santiago's immigrants are Arab but many are of European descent too. Pedro's family were very European in nature. They looked European with white faces and brown hair. They were very poor compared to the average European and it was strange sitting around their hut, beside a fire. There was no electricity and wood was cheaper than gas. Water came from a well. But to me they did not seem poor. Pedro ran his own business with his wife. His family seemed close. They would go in to Santiago every once in a while. And otherwise they sat round the fire and talked or listened to the radio with the odd Friday night party thrown in. It was rather like how I imagined 1950s British life to be.

The scrub continued to Termas de Rio Hondo but it was a lovely ride. There was no traffic. We saw a car a day and the odd horseman, and we felt very cosy in the monte. After the openness of the pampas, its density was comforting, and there was plenty to tie the horses to. But the major excitement was that we were starting to go up and down. After weeks in the pampas, we had reached hills, although they were so small that initially I could not understand what was different. We travelled so slowly and quietly that we drifted from one place to another, without major changes becoming instantly apparent. I suppose hills are pretty major but these were really just bumps – the 'toe' hills of the Andes.

Termas is a tourist and retirement spot – the Eastbourne of Argentina. There were rows and rows of deckchairs in front of the hotels, which loudly advertised thermal water in every room. Every hotel and house in Termas relies on the thermal springs below for hot water and heating. Being the sort of tourist that the town did not cater for, it took me a long time to find help from the inhabitants. The woman in the Tourist Office seemed convinced that the horses could stay in a hotel and gave out a list as she had done to every tourist coming in to ask for help.

Eventually an ex-cop lent me a corral, after his son had taken us in hand. The son worked giving pony rides to the youthful section of town at a campsite down by the river. There was such competition that the campsite owner, who had said we could stay for a pretty exorbitant fee, accused Mario of being a liar, cheat and a thief.

'He will steal your horses,' he said, making the Latin gesture of grabbing an imaginary object from the air and putting it in his pocket.

The corral was beautiful, shady and quiet, and I trusted Mario implicitly, even when he had guided us off across a wasteland and through a minor shanty town. I had been worried but only in a paranoid way. I stayed in one of the cheaper hotels and bathed a lot. A huge stone tub led off from my room and I spent hours soaking in the steamy, eggy water piped from below.

I decided to go on a bus tour of the area. The bus had been converted to look like a train and first we drove around the town. The commentary went something like this:

> Termas de Rio Hondo was founded in ... by such and such. Here on the left is the Ambassador Hotel, Five Star and $US15 a night. Over the junction you can see the Plaza Hotel, Four Star and $US10. Behind you to the left is the Hotel Libertador, the most expensive here in Termas.

Questions came:

'How much did you say the Continental was?'

'How many stars does Hotel Europa have?'

'Which do you like best?'

The town was full of old folk who never sat on the deck-chairs and played the Argentine equivalent of boules all day. The water was supposed to have recuperative powers and many parents had brought their disabled children, who dragged them round the amusements. There were cafés and restaurants galore, many shops selling alfajores (two maize biscuits sandwiching dulce de leche), and a casino.

It was full by the time I arrived at 8 pm. The gambling took place in a high neon-lit barn and I was the youngest there by about ninety years. I had hoped to slide into a dark smoky atmosphere of red and clicking chips, but the only game played was roulette, which I find extremely boring. I put some money on the numbers of horses I had ridden to win in steeplechases – 11, 17 and 36 – and lost the lot. I left to eat at 'The Crazy Sausage'.

Gambling is legal in certain state-controlled casinos but the Argentinians have made every attempt to make the experience as gloomy as possible. Roulette only, and neon lights that show every emotion on pasty faces. They did not seem to me to be great gamblers, wagering a few australes on tabas, but a 10 australes bet was treated as a man-against-man, life deciding event, and everyone got very excited. It was great fun and I became just as caught-up in the game, trying to spin the knuckle bone so that it landed the right way up.

My notes record my verdict of Termas: 'Expensive town, but great baths – the first for five months.'

Termas led us into sugar cane country and we were lucky to be travelling at harvest time. Huge fires lit the horizon at night as the cane's superfluous leaves were burnt off. I learned this to my embarrassment when I galloped into a farmer's yard shouting: 'Your field's on fire, Señor! Your field's on fire!' It was like complaining to a cinema manager that the lights had gone out.

We met cart after cart on the track, often dragged by up to eight mules, taking the loaded sugar cane to lorry pick-up points. There were mule-powered cranes to lift the cane, bound by a chain to make a cylinder the size of a modern hay bale. The mules were attached to a wheel, and walking round would slowly raise the cane into the air. My horses loved the cane, chomping their way through the odd stalk, and were also learning to bone maize from the cob.

There was one particular farm I visited, which was a small farm and needed only one extra hand. Luckily the work-hand had no family, as only his board and keep were provided. He came to the house to eat after us and was fed a second-rate version of what we had just eaten: a small meal of soup, spaghetti and meat. I asked what he was paid, and was told 'nothing'. He worked all day for bread alone. It was the closest thing to slavery that I have ever seen.

Kids were trying to earn more money for their families at the entrance to the city of Tucuman, population 1,000,000. They guarded the city like sentries, with teepee piles of sugar cane that they sold to passing motorists.

The Club Hippico welcomed my horses and again I made for the most expensive hotel. This time I really was dirty and probably very smelly, and the hotel was very up-market. I thought that they would not allow me in, but once booked in I waited for an empty lift as I felt I could not trap someone in the lift with the smell of horses, shit and sweat. I struggled into my room ($US15 a night) and switched on the complimentary television to catch the end of a dubbed version of *The Dambusters*.

The next day, having made sure the horses were comfortable and given detailed instructions for their care, I left for Buenos Aires – two hours away by plane. Carina was flying in to spend a month or so of her summer holidays in Argentina. The plan had been for her to meet me wherever I was with the horses but I could not wait to see her after four months apart and wanted to show her Buenos Aires, Rosario and go to the falls at Iguazu.

I cannot tell you how good it was to see her as she came through customs. I was rather gratified to see that she was in tears, obviously

99

overcome at the thought of seeing me. Actually she was upset because the airline had lost all my mail from home and a video camera that I was going to use to film parts of the trip. Carina was distraught, but I tried as hard as I could to assure her that no amount of lost mail or video cameras would detract from seeing her. After four months I had become accustomed to Argentine beauty and I had forgotten quite how beautiful Carina is. I was blown away by her, and gulped in her smell. I still feel like this every time we are apart for longer than ten hours.

We nosed around Buenos Aires for a week. George and Bridget organised a party for my birthday, and Carina and I checked out the centre of Buenos Aires, La Boca and then flew off to the Iguazu Falls. Iguazu lies on the border between Argentina and Brazil and is hot, sticky and humid. I was very surprised and totally unprepared to see torrential rain on arrival. A taxi took us along red dirt roads to the International Hotel, the most expensive I have ever stayed in but in a perfect location. We had a balcony that overlooked the falls themselves, which plunge over sixty metres, throwing up a thick spray laced with rainbows.

The falls are one of the most popular tourist attractions in South America, but we were lucky with the weather: the rain, although sweet and soft, poured down, so we had the place to ourselves. We walked through the natural grottos of tropical foliage, watched by toucans. People who had already been to Iguazu talked at length about the power of the falls. Close-up, there was a huge roar of water as it charged to the sea, but it was one of the most relaxing environments I have ever been in. It was not frightening as I had been told, but incredibly comforting.

But this may have been because I was with Carina for the first time for so long. Her ideas and energy were so fluid compared to Argentine women, many of whom centre their conversation on Miami (latest shopping trip or desire to go) and the exchange rate. She made me laugh and feel so relaxed. When alone, I had the tendency to keep as busy as possible, always rushing around afraid of sloth and afraid of my own company but with Carina I could feel the tension slip away and a positiveness emerging.

We flew back to Buenos Aires in time for the Sociedad Rural show in Palermo, Buenos Aires. The show is the main agricultural fair of Argentina and includes cattle, sheep, pigs, demonstrations and stands. The main attraction are the cattle and every breed has its own section: Charollais, Aberdeen Angus, Cebu, etc. Oddly, overlooking each breed of cattle was a restaurant that served that particular type of meat. We ate in the Aberdeen Angus restaurant, like good patriots, and watched the attendants groom, wash and muck out their charges. Huge beasts, they had been buffed until they shone like a classic American car. They seemed unperturbed by the vast quantities of their colleagues that were being eaten only twenty metres away.

Before Carina and I left for Tucuman in order to do some riding together, we had a final lunch at San Isidro and said goodbye to George and Bridget, and Alex. It was particularly awful to say goodbye to Alex as he had become such a good friend and adviser within a day of my setting foot in Argentina. I knew I would see George again but it was unlikely that I would see Alex again for some time, and I shed tears. I had always been scrounging lights off him and as we were waiting for the bus to take us north to the horses, Alex disappeared. He came back, smiling and said: 'I have a present for you,' and deposited ten lighters in my hand.

We gave each other the Argentine hug – arms round with much back-slapping – and then Carina and I were away.

We changed to a train in Rosario and travelled to Tucuman. The train passed through many of the villages the horses and I had seen. From the window I barely recognised them. They seemed homogenous, with a run-down rail halt and their symmetrical dusty streets. They seemed, no longer, to contain the people I had met – the Marcellos, Marias and Pablos – just Lowry-type stick figures.

It was good to be back in Tucuman and we went to stay with some friends I had made, in a smart apartment a few blocks from the centre. They were all medical students and one day they insisted that I came into the medical school with them. Our destination was the morgue and once they had slipped the attendant a few australes, I was led in. Huge tanks filled the room and in each tank there was a jumble of heads, legs, arms and torsos that had been turned brown by the preserving fluids. It was a picture of hell. Every way I turned there was a face, with the lips dragged back from the teeth, snarling at me. An errant eye from a skull chopped in half caught my own, and I saw a back that had pushed its way out of the tank, exposing it to the air, that was covered in mould. The most disturbing sight was a woman who was whole and had a tank to herself. She was perfectly preserved beneath the surface and it was hard to believe she was dead. She was smiling and had her hand over her crutch.

The rest of the time we spent in Tucuman we prepared for our departure. Carina tried Viento Norte first and he was very badly behaved. However she fell in love with el Chapeton who was the perfect smarmy gent to her, displaying impeccable manners and great charm.

Our friends took us by car into the hills that I thought I had seen from the plains when entering Tucuman. My eyes and mind had refused to accept that they were hills, having spent so much time in the pampas. 'They're clouds,' I screamed as I screwed up my eyes to find a meaning in the shapes on the horizon. They rose sharply away from the plains. We climbed to the top and looked back. We could see the whole of the city of Tucuman stretched out like a chess board, and felt we could have seen to the sea if there had not been a haze clouding the atmosphere. We drove on to a lake called El Cadillal and watched it swallow the sun before driving back.

George flew in for a few days and we had dinner with a very high-ranking judge, a very fortuitous meeting as it turned out later, at the border. He insisted that I eat locro, a gluey soup of pigs' trotters and maize. We also ate 'open your legs' empanadas, so named because as you bite into the pastry casing of meat, egg, pepper and olive, if you do not open your legs you get juice all over them. Carina was very embarrassed when the judge explained this to her, as she did not understand clearly and came away with a totally lewd interpretation.

Carina became very impatient, waiting to leave from Tucuman, and I could see her point. It was really a matter of changing the shoes and slapping on saddles. But in reality, for a trip of this length, it was more than that. Every single piece of kit had to be in perfect nick. Every shoe had to fit perfectly. With lameness, colic or a saddle sore you might sometimes get a second chance but it was not worth the risk. There was also the need to gain as much information as possible about the route forward. I found that the best way to proceed was to be dragged forward by the expedition. Once I was prepared, had gained plenty of facts in advance and reached a state of anticipation and excitement, my legs and horses were obliged to start working.

After a week in Tucuman we were ready to go and as ever I was sad to leave. Tucuman had a faster beat than Santiago but still emanated an atmosphere of tranquillity, self-confidence and self-containment through its plaza, colonial buildings, park and people.

We had decided that I would ride the horses out to El Cadillal and Carina and our friends would drive out to meet us with an asado. For the first time since leaving, the hills really began to undulate and the trees were indigenous and tall. Huge water sprayers irrigated many of the fields and the horses snorted with pleasure as we rode under one of these artificial rainfalls. We stopped at a café for lunch and for the ninety-fifth time in the last two weeks were treated to the Gypsy Kings. I must have listened to them another ninety-five times within the next two weeks.

I parked the horses in a campsite and waited for the party to arrive. They came, eventually, having bought most of the meat market in Tucuman; and we ate sausages, general innards, steak and avocados while the horses grazed around people's camper-vans and tents.

Carina and I meant to get an early start but of course were invited to lunch by some of our fellow campers. Argentine hospitality is so generous and spontaneous that I had become rather adept at turning it down, but it was all new to Carina and she wanted to stay. By the time we were able to set off we'd had rather too much to drink, and circumnavigated the lake on a series of tracks that hugged the cliff walls in roller-coaster fashion. The horses seemed to have no concept of height and insisted on walking on the edge.

The views were spectacular, and we rode for several hours before halting, tying the horses to a fence and putting up the tent. I had been too drunk to remember food when we left El Cadillal, and we had between us a few tea bags and two oranges. The weather changed to damp cold the following morning so we were extremely hungry when we dropped in on the Maya family, to whom I had been told to say hello. They were cooking a whole pig and we managed to eat half of it. It was a real 'criollo' family: the men sat at a table and were waited on by the mother, wives and daughters. Carina's presence created an etiquette problem solved by placing us at a separate table. After pig, there was plenty of singing to a guitar and as usual I sang 'Yesterday' and 'I only wanna be with you', my staples when asked to sing.

We continued on. The skies became more overcast and the hills on either side took on a monochrome brown-grey that faded as they retreated. I was reminded of the hills and corresponding views in Edinburgh. The land was scrubbier and predominantly uncleared, so different from the plains of beef and dairy cattle. Even the monte of Santiago was better populated than these hills and we rode a longish day, always expecting to find a village or homestead but never arriving at one. We crossed the river and decided to camp. For the second night on the trot there was no food for the horses and I felt harassed although Carina seemed hardier about their welfare. I tied them to a fence again and they ate every scrap of twig in their seven-metre semi-circle. I was worried that they'd had so little to eat but they had eaten at lunch-time, were pig-fat, and it was about time I started giving them a few tests. Throughout the trip they had eaten incredibly well: alfalfa, grass, hay and several kilos of wheat, barley or maize a day.

Carina cooked up a delicious mince, onion and tomato hash which we ate with bread and rice. As Carina was with me we were carrying more gear. We had the tent as I thought it would be best if we had our own accommodation when staying with people. Apart from the fact that we were unmarried, I wanted comfort for her rather than the dossing spots I was used to. And above all, I wanted as much time alone with Carina as possible.

We had the world to ourselves that night as I put up the tent, and the fire lit our own space of ten metres. It always amazes me how you can arrive in a spot, unremarkable and devoid of human contact, and by erecting a tent it becomes so familiar. Every tree, every bird, every blade of grass becomes your own. We only had one pot and somehow only one spoon as I had been obsessive about weight before leaving Tucuman. One of us used the top of a pot of moisturising cream to scoop out the food. It was delicious, and our North Face tent snug, although we only had the ponchos that lay under the horses' saddles for covering.

I woke with a start in the night to hear a crash of hooves but when I poked my head out I could just make out two equine shapes. In the morning I was rather disgusted to see that Viento Norte was eating his droppings, and looked across to el Chapeton's patch which was completely bare. He had eaten his long ago.

They did not have to wait for long for a hefty lunch, although we had had a hard morning. As we were breaking camp, a routine that was so smooth after only three days, a tractor appeared from nowhere and its rather surly driver told us that the track that we were taking was blocked ahead by a locked gate. Like a fool I believed him. Often, on my own, I disbelieved much of the advice I was given and often proved myself right. But with Carina, I did not want to risk a long ride to a dead end.

We dropped back down into a valley where the wind never reached. It was hot, muggy, and stank of decay as someone was using it as a dumping ground for dead animals. We rode in silence past horns, bones, and rotting flesh. I was used to this sight and its accompanying vultures, but it unnerved Carina as it had me the first few times. We got lost, and eventually followed a telegraph wire that led us over a series of switchback hills, on and on all morning. The horses did well, scrambling up steep boulder-covered mounds, and I was pleased to see that the Easy Glu shoes were totally unaffected by the rougher terrain. It boded well for the future.

We eventually tumbled out into the green, fertile, cleared valley of Choromara and were able to water the horses for the first time in twenty-four hours. I had given up, fairly early on in the trip, the habit of watering the horses at midday if it meant a search for water. They coped well with a long drink when we stopped at night and in the morning. Obviously, when we passed a stream or trough I would let them drink a little; Viento Norte, especially so, as he drank almost twice as much as el Chapeton – about three buckets a day.

I asked a farmer if we could graze the horses for a while but he turned us away. He went back into his house, and probably received a bollocking from his wife as he started yelling at the top of his voice and waving at us as we continued. We decided to turn back, and were invited in for lunch. We were lucky as another pig had been recently killed and we were again fattened and wined up.

Most rural households breed a few pigs and a few chickens. They cure hams and make the most delicious sausages, which came in two varieties: blood and fat. Both are tasty and early on I had overcome my fear and loathing of fresh blood packed into a skin. When you pierce one of these sausages with a knife, they are rather inclined to explode in a mess of blood. People laughed heartily when I explained that sausages in Britain are predominantly potato. When I said that good meat costs about $US12 a kilo in Britain I was stared at with horror and great sympathy. In Argentina a kilo of best beef retails for about 50 US cents – and I mean best beef. The marbling is superb, and the fat trickles through the meat giving a sweet flavour that enables the eater to gobble a kilo with ease in a good sitting.

The one type of food I really missed in Argentina was dairy products. For many kilometres we had passed through the dairy lands of Santa Fe but milk, cheese and butter were almost impossible to come by. The Argentines do not eat butter with their bread. They do eat cheese, but it is usually of the plastic variety, although the cheeses in Buenos Aires were sometimes excellent, fresh, French copies. That night, however, Carina and I struck lucky and had an orgy of cholesterol: eggs and butter.

We crossed the border into the province of Salta. A police checkpoint station was positioned on the Tucuman side and I presented our papers which consisted of our passports and the horses' health certificates. We had borrowed another video camera from friends in Buenos Aires and told the official we were making a film. As the camera was pointed in his direction he changed visibly. The shoulders came up, his uniform fell back in place and a hand through his black locks caught a stray hair. He had seen the films.

We walked to his office, a standard three-roomed breeze-block affair painted a brightish green. The flag swung in the breeze. The passports and papers were checked, although it was clear that he had little or no idea of what he was supposed to be checking. But then nor did I. He made me sign a register detailing 'Where from', 'Where to', and the mode of transport. I wrote 'horse' in the latter and we shook hands.

The crossing from Tucuman to Salta was a natural border, the river Sali, and we then entered the village of Tala. To me it was not a good start to Salta. Prefabricated blocks of housing had been erected around a centre that was rapidly falling apart. People, comatose in the heat, watched us ride into town with little acknowledgement of our greetings, and we stopped to buy food at the one store, for a possible night out. As we were leaving, the shopkeeper suggested we stay at the hotel.

I knew that Carina wanted a bed badly and we trailed after a self-appointed guide to a bar-restaurant-hotel on the road. They had beds and space, and they could have prepared food but they just could not be bothered and turned us away. This put me in a foul mood and we crawled back to the house of our guide, who said we could stay with his family. Grudgingly and with bad humour, I accepted. At the end of the day, if I thought we had finished, my body would immediately shut down and start recuperating, resting. If in reality it was tricked and we were forced to go on, it complained vigorously and every further step was a nightmare.

The house of our guide confirmed all of my opinions about Tala. There were three rooms, all of which were decorated with peeling wallpaper, mould and falling bits of ply-board. To me it was all too familiar and, for the first time, depressing. Some of my feelings were selfish as I had wanted to show Carina what a great place Argentina was – and we had ended up in this dump. I wanted to show her what an interesting, beautiful life I was having, and to me there never has, never is, never will be anything interesting or beautiful about poverty.

I chatted for a while to the father of the household. There was no work and any income was decimated by inflation. We handed over the food that we had bought for ourselves and I went out to help the father bake bread. We fired up the beehive-shaped oven, by putting and igniting wood inside its metre-wide, metre-high space. A good fire was soon blazing and after the wood had been removed, bread dough was popped in and the openings shut off. The heat retained by the bricks was, remarkably, enough to bake the bread for the household and their neighbours, who took it in turn to do the baking.

Going back into the house I was aware that our supplies, sufficient for Carina and me for one day, had been miraculously turned into supper for us and the family of about six. We had a scrap of meat each, floating in a watery tomato broth, and spaghetti with a smidgen of butter. The way in which our hosts tucked in made me think it was a feast.

Depressed as hell by the whole scene, I left to go and sort out more food for the horses. Crawling round the village, I managed to scrape up a little alfalfa and some maize. My guide professed himself to be a communist and had been fed some serious misinformation, as he regarded the Falkland Islands as being Argentina's most valuable resource. I dreaded returning to the house and we delayed in a run-down boliche to finish off the last remaining bottle of beer. At last, I could delay it no longer and prepared myself for the squalor of spirits we were staying with, and walked back to the house.

It was like walking into a different world. The atmosphere was charged and excited. The air was fresh and there was great activity. It was totally different from an hour before, like walking into a party in full swing.

Carina had transformed the place. The children were all drawing at the table with crayons that she had been carrying in her bag. The mother was talking at top speed to Carina and as she did so, was beavering away, clearing up the mess and pinning wallpaper back on to the walls that were already covered with children's pictures. The father of the house was sitting in a chair puffing on a pipe, reading the newspaper and glancing up every once in a while with obvious satisfaction at his transformed brood.

I was amazed. For the first time I really saw the deep power that Carina has to change people's lives for the better; the energy and glow to activate dormant creativity and self-expression. Since I had met her two years ago, she had always had this effect on people (myself included), but in this hole in Argentina I saw it for the first time clearly and openly. I loved her so much.

The family obviously did too as there were tears and present-giving when we left the next morning. I was completely ignored but Carina received pictures, addresses, plastic flowers for el Chapeton's reins and beseeching demands to return.

She impressed me even further that day as we had a long ride to make up for stopping short at Tala. It was a hot day and we rode for eight hours, stopping in the middle for an hour's break at the entrance to a finca (the Tucumanos name for an estancia). As we were leaving after our lunch of salami, bread and water, the owner of the finca came cantering down his drive, highly annoyed that we had not gone up to the house and invited ourselves in for lunch. The trouble with inviting myself for lunch, I had found, was that I ended up staying half the day and leaving drunk as a fart, if at all. Although the Argentines are moderate drinkers, my presence always seemed to be an excuse for a piss-up.

Our destination was Arenal, the finca of a friend of George's called Luciano de Tella. It was late when we arrived and we were both tired, resulting in a blazing row when Carina dropped her reins into a stream and accused me of thinking more about the horses than her: I had organised a magnificent field for them and a makeshift campsite for ourselves.

The campsite situation was soon rectified as José Leal, the manager of the Arenal, said that of course we must stay in the big house. It was stunningly beautiful, laid out around a cavernous hall decorated with a long table, lit by candles. One of the men rushed around providing sheets, towels and hot water and installed us in one of the spare bedrooms. We had luxurious baths and ate and drank ourselves into a state of ecstasy. I suppose that the differences in accommodation for the first two nights in Salta would be like comparing a squat with a stately home.

Our final day riding together was into the town of Rosario de la Frontera. We were riding along the old road which was beautiful as there was no traffic. There were certain sorts of food that we craved, having been in the countryside for a while, and we talked about the huge plates that we were going to have on arrival. Toasted cheese and ham sandwiches featured highly, for some reason, on our serious desire list.

The entrance to Rosario de la Frontera is long, straight and dusty and, riding down it, I knew that it was the last section of Carina riding with me, and I was very depressed. Carina's water bottle strap broke and the water bottle squelched to the ground. Tiny events like this always seem hugely symbolic. I was never quite sure what they meant but nevertheless they seemed important.

We loosed the horses in an enormous water meadow, bare of grass, but great for rolling and relaxing, and walked back to the plaza to find a hotel and some toasted ham and cheese sandwiches. The hotel was clean, functional and pleasant, laid out around a courtyard. The café was typical of small town restaurants. Waiters dressed in bow ties and red jackets supplied poor food, sandwiches, coffees, beer and chocolate bars at the speed of a snail with ingrowing toenails.

Carina and I had a rest morning and afternoon before she was due to leave for Buenos Aires, and the UK. We were busy organising the kit, writing a few last minute letters and being together.

She got on the bus at around 4 pm and I waved until I could see the bus no longer. I was left standing in the deserted bus station, wearing clothes she had helped me buy, ready for the next part of the trip, alone and in tears. I knew then that I wanted to marry her. I suppose I had always wanted to be with Carina for the rest of my life ever since I had met her.

I wrote in my diary: 'I went back to my room and it seemed like a monk's cell. I could see the nights stretching away forever. I longed to see her, to hold her, to have her in my arms. Every detail was a reminder of her and the difference she had made in my life. I know that I want to be with her. Is riding two horses across South America worth one moment of being apart? I love her.'

I had arranged to meet José Leal from Arenal that evening, which was a godsend. We talked about Argentina, as usual, but José Leal surprised me by saying that he was non-political, the first person in Argentina to do so. Not that I believed him. However he did not surprise me when he told me that one of the qualifications he had was in artificial insemination. He was the thirty-fourth qualified artificial inseminator I had met to date.

We left early the next morning. The horses were particularly badly behaved. El Chapeton had gone completely mad. When I tied him up he would often pull back on his headcollar with all his strength. As my headcollars were made from rawhide this just meant he dug himself into the ground. He would then start leaping around sideways. He was impossible to saddle if tied. He went berserk, so I always untied him and treated him very gently. When shoeing him or picking out his feet, I had to go as gently as possible. Viento Norte, on the other hand, was as quiet as a lamb despite his fear of humans that receded every day. He was still thinner than el Chapeton but was building up into the most fantastic horse.

El Chapeton was seriously pissed off about everything and nearly trampled me as we pirouetted around together while I did up the girths. He was bolshy all day and I think that he missed Carina as much as I did. Viento Norte had been seething with rage throughout Carina's stay, as he received far less attention than usual. A real prima donna, he had quietly sulked.

As the pack animal that day he carried nothing and my inventory was as follows (all fitting on to the lead horse):

1 foam saddle pad	1 pair of socks
1 blanket	1 pair boxer shorts
1 poncho	1 diary
1 saddle	1 set of papers
2 headcollars (1 lead rein)	1 water bottle
1 file and horseshoes	1 camera

I loved travelling light and was always thinking of ways to make things double up. The foam, blanket and poncho were my bed and I was thinking of designing a headcollar that was made of crucial but rarely used items such as hobbles. Saddling now took me ten minutes in the morning.

Hectic winds and some serious grass fires took us to the other house of the de Tella family. We pulled in and the manager of the farm was incredibly excited as there was already another Briton staying on the farm. Giles, a mathematician and a cousin of Luciano's, was helping out at the finca for a few months, having graduated from Bristol University, deciding whether to become a farmer. We greeted each other in the usual manner of two Britons abroad: handshakes, rushes of words followed by silence, and strict avoidance of eye contact. The dairy workers watched with slight disbelief our sang-froid.

We went back to Rosario de la Frontera that night and had a drink while watching President Menem play basketball on television. The charismatic premier of Argentina started political office with a round of highly publicised, highly watched games of football and basketball, playing with and against the national teams.

There was much macho slapping of backs and: 'I'd love to see La Thatcher play basketball,' from the locals. So would I, mate, so would I.

Giles left the next day for a few days in Tucuman and I spent two days eating and reading books. The horses ran wild with the dairy cattle for a while and I would occasionally see them from the verandah being herded past by a few gauchos. When I say 'ran wild' I mean they ambled about from one choice bit of grass to another.

Leaving, the ground became more undulating and we ploughed on towards the town of Salta, skirting Metán, where I parked the horses in a lorry park and made use of a truckers' café. I did not look too out of place in my riding gear as the party at the next door table was dressed in 'wild west' trucking outfits.

We had left the sandy tracks parallel to the main road and the old road behind, and were forced to scuttle along the verge. On the way up the hills, we would often be travelling faster than the trucks that groaned and spat their way to the top. I would wave at the drivers as we passed. On the downhill sections it was hard to think of the hurtling masses being driven by flesh and blood. Just a roar of dust, oil and machinery. A blank window surrounded by unlit lights.

When travelling on the road I favoured stopping at any of the villages that lined it. It was strange to see the different attitudes that bordering villages had to the road. Some would face towards the road, all economic activities aimed at selling or buying from passing trade. Others would ignore the road and focus on the traditional plaza centre of the village. Shops, boliches and the administration serviced the local inhabitants, reading newspapers, listening to radios and watching the television for news of the outside world, but ignoring the wealth of traffic passing their doorsteps.

I liked both types of place. In the former there were always delicacies and chocolate bars, fruit, cheese and cold meats, unavailable elsewhere. There were always restaurants and sometimes even a hotel. In the latter the pace of life was calmer. People were friendlier and more open to a chat. I could always find a roof in the police station or municipal compound, many of which seemed to have a room specifically for errant travellers.

Vergilio Tedin, however, was completely devoid of hotels, restaurants, rooms, shops and almost devoid of people. We had crossed the River Juramento and were looking for a place for the night. Vergilio Tedin was some way off the road – I calculated about five kilometres – but as there was nowhere else, I decided to go for it.

The trip off the road showed that I was becoming slightly paranoid or mad or both. The track was horse-knee-high in dust, surrounded by monte scrub and, having left the road, our progress was eerily quiet. There was no clip-clop as the horses' feet were muffled by the dust. As the track twisted and turned I soon lost my sense of direction completely. A snake spermed its way across our path and into the bush. I could hear machinery in the direction I thought we were going. It got louder and sounded like fork-lifts.

This is when my mind became over-imaginative. I knew that Vergilio Tedin was on a railway line and I knew that we were getting closer to the cocaine industry. The scene that I conjured up for myself was that of a cocaine distribution point. Fork-lift trucks were removing pallets of packaged coke from a train that had illegally come in from Bolivia or from a few carriages that had been dropped off surreptitiously. Guards, armed with automatic weapons, were overseeing the work and would not be disposed to someone blundering into the middle of the operation. The scenario in my mind got worse and worse as I approached, but we kept going. First, there was nowhere else to spend the night as I had no water and no food. And secondly, I suppose I wanted to see if I was right or wrong.

I heard a truck start up and come closer. I got off el Chapeton and dragged both the horses off the track and into the scrub. It passed apparently without seeing us. There was no reason for a truck to be here. For the first time I untied the second horse and held the lead rein loosely in my hand, if necessary to drop and scarper on the riding horse.

My fears, of course, were totally ridiculous and totally unfounded. When I arrived at the bottom of the hill, there were no fork-lifts, only a bulldozer working around a bridge that had collapsed.

Astride el Chapeton, I watched the bulldozer and driver for a while until he saw, with obvious amazement, me watching him. He paused in his work for a second and beckoned me over. I tied up the horses, walked over and hopped into the cab. He motioned me into a passenger seat and blipped the engine. The noise was so loud we made no attempt to speak. We sped about from the bridge to a dumping ground for the waste.

He was good. Sliding levers and switches the Russian bulldozer sped about, picked up and spewed down. The driver, with whom I had still not spoken a word, handed me some rolling papers and tobacco. I rolled up a couple of cigarettes and we puffed away for a while. At last he stopped the engine, turned towards me with his hand outstretched and said: 'Bazam.'

I was not sure if that was his name or he had called his hand after one of Superman's, but I got in my usual questions about being able to stay, get food and water for my horses and he said sure.

'But there's nothing here,' he said, pointing to a hut and some railway carriages. There was, however, water from a well and some scratchy pickings for the horses.

I went back to organise them and found, to my horror, that they and the man-driven rail-cart, to which I had tied them, had disappeared. I found them about 200 yards down the line, still attached to the cart.

I staked them out for the night and went back to find Bazam. He had parked his bulldozer for the night and was preparing the stove.

He and an accomplice lived in a converted cattle truck. They had a stove, an eating table, a four-bunk bedroom, a stockroom and pantry. A flat-bed wagon was attached to theirs, and on this travelled the bulldozer. They were basically bulldozer troubleshooters. Wherever they were needed, they were driven by attaching their house and bulldozer to a passing passenger or goods train. Off they went to the desired destination and were dropped in a siding, home, bulldozer and all.

Bazam's assistant returned with a shotgun as Bazam and I were settling into a large flagon of wine. He climbed into the wagon, said hello and threw me a coconut. This surprised me, as by my reckoning we were about 2000 kilometres from the nearest palm tree.

'What do you think that is?' asked Bazam.

'A coconut,' I said. They both laughed. It was certainly the size and shape of a coconut. Brown, round and slightly hairy, its side was etched with three distinct grooves, rather like a tennis ball. I turned it in my hands looking for a clue. It moved. It was alive. I quickly passed it back to Bazam.

'It's an armadillo,' said Bazam. He opened up the shell a little and out appeared a whiskery little nose and frightened eyes. Its defence was insufficient against man and Bazam efficiently drove a knife through the back of its exposed neck.

Roast Armadillo (Serves 3)

1 Kill.
2 Unravel and gut.
3 Hold open with stick and sprinkle inside with garlic, pepper and salt.
4 Cook for forty minutes in wood-fired stove (say, gas mark 5).
5 Serve in shell.

The correct method of eating is to tear the carcase from the inside of the shell and to pick the meat from the bones. Should be accompanied by bread, potatoes, a few steamed vegetables and large quantities of red wine.

Comment: Fatty and full flavoured meat. A delicious, gamey pork flavour.

That armadillo was one of the most delicious meals I have eaten. The smell and taste were exquisite. It had been cooked to perfection and we scooped out the shell with the remains of our bread so that the fat ran into the joints of our fingers.

Our entrance to Salta was not as clean as I would have wished. I was aiming to get within twenty or thirty kilometres by stopping at a finca, to which I had been recommended, spending the night and making the short hop into the city the following day. It did not quite work out as planned.

First, I could not find the finca. Secondly, I was completely lost. We had had a late start and darkness came down as we were still in the middle of the country. I was trying to cut across from one road to another and took a wrong turning. We ended up trudging around all night until I felt too tired to go on any longer. I staked down the horses and crashed out. We had been on the move for about fourteen hours and I was knackered. The horses coped with travelling in the dark, as if they did it every night, which I suppose they did. I am terrified of the dark and jumped a mile at every twig crackle. It was a very dark night and I could not see the road ahead at all and was always stumbling on stones and falling into potholes. The horses were very sure-footed but I walked leading them most of the time as I was terrified that I would fall off and lose them in the dark.

We came to one house at about 2 am. The dogs, resident at all houses, whose purpose is to scare anyone arriving, succeeded. Due to mild exhaustion, I had forgotten that they would come tearing out of their hutches and was still standing on the ground. Mild exhaustion notwithstanding, I do not think that I have ever leapt on to a horse so fast in my life. The barking failed to raise the inhabitants so I bashed on the door. Lights appeared and then a shotgun nuzzled around the front door. I asked if I could stay the night and was told, in no uncertain terms, to bugger off. I said that I was lost and had no idea in which direction to bugger off. The shotgun was waved around a bit so I left. In the morning I found that we had been travelling in exactly the right direction and were only a few hundred yards from the main road.

The place I wanted to put up the horses was the Club Hippico in Salta, which has as its members some of the smartest members of society. The problem was that not only had I not washed since leaving Rosario de La Frontera but also I had slipped off my poncho in my few hours of sleep and had lain in a bath of dust. I tried to wash as best I could in a roadside café, but only succeeded in turning the dust to mud, showing clearly how dirty I was.

The entrance to Salta from the south is beautiful. We wound our way through the gentle green hills that approach the town and came to a rise topped by a restaurant and a cross. The city, gridded like the bars of a cell and barren, stretched before us. I drank a coke in the restaurant and looked down over the town. Another arrival, another place to be crossed off. I felt great, another sense of achievement and I looked forward to a few slap-up meals.

We were fortunate to arrive at the Club Hippico at the same time as the President, and he made us feel very welcome. The Club Hippico is part of a racecourse and a sportsground complex and I had asked some rugby players for directions. Rugby is a fierce religion in Argentina, played by upper-middle-class students. They were all standing around their cars drinking beer, and insisted that I join them. They had their beautiful girlfriends in attendance and it was hard not to flirt. The contrast between the camp, riding all day, dust, horse sweat and water, and beautiful people, smart clothes and beer seemed enormous.

The Hotel Plaza, where I stayed, was another cracker. It was dirt cheap, had a huge double bed and looked out over the plaza. I had a telephone, room service and all the functions of a business hotel for about $3 a night. It also had the colonial and New World charm that pervades the centre of Salta.

I was lucky to get a room at all as we had arrived a few days before Salta's main festival. On 13th September 1692, the statues of the Virgin Mary and Christ were paraded through the streets. A supposed miracle occurred as they were passing by. An earthquake started and was immediately halted, according to bystanders, by the power of the Virgin Mary and Christ. A festival celebrates this event every year and thousands of pilgrims pour into the town. I did not take much part in the festivities but they were hard to ignore. The Hotel Plaza was directly next to the cathedral and day and night a succession of priests said mass, with bells ringing to emphasise a particularly good point, that was broadcast over the Plaza.

My time in Salta, ten days in all, was spent mainly eating and watching the horses eat. They were cared for immaculately and nothing gave me greater pleasure than taking a taxi to the Club and watching them snooze in the shade of a tree. They were having a truly superb time.

I was fortunate to have some excellent contacts in Salta, which I made full use of. As they were probably three of the most powerful families in Salta, I was very well looked after.

Luciano and Joanna de Tella, whose estancias we had stayed on, I met at last. Luciano had studied at Oxford and, therefore, spoke perfect English in that rather slow, classical, fruity way that some people seem to emerge from Oxford with. He is supremely intelligent and therefore has not followed his father into the world of Peronist politics, but spends his time running the estancias. He met Joanna in England, as she lived in Oxford.

I was very impressed by the estancias of the de Tella family, especially the cheese factory at Yatasto. Luciano had set up a small factory that employed about ten people. The factory produced high quality cheeses that were sold both in the local market and major urban centres such as Buenos Aires. The cheeses were expensive but output totally failed to satisfy demand. First, cheese is rare, and secondly, good cheese is unavailable outside Buenos Aires.

Luciano's cheese factory is, to my mind, an excellent example of the way forward for Argentina. Small, intermediate technological, labour-intensive concerns aimed at satisfying a strong domestic and local market: cheese, clothes, shoes, and foodstuffs desperately needed by the local population rather than cars and ships.

We soon got on to the subject of Luciano's estates up in the north. It was covered in monte scrub which Luciano was clearing at top speed with bulldozers and converting to productive agricultural land. This to the 'green' sentiments of Joanna and her mother was sacrilege; to them he was devastating large areas of natural scrubland.

For many South American countries development can be attained only through the exploitation of their natural reserves. Luciano's land should in the future create wealth that can be used for investment and a general raising of the standard of living for his people: a standard of living that most of us in the West have attained already.

Salta brought me for the first time into contact with cocaine. I was to see and hear a lot about the white powder in Bolivia and Peru, but Salta was the first contact.

A friend took me to a particularly rough bar and, while I waited around attempting to hide between the pinball machines, he went into the baño and emerged, clutching a piece of chewing gum paper wrapped around on itself. He laid out some lines on the dashboard of his car and then blew them off as a police car passed by. The lines were laid again and we both snorted a couple. He then took me off on a tour of the red light district.

We cruised around one of the roughest areas initially. Women were standing around the doors of their 'offices' which were lit by single red bulbs. I could see through the doorways into rooms that boasted a bed and a bucket. Every once in a while a man would emerge from out of a closed door followed by a prostitute who would slop out the bucket in the wake of his departure.

Our first stop was at a strip joint that had been closed down. My guide for the night was convinced that it was still open and nearly picked a fight demanding to be let in. I extricated him and took him back to the car where he laid out more lines. Another strip joint out towards the racecourse was open. Situated in the heart of an industrial estate, it was more of an aircraft hangar than the friendly red atmosphere of strip joints I have been to before. A number of girls took off their clothes to James Brown tracks, displaying expressions of infinite boredom to clientele obviously as bored as they were. Once they had finished their routine, their job was to sit on the laps of the 'guests' and persuade them to drink as many watered down whiskys as they could.

At last, I was taken back to my hotel, and declined another puff of powder.

'Great night, eh?' said Pedro, before driving off.

'One of the worst of my time in Argentina,' I said to his departing brake lights.

Unfortunately, that night remains my strongest memory of Salta. The town is beautiful, the people incredibly friendly and helpful and all I can remember is a lousy night snorting ineffectual cocaine and wanting to go home.

Leaving Salta with all my kit repaired, I felt that I was really making tracks towards the border. Jujuy, only three days' ride away, was the last major town before the Bolivian border, a further three weeks' ride. At the beginning of the expedition the border had seemed an impossibility – so far away – and now it was close.

There were two roads to Jujuy. The shortest one was devoid of traffic so was perfect. It took us an hour to cross Salta, as the Club Hippico was the wrong side of town, and we clattered past startled faces peering from fume-laden cars. Then we were out on the old road. A side verge led along the deserted two-laned road, and the weather was beautiful.

We entered a wide valley and passed through village after village that looked as if they were all competing for the 'Best Kept Village in Argentina' award. Flowers spilled from hanging baskets and the gardens down to the roadside. One house was so covered it was hard to see windows and doors.

The horses were in excellent form after a ten-day rest and ploughed through the kilometres. Our average speed through the expedition so far had been between five and six kilometres per hour, walking. Five kilometres per hour is slow but is the very essence of travelling by horse; there is plenty of time.

Luciano and Joanne Tella had driven out for the day and we met at the town of La Caldera for an asado. By the time I arrived at the meeting point, Luciano had ignited a small fire, and was positioning pieces of meat on the grill. I loosed the horses using one hobble. I found that if I hobbled one of the horses he would hop around like a carousel horse and the other would stay close.

The de Tellas had brought a vast supply of wine and this sharpened our appetite for the traditional asado. First, we had sausages of two kinds, blood and fat. The second round usually consists of kidneys, liver and intestines. The intestines are rather strange as they consist of a thick, rubbery tube, packed with a strong goo with the consistency and taste of pâté. I did not go a big bundle on intestines and would usually wait after a few kidneys, for round three.

Round three was the meat course and could be chicken, pork or beef. Luciano had supplied two different cuts of beef: asado strips and a fillet. A good asado cook like Luciano puts all three courses on the fire as soon as it is going. Round one and two cook the fastest and are eaten when ready. The asado strip of rib bones cooks quicker than the fillet, and correspondingly is eaten when ready. The fillet is eaten as it cooks. The correct form is to take your knife and slice off a piece from the outside, exposing uncooked red meat to brown up.

All this was washed down with red and white wine and eaten with salad and bread. Some friends of Luciano failed to turn up until after we had finished the asado, including their portions. I asked Luciano how much we had eaten and was surprised to find that Luciano, myself, Joanna and her mum had eaten four kilos of meat between us. This meant that Luciano and I had put away well over two pounds of meat each.

'Asado de cuero' is a side or quarter of beef, cooked on an open fire with its skin and hair intact. The skin retains the fat and the flavour and the cooking process is very exact, ensuring that the skin remains undamaged by the heat. The asado de cuero is the height of asado cooking and President Menem had gained kudos by taking an asado de cuero chef with him on election campaigns.

The de Tellas piled back into their car and I crawled back on the horses. We said goodbye and, as with so many people I had met, I was sad to see them go. The closer we got to Bolivia, the more sporadic became my line of contacts. We were getting further away from the comfort of home, family and friends, further away from the help of George and Buenos Aires. It seemed like standing on a high board, as though we were about to make a plunge although we were actually climbing into the Andes. But then the physical process of riding the kilometres would always come through. As we rode from the asado spot, I felt full of food, warmed by the sun and very happy. The movement of my horse helped digestion and all was quiet as we plodded up a track to the house of the Romeros, just outside La Caldera.

Marcello Romero had taken great care of me in Salta, showing me round and buying me a delicious lunch. He was very proud of Salta, his father having been instrumental in building many of its landmarks during his time as governor. The family owned the main newspaper, *El Tribuno* and were prominent in the town. *El Tribuno* had printed an article on my journey and had given the impression that Marcello was to accompany me. Marcello was actually going to study at university, but his father, seeing a copy of the paper in Buenos Aires, freaked out and caught the next aeroplane to Salta to forbid him 'to join El Ingles on his trip'.

I arrived on a Saturday and had the place to myself. There was to be a birthday party for Marcello on the Sunday, but the family was not turning up until the following day. The Romero finca was very lovely. A main block, with large dining and sitting rooms, looked out on the garden and ornamental pond. There were further outhouses for the kitchen and guest sleeping areas. The estancia had been founded and developed by an Englishman who had sold out to the Romeros as the hills, in which it was set, became too much for him. His maid had stayed on and spoke of him very fondly. She clapped her hands with glee when she learnt that I was British and promised to make me a real British dinner 'just like old times'.

I went off to have a bath and came back mighty hungry and ready for bangers and mash, or steak and kidney pie, or roast beef and Yorkshire pudding. Eating so much meat seems to make you continually hungry. Sitting on the kitchen table, where I was to eat, were an omelette, a glass and a bottle of whisky – Breeder's Choice. The maid was beaming with pleasure.

'El Ingles ate this every night,' she said.

I sat down and started on the omelette as she poured me a tumbler full of Breeder's Choice, neat. I polished off the omelette in four seconds and sat back waiting for the next course. But that was it, apart from whisky.

'He used to drink a lot of whisky,' said the maid wistfully, and was obviously rather upset that I only drank a quarter of the bottle. I wanted to tell her that not all the British drink huge quantities of whisky, but she was in a different age – when 'Los Ingleses' ruled this farm, had tea at 4.30 and omelettes and whisky for dinner.

The Romero tribe arrived the next day and I was given a grilling and a tour of the estancia by Papa Romero. He explained what had been added on and showed me the hydro-electricity supply. A small stream about a metre across and 50 cm deep could be dammed and dropped about five metres to power a turbine that in turn generated enough electricity for the needs of thirty people.

We sat at a long table in one of the barns for lunch and I felt very privileged to be present as the company was made up entirely of the Romero family, spouses and children.

Fortified by wine, we took to the croquet lawn, a legacy of 'El Ingles'. The hoops had been spaced at a distance the Croquet Association would have disapproved of. They certainly would have disapproved of the style in which we played. The object of the Romero game was not to pass through the hoops in an orderly fashion, arriving at the central post first, but to croquet and clobber your opponents as viciously and vindictively as possible. A good stroke was when the croqueted ball landed in a prickly and inaccessible shrub.

The rules were a little vague and disputed hotly. I was partnered with Papa Senator Romero who cheated every shot. As he was on my side, I did not tell him that pushing his ball along the ground with his mallet, like a hockey player dribbling the ball, was illegal. His two eldest sons, Juan Carlos and Tito, did protest but to no avail and when I was caught cheating, moving my ball with my foot, Papa Romero silenced all suggestions of missing a turn.

Tito asked me: 'Is that an Argentine trick or a British trick?' referring to moving my foot.

'Well,' I thought and said, 'a British trick, but in Britain I would not have been caught.'

Spending the day with the Romero family was rather like being caught up in a Gerald Durrell book. Papa Romero presided over the whole gathering, while Marcello spent most of the day pursuing his current girlfriend who was playing hard-to-get. Juan Carlos, also a politician, was into guns and had bought a new rifle the previous week. Every two seconds there was a huge explosion as he loosed off another round. We all were made to have a go shooting at rocks in the river. Every once in a while, Juan Carlos would lose his patience and fire off a magazine as fast as possible. Tito, one of the nicest people I have ever met, mingled round making sure that everyone was happy. The sisters and Mama – and I must have begun to be affected by Argentine chauvinism as I have no recollection of their names – sat round with the spouses, chatting.

Later in the afternoon we started the rodeo. One of the peons had rounded up some cattle and enclosed them in a corral. He would lasso the bull to be ridden from his horse, pass the lasso round a post and ride off until the bull had its neck jammed against the post and was trapped. Another peon would run in and tie a strap around the bull's middle, just behind the front legs. The rider then jumped on the bull and twisted his hands under the strap until he had a good hold. He hooked his legs under the bull's armpits, the bull was loosed and away he went. The correct procedure was for the rider to lean back as hard as possible, balanced by his hands and feet in their semi-secure hand and foot-holds.

The animals varied greatly in their response to the unaccustomed weight on their backs. Some would get wild in a true 'Wild West' fashion, swerving around, bucking and jumping. Some would trot off and then go wild. Some, like the one I rode, just trotted quietly off to the nearest post and attempted to tear the rider's legs off. Papa Romero had been adamant that I should not ride and risk the expedition. But there were a lot of people watching and my 'machismo' sensibilities were aroused. He was right. Having my leg half-torn off on a post was excruciatingly painful.

In the evening we had spaghetti and butter and finished off the wine. Someone had a guitar and we sang songs to each other.

The following morning I said goodbye to the Romeros and back-footed down to La Caldera to buy supplies in the shop. Like most country shops it stocked a variety of the basics: bread, wine, maté, rice, maize, spaghetti, eggs, soup and chocolate. As usual I bought some ham and bread which formed the staple of my diet when out in the camp. It was a lucky break stopping at the shop, as they gave me directions to an even older road than the old route on which we were travelling.

The road was one of the few surviving pieces of the old colonial road down from the Andes. It followed the valley floor and was virtually impossible to travel by motor vehicle as it dipped in and out of the river. The riding was spectacular as there was not a soul in sight and the evening was beautiful.

As the valley seemed so perfect I decided not to go on to the town of San Lorenzo but to camp out. There was one house, and I considered going to knock on the door, but my romantic spirit got the better of me. I loosed the horses, hobbling one, and they went off together. Lighting a fire was easy and I put together a dinner of sausages, eggs and coffee, throwing the remains of my coffee on the ground like they do in the movies. I laid the poncho from my saddle out on the ground and lay dozing in perfect harmony with nature, or so I thought; until I noticed little birds flitting across the rock-face under which I had parked myself. I watched them for a while, wondering what sort they were, with the niggling doubt at the back of my brain that they were flying too fast for birds.

'Bats!' I thought suddenly, and felt a shudder of revulsion.

Everyone I know says bats are very sweet animals but the thought that they were possibly vampires was too much. I had been told, and had seen on television, how vampire bats crawl along the ground towards an exposed part of their victim and quietly suck blood. I was still wearing my boots so my feet were OK, but I swiftly withdrew my nose and fingers under the poncho to join the rest of my body. But my poncho was inclined to slip off in the night, and the fear of being bitten – they were zipping only a few feet above my face – drove me, with the foam and poncho, out into the open.

I had lain down for about five minutes when the rain started. I considered going back to the shelter of the bats' rock-face, but the thought of having my fingers sucked for their blood rooted me to the spot.

In the morning I appeared bedraggled from my poncho, which had kept most of the rain off in the night, and saddled up. As I passed the house, a lady called me over.

'It rained in the night,' she said.

'I know.'

'I couldn't sleep as I thought that at any moment you would come over and I wanted to be ready to let you in.'

'Thanks,' I said, still in my damp clothes.

'You're English, right?' she said. Most people thought I was American, Irish, Italian, French; anything but British.

'Yes,' I said.

She tapped her temples. 'Crazy,' she said. 'You English are strange. You love the rain.'

Riding into Jujuy, I spent the whole day thinking about the possibilities of setting up a dude ranch in Argentina. They seemed endless. Horses are cheap, land relatively so. The scenery in the north is spectacular and would gladden the heart of any armchair gaucho. My tourists would live in family huts that were spaced around the central meeting and eating point, at a radius of a kilometre, so that they were forced to ride everywhere. They would learn to break horses, herd cattle, lasso, cook asados de cuero and live like true criollos for their one or two week stay.

We were forced to cross the centre of the town of Jujuy, pronounced

Hoo-Hooey, in the pouring rain to arrive at the horses' hotel, the Sociedad Rural de Argentina. A friend had promised to warn the President in the Sociedad Rural of my arrival. However, no one knew who the hell I was and I was nearly turned away. Close to tears, I begged that the horses be allowed to stay in one of the outside corrals.

The big fear in the club was that my horses carried equine infectious anaemia, a blood disorder resulting in fever and sometimes death, usually spread by flies. Equine infectious anaemia is a major plague in many Latin American countries and its control and eradication is a time-consuming business. Equine infectious anaemia is not the only animal disease in Argentina. Perhaps the most serious of all is foot-and-mouth in cattle, which is present in all areas north of the Patagonian region. The problem to the Argentines is that, come 1992, the EC will refuse to import any beef from areas that are not completely free of foot-and-mouth, which rules out most of Argentina.

By promising to separate my horses from the horses in the club, the members were appeased and, as ever, once the horses were in they could stay as long as they wanted. The first hotel that I went to for myself was a rip-off. I was charged $15 for a rabbit hutch in a conference-type hotel. Getting there had been a nightmare as the stables were about 5 km from the town centre and I was unable to get a taxi. It poured with rain as I waited for an hour under a memorial to the Jujuy Malvinas dead. At last I walked, and was in no mood to search around for a better hotel until the following morning.

Although we had only been out in the countryside for four days, I followed the arriving-in-town sequence. Ring Carina, buy an English book, read, and stuff myself for two days.

Jujuy was our last major stop before arriving at the border and, correspondingly, I spent more time than I needed to getting ready. The horses had to be tested for equine infectious anaemia by Coggins testing them, and I bought a few more certificates from the local vet by testing the horses for diseases I knew they would not have, and having their papers stamped 'clean'. As for myself, I got into a 'border panic state', thinking that this would be the last chance to buy anything; that once we had crossed the border there would be nothing available. This state of mind arose not only from fear that Bolivia would be devoid of most goods but also from a natural fear: whenever travelling to the Continent, I have to remind myself that the French, Germans, etc., do have toothpaste, batteries and medicines.

I bought myself a new knife and had a saddlery-maker run up a sheath. I bought new foam pads for the horses. I also came within seconds of buying a gun. There were a couple of gunsmiths in Jujuy and I spent ages looking at their stock. I decided that if I was going to carry a weapon, a small .22 revolver I could wear on my body at all times would be the most appropriate. It would be no use in the bottom of one of my packs.

I changed some money – it was going to cost about $30 – and went back to one of the gunsmiths. I said that I wanted to try the gun out and did they have somewhere to practise. I was taken out the back and felt rather excited about trying the revolver for short-range accuracy. I was shown a tube about a metre long and with the circumference of a drainpipe. Rather taken aback I said to the assistant, 'I was expecting a range.'

'No, no. You try the gun here,' he said, and taking the gun from me, loaded it with six shells and fired them off into the tube to demonstrate that it worked. At the last moment (I had the money on the counter) I chickened out and, deeply embarrassed, said that I had changed my mind and scurried out of the shop.

Out on the street, I felt a deep sense of relief that I had decided not to buy it. I remembered talking to my father before leaving the UK.

'Are you going to carry a gun?' he had asked.

'I don't know,' I had replied, although to everyone else who had asked the question, which was everyone who had asked about the expedition, I had categorically said no.

'No guns, big smile.'

'Do you think that you will need one?' asked my father.

'I honestly don't know.' Tschiffely at one point was carrying four weapons, and shot someone on his trip.

'Can you envisage pointing your gun at someone with the intention of killing them?'

'No,' I said. 'I would hope to wound them or frighten them but certainly not kill.'

'Well,' said my father, 'let me give you a piece of advice. Unless you think that you are capable of killing, do not carry a gun. It'll be more trouble than it's worth. If you produce a gun you have got to use it, because if you don't someone will use theirs and you're dead.'

As my money lay on the counter in the gun shop in Jujuy, I realised that I was still incapable of killing. I remembered talking to a man who had undertaken an expedition through Chile, and his chilling story of shooting one of his horses by mistake as his girlfriend sat on it. I felt very relieved to be without a gun, but I decided to sharpen my knife.

Jujuy, the capital of the province of Jujuy, is another colonial town. The administrative centre is grouped around the Plaza Belgrano and the commercial and café centre to the town is along Calle Belgrano. I spent most of my time in the centre browsing through the shabby selection of shops and eating in the cafés. Jujuy itself, to my mind, is rather a dull ugly town, its saving grace being the spectacular views to the hills, punctuating the end of each street.

Its economy is very much dependent on the throughflow of goods between Bolivia and Argentina and many people told me that Jujuy benefits from the cocaine trade. Before leaving the UK, I had not realised Argentina's position in the cocaine industry. I had been led to believe that virtually all the coke left South America through Colombia and the north end of the sub-continent. However, Argentina's export business to the rest of the world means that the country's trade routes are often used for transporting cocaine to the end-user markets.

Jujuy had a border town feel. Salta, Tucuman and Rosario are all positioned in the agricultural heart of Argentina, the heart that supports and fuels the whole country. From this geographical advantage, they were lent importance and a sense of purpose. Buenos Aires, as the capital, has its nose stuck higher in the air than anywhere else but Jujuy just dangles from the end of the country. It is functional and useful but rather unsavoury compared to the other provincial capitals in Argentina. Something like a big toe.

For the first time I saw Andean blood in the people and initially found them colder than the Italian, Spanish and Arab-blooded Argentines that I had been meeting to date. On the third day in Jujuy, however, I was fortunate to meet Andy Pedrazza, who had a couple of horses in the Sociedad Rural. We got on well immediately and I liked the way that he treated his horses, not as competitive machines, but as animals to be with and around. He is the rebellious son of a famous aviation couple, and at that time was building up a trucking business from scratch, having lost his house and business to his first wife. He invited me to his home and I ended up eating virtually every meal with the remains of his family and his beautiful girlfriend, Alicia. In many ways they embodied all the good things about the Argentine people: they were enthusiastic, full of life, ambitious, hospitable, open and hesitant about the future of their country.

The Argentines are often criticised by foreigners for being arrogant. This partly stems from their behaviour when abroad, but then all nations are usually obnoxious abroad. In any case, they have everything to be arrogant about. They live in a beautiful country. As one of the world's developing countries, they have more future than westerners; certainly more future that they will be able to see in their own lifetimes.

Andy and Alicia were moaning that all the Argentines were ever able to do was make mistakes. Some of the mistakes have been horrific, such as the persecution and social unrest of the 1970s military government. But the mistakes that they were referring to were the succession of economic cock-ups that have deprived Argentina of holding a position in the First World. However, there is little starvation in Argentina and the country is lightyears beyond the state of many of the Third World nations. I argued with them that Argentina had time to make mistakes, and those mistakes were crucial to getting development and progress right. They can afford to take and borrow ideas from the West. Unfortunately, they have borrowed a lot of the bad by attempting to copy instead of selecting. But I got the feeling during my time in Argentina that focus has turned inwards, a legacy of the Falklands War, a beneficial legacy. Also, they have time because however badly the Argentines make a mess of things, they cannot actually stop the wealth, e.g. cattle, crops growing.

They have the chance to live in a beautiful country and exploit its wealth without destroying it. They have the chance of coming as close to Utopia as any country I know.

Andy helped me enormously in providing food for the horses in the Humahuaca valley, from Jujuy to the border at La Quiaca. His business was based on two trucks transporting goods for export from Jujuy to the border. He ensured that they always returned empty, however, because as he said: 'You never know what they might be carrying', referring to the narcotics trade. He took me to a fodder merchant and we bought some bales of hay and a sack of grain. I split the sack into two-horse ration bags and we loaded the whole lot on to one of his trucks. I had a good idea where we would stop and the driver dropped off a supply at the local cop-shop, if there was one.

Andy decided to accompany me on one of his horses and we rode out of Jujuy on 17th September. The weather was perfect for riding, sunny but with a breeze. I was rather startled to see snow on the hills which looked as if they were just above us, but Andy said they were a couple of thousand metres higher.

It was great to be riding with a friend again. Further back on the trip horse and trap riders and horsemen had ridden with me for a few kilometres. We would ask what the others were up to, where they were going and where they had come from but I was usually glad when they pulled off. I loved travelling alone with my horses, my thoughts and Argentina. There was plenty of time to talk and meet people in towns and villages but I hated sharing the pleasure of riding alone with strangers.

Andy talked so fast with such volume that I was only required to listen, which suited me fine. Like a true Argentine, he talked about himself mainly and his upbringing, marriage and current life. Devoid of self-consciousness and social pressure to hold back, the Argentine people, talking about themselves, painted a picture of their country, as a whole, more vividly than if that had been their intention.

Alicia met us with an asado which we ate in a wood surrounded by other day-trippers. We pigged out, drank a lot of wine and lay in the sun. Unfortunately, Andy's horse had gone lame so he borrowed a corral, and took my pack on to our first step out of Jujuy, Ana Maria Barcena's place in Volcan.

We sat in the vast kitchen of her hacienda which she refused to have lit by electricity, bathed in the glow and hiss of her kerosene lamps. She ran trekking tours, predominantly for foreigners who rode up into the hills for several days to a height of 5000 metres above sea level. There was a tour operator staying to discuss business and, talking to him, I was surprised to hear the sophistication of the Argentine tourist industry. My idea of a Western-style dude ranch was in no way new as there were numerous trekking and riding centres throughout Argentina. The tour operator's job was that of one of the many middlemen in the tourist industry, putting the end-user, the tourist, in touch with the provider of tours, for example Ana Maria.

The horses were put out in a vast field with about twenty of Ana Maria's ponies. It always surprised me that, when they had the chance to fraternise with other horses or ponies, my horses would take themselves off away from the crowd and stick very close to-gether. When alone together, they would bicker with one another, make faces and pretend that they were not friends in a rather adolesc-ent way. But when there were other horses around, they made a rock steady pair, never drifting further than a few metres from each other.

One piece of behaviour that really endeared them to me occurred when I camped out at night. Often I would loose them to wander around freely, although one of them always wore the thick leather hobble, so thick that it never even scraped one hair off their legs. Horses do sleep and their pattern in the night is to graze for a while and then sleep, graze, sleep. I woke up a number of times in the night to find myself surrounded by horse flesh. El Chapeton would be one side and Viento Norte on the other. They would be nodding away, snoozing so close that I could touch them. I always felt that they were standing over me like sentries, but I do not know who got the greatest sense of security from being close, me or the horses.

Andy and Alicia left that night and we made a plan to meet up later. My link with what had gone before had still not been broken. People would not let go and I was glad. I wanted to be alone, but not that alone.

Leaving Ana Maria's place, we carried a pack-saddle again for the first time for a few months. I had thrown out most of the stuff that I thought was superfluous, like my sleeping bag, and was very pleased with the way that the pack fitted. We wandered down to the village of Volcan and I bought some empanadas.

The weather was excellent again and we rode through the numerous valleys that make up the whole of the Humahuaca valley. As we rode the peaks on either side came down to meet us. In one stretch of the valley the sides are coloured like a rainbow, where rich ores have been exposed to the elements and oxidised. Full of hot, greasy empanada I felt again as if the expedition was just starting. I love starts with their promise of novelty and knowledge. We were also more self-sufficient, carrying everything that was necessary in the packs. I was reminded of a game that my sister and I used to play on long drives. Whoever saw a caravan first had to lean out of the window and, as loudly as possible, scream, *'SNAIL!'* at the poor, unsuspecting driver.

I slept under a cart that night and was given permission to cut green barley from a field for the horses. I bought eggs and potatoes and fried them up on the stove. Viento Norte escaped in the night and I heard him crashing around in the barley field.

The farms up the rich valley floor were all beautifully cared for, and the ploughing was all done with horses. I found it hard to believe that we were in the same country that boasted the mechanical efficiency of Santa Fe.

We crossed the Tropic of Capricorn and I took a picture. There was less difference in the land either side of the sign than there had been at the state boundary crossings. It meant nothing.

In the village of Huacalera I had been given a contact by Tito Romero from Salta. Unfortunately, the contact was away and his father suggested that I try the hotel for the night. I walked the horses over and was surprised to see many locals hanging around the entrance, and further surprised by their complete lack of interest in me and the horses. The landlady said that I could stay the night and I put the horses into the overgrown tennis court. The locals were still standing around, staring down at the road as I took off the saddlery. They were waiting for something.

All was explained when a huge red truck that had been converted to a bus, towing a containerised trailer, rolled in. Out poured thirty-two European adventure tourists. I could see why the locals showed no interest in me and my horses, when there was a far better show on offer.

The bus/truck was disembowelled of its rucksacks, and a lean-to canopy was drawn out from the side of the trailer, covering from sight what looked like a giant pigeon-carrying wagon. The Europeans were rushing into the hotel at top speed with their rucksacks and I found the whole scene fascinating. I was amazed how loudly they talked, how large they were and how much space they took up. They also seemed not to notice me and, to assert that I actually existed and had not vaporised on crossing the Tropic of Capricorn, I went to talk to the locals.

'You're lucky, paysano,' said one, 'the hotel is only open once every two months and tonight is the night that the Germans arrive.'

'They're Germans?'

'Yes, Germans. Every two months, for one night they stay in Huacalera,' he said proudly.

'Oh no, Germans,' I thought and rushed into the hotel. But I was too late. The Germans had already got to the hot water, and I had a cold shower that I shared with a dead frog.

Spick and span, that is washed with slicked back hair and the same filthy clothes, I went through to the bar and chatted to Christina, the very beautiful landlady. The Germans began to appear and as neither they nor their guide spoke any Spanish, I ended up translating between them and Christina.

A set meal had been prepared and 1/33rd was taken from each German's meal so that I too could have one. We all trooped through into the dining room to find a long table set for thirty-two and a small one set for one. I was surprised not to be invited over. For the whole expedition, it had been virtually impossible to eat alone in a restaurant as someone would think that I was lonely and demand that I eat with his party.

In between courses I was visited by a few of the Adventurers. They told me all about their route, and sang great eulogies about the company that had arranged their tour. When I enquired, they seemed to have no impressions of Argentina, but explained that their bus was excellent and that they never had to sleep in a hotel.

Unprompted, I explained what I was doing which provoked zero interest, apart from one woman who asked, 'Are you going into the mountains to find yourself?'

At the time I thought, 'what a bloody stupid question' although I am sure that I could have rattled off, quite happily, a good answer at a Berlin dinner party table.

'Going into the mountains to find myself?' I repeated. 'At the moment, I am here and when I am in the mountains I will be there,' I said truthfully if a little pretentiously. I could not make head or tail of what she was talking about, and she did not have a clue what I was saying.

The conversation died and they went back to their table. I realised, when left alone, that I had forgotten how to communicate with Europeans, people from my own home.

At the end of the meal, five rather frightened colla (Quechuan Indian) children came in and started to play Andean wind instruments. I was sitting closest to them and the first seconds of that melancholic, haunting, all-knowing sound leapt straight at my heart. That feeling lasted no longer, as I found myself virtually swept from my table by a tide of Germans attempting to get a better photo position. There were camcorders and cameras of every size and description. As the room was filled with flashes, the children seemed to sink into themselves even further.

I saw them later outside having finished their performance and having passed round the hat. They were handing the money over to ecstatic parents, who counted out australes and dollars that two men would have had to have worked for two months to earn. Good for the families, good on the Germans. Good all round? Who knows?

I sat on the steps outside and watched the Germans going to bed. The reason that they never slept in a hotel was that they slept in the pigeon wagon. The guide explained in perfect English that the wagon contained eleven columns of three cubicles, two metres by 750 cm by 750 cm; a German slotted into each one. I said goodnight and went back to my six metres by six metres by two metres double room.

As I lay in bed, squirming as ever with sexual frustration, I heard a knock on the door.

'Who is it?' I said.

'Christina,' came the reply.

'Come in.' I thought that she had come to seduce me and wished that I had washed my feet slightly more thoroughly.

She did not want me, however; she wanted to make sure that I did not leave without paying. I had thought that she was going to let me off, as I had translated, and by my reckoning she was making 3000 per cent profit on the Germans' food.

Most of the people that I passed during the days were colla, as the Argentines call them. The women, dressed in hats and multi-petticoated dresses, were always extraordinarily friendly and waved and said hello. We usually met in the middle of nowhere and I could never understand what they were doing, and why they always chose to wear such unsuitable footwear, such as plastic loafers.

Finding a place for the horses in the town of Humahuaca was a bureaucratic nightmare. I wanted to put them in the corrals of the municipal slaughterhouse and was passed from the police to the chief clerk to the mayor, who had the superb name of Geronimo Cruz (pronounced Cruise).

Humahuaca gave me my first taste of an Andean town. Tiny pedestrian streets led to the plaza. I stayed in an excellent hotel and was kept awake most of the night by drunken students who were getting ready for the official start of spring, marked by a procession of floats. The town had a number of attractions, including the national monument to Argentine Independence, and the statue of Saint Francis. At around a quarter to twelve midday, hundreds of tourists, mainly Argentine, were herded off their buses and into the plaza. Most of the buses had come from the south, and the tourists were dressed, like tourists anywhere in the world, in colourful T-shirts, shorts and silly hats. The major difference was that they all sported the type of disposable camera that you buy in airports. Except these were not disposable. Like the Germans' Nikon and Pentaxes, these were the Argentines' record keepers.

The anticipation heightened as the time crawled towards twelve. At midday on the nail we were guaranteed the joy of seeing a 'sight'. As the municipal clock tower struck twelve, a door in the wall of the tower swung open and the statue of Saint Francis was visible. The sequence was as follows:

1 Door opens.
2 Arm raising cross is lowered.
3 Arm with pointing finger is raised.
4 Arm holding cross is raised.
5 Arm with pointing finger is lowered.
6 Head nods.
7 Door closes.

Everybody clapped like mad and sped off to their reserved tables at the local restaurants. Unfortunately, we left Humahuaca the following day so I was unable to see the Saint Francis sequence again.

The horses were fast asleep in the slaughterhouse when I went to fetch them. They often stayed in slaughterhouses as the corrals were good and usually central to the town. Such a location always worried me and I spent many a sleepless night wondering if el Chapeton's sightless eyes would stare at me from his severed head, as his plump body was turned into steak and sausages. But they were fine and becoming used to the stench and feel of death. Initially it had disturbed them and although they realised it was part of the routine, they never really relaxed fully when staying in the slaughterhouses.

The day's riding from Humahuaca was one of the best of the expedition. The vegetation began to thin as we climbed higher and there was a strong north wind to keep us cool and mad, in the true tradition of the Viento Norte. We stopped for lunch, sheltering in the lee of a high-walled graveyard that looked as if it had been the site of a good party the night before. The air of finality, decay and rubbish was enhanced by the paper flowers that flapped from each cross. The view was spectacular as the graveyard, like most in the region, was at the top of a hill. A great place to be buried.

In the afternoon, my diary records that 'we walked into a few hours of paradise. The mountains were lower, friendly and looked like chocolate mousse and cream dollopped on the edge of a plate. We were in the middle of a flat, open plain. The altiplano was coming closer. I was listening to Pink Floyd's *Wish You Were Here* on my Walkman. The horses were going well. Every once in a while, men are given the chance to see the beauty of their own lives. For me it was one of those times.'

We did not actually reach the altiplano for another few days. Andy had arranged that we would meet at the Minerva de Aguilar mining company at Tres Cruces. Originally American-owned, it had been sold to the Bolivians and accounted for eighty per cent of Argentina's lead. They had a base at Tres Cruces, from which the ore was railroaded south and people were sent up a few thousand metres more to the mine itself.

A friend of Andy's used to be an engineer at the company, and dropping his name provided an excellent corral for the horses and a room for myself. Although we were twenty kilometres from the mine, all the employees of Aguilar and therefore of Tres Cruces were required to wear hard helmets. They could not have been more hospitable and at one point there were four men in my room, lighting and stoking the wood-burning stove – all wearing hard helmets. When I went to collect the horses' feed from the police station, the police all jumped to attention and called me 'sir'. It was all very strange.

The nights were starting to get cold, and Andy and Alicia spent a miserable night in a local hospedaje. I, on the other hand, was forced to strip naked as the fire had been stoked to sauna level. Of course, I fell fast asleep and woke, like a shrivelled penis, when the temperature had dropped below zero.

We entered a different world the following day, when we rode out of Tres Cruces and up over the pass on to the altiplano. It felt like being in an aeroplane, climbing and breaking through the cloud cover. All was flat and had a calmness that hid its hostility. We came over the pass and before us stretched kilometre after kilometre of altiplano. We had reached one of the higher steps on the staircase to the top of the Andes. The road had lost its wiggles and led forward unswervingly. It all seemed rather comforting, the lack of human presence. We were the only presence and I felt as though the land accepted us, but no more. The wind was strong and comfortable, but if it rose we would be miserable. If we were stuck out at night, we would be frozen. But for the moment, I felt safe.

Arriving in Abra Pampa heightened my feelings of having entered another country as every inhabitant of the town seemed to be completely drunk. The horses were lodged in a field behind the restaurant of a man called Saavendra, to whom the horse rations had been delivered. I walked the kilometre or so into town and found a room in the only hotel, which was a fleapit. I walked out into the streets and, for the first time, felt exposed as an individual, not just as a weirdo riding through. The women of the town were all wearing many-layered dresses, hats, and mantas, intricately-woven blankets, on their backs; the men were in work clothes and baseball caps. There was very little European blood, if any, so I was a physical anomaly for starters. I was also sober.

Abra Pampa felt so different from the Argentina that I had slid into for the last five months that I decided to stay a day to acclimatise. At least it would be a weekday and there would be more sobriety.

Saavendra told me the story of his grandfather, which was well worth waiting for. In 1932 there had been yet another popular coup in La Paz, Bolivia. The population had taken to the streets and overpowered presidential resistance. The presidential palace, however, did not fall and the crowd stood at the gates howling for the blood of the President. Somehow Saavendra's grandfather managed to get into the palace alone and was ignored by the presidential guard who were busy thinking of ways to save their own skin.

He wandered about the palace corridors, looking into rooms, amazed at the wealth that the President had managed to syphon off for himself. Not that it was going to do him any good as Saavendra, the grandfather, found him lying, unguarded and unconscious, in one of the suites. Saavendra lifted the eyelids of the man, who he thought was the President, and the unseeing eyes confirmed his doubts. The President was known to have blue eyes.

Saavendra dragged the comatose body to a window and, lifting it, showed the man to the crowd.

'What shall I do?' shouted Saavendra.

'Kill him,' yelled some.

'Throw him down,' screamed others.

Saavendra chose the latter course and threw the President out of the window. He landed amongst the mob, was taken off and hanged.

Saavendra junior told me the story with pride and explained that his grandfather, as the sole hero of that particular coup, had had his picture splashed all over the papers. He had been forced to cross the border to Argentina but, wary that the Argentines would throw him back, had settled in Abra Pampa, border no-man's-land.

'My grandfather's trousers are on display in a museum in La Paz,' said Saavendra. 'You must go and see them.'

I promised that I would if I could.

La Paz seemed very far away but we arrived at the border town of La Quiaca within a few days, on 24th September.

Diary entry for 24th September:

'The last day of travelling in Argentina. I decide to ride Viento Norte again as he is fatter than el Chapeton. El Chapeton has lost weight in the climb but he needed to. Viento Norte is building up beautifully.

'We had a hassley morning with Viento Norte going very slowly. I had to push him along all the time and then he dragged on the rope when I was leading them on my feet.

'Saw two "gringos", the first foreigners that I have seen since Buenos Aires apart from the Germans. They had obviously just entered Argentina on their motorbikes. I was a long way off the road but we stared at each other very hard and, in true westerner style, made no attempts at acknowledgement. I was jealous of them. I sat with my back to Bolivia at lunch and looked back over Argentina. Back to Buenos Aires and the start of the trip. Back over the trip. I was very sad – almost in tears. Argentina has been my home for the last six months: home in the sense that I have been welcomed in and treated as part of the family.

'Argentina is a new country. It has started so slowly and continues so slowly that it has the opportunity, and is creating the opportunities to build a country that will be a world leader. Not necessarily in monetary wealth. Money will form a lesser part of the wealth formula in the next decades. But in its respect for the individual, and life with a capital L.

'The feeling of terror returned at lunch. The terror of failure. What would I do if I failed? The thought of a job does not appeal. The freedom that I have been given – although probably in my life I have never been so tied down or worked so hard – is very valuable.

'Failure to a Brit is acceptable; something to pontificate about at length at parties: how the business went down the tube, why the relationship failed. Failure is not acceptable to me but I am not talking about failure, in any case. I'm talking about the fear of failure.'

I was very sad to be leaving Argentina and frightened of Bolivia at the same time. I was used to Argentina. Bolivia seemed so alien and impossible. Stronger than the fear of the expedition itself was the fear of having an accident or being robbed or shot. But somehow, these latter possibilities seemed unlikely. 'Not to me, they won't happen to me.' But first I had to cross the border.

I went down to the gendarmeria and wangled my way into the chief's office. Their role was to maintain the border and to control contraband, especially cocaine, entering Argentina. Outside the gendarmeria there was a car park, containing about eighty vehicles, ranging from vintage buses to brand new BMWs. To add a bit of dash, several were stitched down their sides by bullet holes and many had had their windscreens blown out. The Gendarmeria's reputation had been slightly punctured when another unit, back down the road at Tres Cruces, had stopped a truck belonging to the border unit, and found it to be stuffed with cocaine. Rather than the expected cover-up, the border unit had been removed and replaced.

The new chief struck me as a particularly impressive and steady man. More than regulation height, but in regulation uniform, he asked me about the expedition and assured me of every assistance in crossing the border. He also gave me permission to corral the horses in the gendarmeria's mule corral; mules were used for border patrols.

He allocated me one of his men and told him to accompany me to the customs house. Unfortunately, the soldier had a brother who had been shot during the Falklands/Malvinas War and had spent the remaining years in and out of various mental asylums. I was told all this very matter-of-factly and he could not have been more helpful.

The first man whom we saw at the customs house took one look at my papers and told me to wait for the boss. I was very nervous, as I had all the papers that the Argentine mission in London had told me that I would need, but was still unsure of their validity, and paced the waiting room floor like a nervous father waiting for the birth of his first child.

At last a ferrety-looking man, with black greased-back hair and overcoat appeared. He reminded me of the suburban commuters that pour in and out of London every day. He had a commuter face and a commuter personality, which is very unfair to commuters the world over. He did not even look at my papers, but upon hearing about my expedition, went nuts. Apparently, two French people had brought horses from Bolivia and, devoid of the correct papers, had been refused permission to enter Argentina. They had immediately spoken to television, radio and the press complaining loudly about Argentina and Mr Customs Man, who had received a lot of flak from the authorities, although by the book he had been perfectly correct in refusing the French entry. Fortunately for the French (and unfortunately for Mr Customs Man), individuals are more important than the book to the Argentines. The French were allowed through and Mr Customs Man had a hatred of horses crossing the border.

I had impressed the chief of the Gendarmeria with a heavyweight recommendation from one of the country's top politicians. The chief sent his second-in-command around to deal with Mr Customs Man. They went into an office together, leaving me, the distressed father, outside, and argued for an hour. Apparently I was missing an important paper, which the Argentines in London had said was not necessary for horses, only mules.

The second-in-command at last appeared and, taking me aside, said, 'It's all under control, James. Relax. Your contact [the high-ranking judge] rang a very influential man in Jujuy, who rang the Gendarmeria and we have squared the customs. You can cross.'

The Gendarmeria also helped greatly with my dealings on the Bolivian side of the border. They introduced me to the Bolivian consul in La Quiaca, who either owed the Argentines a favour or two or needed to smarm up to them. He gave me a sidekick who accompanied me to Argentine immigration, where I officially left Argentina, and on to Bolivian immigration, where I officially entered Bolivia. We then crossed back to Argentina, where, officially, I was now an illegal alien.

I spent the next couple of days zipping backwards and forwards over the border on foot. The border is marked by a stream, over which a road bridge and a rail bridge have been built. All cross-border traffic is supposed to pass through customs on the bridges but as the stream can be crossed on foot there are a number of crossings.

La Quiaca, on the Argentine side, and Villazon, on the Bolivian side, are both dependent on the flow of goods between Argentina and Bolivia. Basic foodstuffs are shipped from all over Argentina to wholesalers in La Quiaca, to be sold to wholesalers in Villazon, who distribute them to the Bolivian population. Hundreds of Quechuans are employed to carry great loads of cheese, yoghurt, cooking oil and pasta on their backs from La Quiaca to Villazon. The loads are enormous by any estimation, forty kilos and upwards and are strapped on to men's, mules, and women's backs. The sight of many hundreds of campesinos in full costume staggering across the bridges was extraordinary.

Extra money is made, of course, from taking a risk with contraband which ranges from auto accessories to cocaine. Contraband crosses the border in all manner of ways. Big risks are often taken using mules. It has to be a big risk because if the plan fouls up, the mule would be confiscated, and mules are worth a great deal of money. A mule, if let loose, will always return to the place where it is fed with unswerving accuracy. Teams of mules are, therefore, fed up on both sides of the border. For a contraband run from Argentina to Bolivia, a Bolivian-fed mule crosses the border to Argentina legally. In La Quiaca it is loaded with contraband, led out on to the street and let go. Everyone then rushes back across the bridges to wait for the mule to pick its way across the illegal crossings, usually at night. If it is stopped by the Gendarmeria, the mule is lost, but is hard to prosecute.

Even more ingenious methods are used for smuggling cocaine. A popular one is dissolving the cocaine and soaking a sheep or llama skin in the solution. Safely on the other side, the skin would be re-soaked, wrung out and the cocaine extracted from the solution.

George had promised that he would make the six-hour plane trip up from Buenos Aires to watch us cross the border and I waited for him to arrive. I sat in my room scribbling letters to friends and to 'the jury'. 'The jury' consisted of sixteen people to whom I sent a one-page update on the expedition at regular intervals. I called them 'the jury' because to me they were the main judges of the expedition in terms of ethics and results. I tried to be as open and as expressive as possible in my reports, at the same time also trying to satisfy the needs of sixteen distinct readers.

'The jury' represented my attempts to justify the expedition. I had gone because I wanted to, but that is insufficient reason in the age of Objective. Any action must be for a purpose. Of course, I had no idea what my goal was; that was why I went. Each member of 'the jury' was connected to a component, e.g. charity work, this book, which made up an intangible whole (probably the value of the expedition to me).

I was thrilled to have passed border formalities, albeit in a mildly devious manner, but I was still nervous as both my horses and I were still on the Argentine side. I had learned in Argentina never to count chickens before they hatch. And I was right, as the 'incubation' of our border crossing was a hard one.

George arrived with Pablo and Andy, which was a great surprise. Pablo had driven the Falcon up from Buenos Aires, a huge journey, and George had flown to Jujuy. Andy had made contact with them in Jujuy and they had all come up together. All three were in fine form, as excited as little boys from their road trip up from Jujuy. It was great to see them and we immediately repaired to the nearest bar, the Terminal Café. Andy had very kindly brought more hay and grain and, as I still had supplies in La Quiaca, we decided that once I had crossed the border with the horses in the morning, we would drive on to Tupiza (the first town in Bolivia) and drop off the supplies.

We had an excellent dinner that night and introduced George to roulette. Pablo, Andy and I lost our money within a few minutes so we persuaded George to have a go. He cashed a couple of dollars for chips, stepped up to the table, put all his money on a number and won. I could not decide if it was a good omen or not.

I was very nervous about the crossing the following morning and slept badly. I arrived early at the gendarmeria and saddled the horses. Because of the paper problems, the horses were, officially, being smuggled out of Argentina while both the Gendarmeria and Aduana turned a blind eye, officially, on the day. A lieutenant at the gendarmeria had been instructed to show me to one of the illegal crossings and to allow myself and the horses across. Unfortunately, he hated me on sight. He was the only person that I met in Argentina who hated me because of my nationality. The first thing he said to me was: 'If it was under my control, I would not allow you over. I would make you go back to Buenos Aires and obtain the correct papers.' Which was fair as I was breaking the rules.

We (me, the horses, George, Pablo, Andy, the lieutenant and a private) all set off on foot towards the border. The animosity of the lieutenant and the fact that I was about to do something illegal created a tense and heavy atmosphere.

A twenty-minute walk took us to an outpost that overlooked the valley and the Bolivian side. It was manned by an official, who had been told nothing of our crossing. If the lieutenant had wished to, he could have overridden the official and we would have been on our way. He did not. We sat on the top of the hill and waited for four hours. The telephone in the outpost had broken so the private was sent back to the gendarmeria. He came back to say that as it was a Sunday, the authorities were off duty and mainly still in bed. They had chickened out and none of them would put their name to the order to let us across. The private was sent back again.

For me it was excruciating as I could see the border 500 metres away. George, a very experienced man, was brilliant, quietly assuring me that everything was going to be OK and to stay calm. We talked about 1992 and the ease with which it is already possible to travel between countries in Europe. He compared the current agreements between South American countries to nineteenth-century Europe.

We waited. Every once in a while, there would be a flurry of exchanges between George, myself, Andy on one side and the lieutenant and the official on the other. George would be rational, I would be emotional, and Andy would be Latin. The combination worked, slowly, but at last the lieutenant relented.

'Go,' he said, 'perhaps the Bolivians will shoot you,' and turned away. There was no chance of this but I was not filled with enthusiasm. Still, we were moving again and, without saying goodbye to anyone, I led the horses away from the outpost and down towards the border. I expected the lieutenant, at any time, to change his mind and call us back. But we got closer to the stream. We were paddling through. We were over. We were in Bolivia.

Now I was afraid that the Bolivians would throw the horses back into Argentina and I would be stuck in Bolivia, unable to return to Argentina myself as my visa had expired. I had also been warned that there were gangs roving the border and ripping people off. We were about twenty metres into Bolivia when I saw four heavy looking youngsters peel off from a wall, from which they had been watching me and the horses.

'Papers,' said one.

'What?' I said, feigning misunderstanding.

'Papers. Show me your papers.'

'I don't understand.'

'Papers. I want to see your papers. Passport. I want to see your passport.'

I was not going to show any papers or passport stuck out in the open. A favourite trick of con-men is demanding to see papers and then ransoming their return. I was sure that these people were hoods.

'Show me yours,' I said.

'What?' replied one of the hoods in surprise.

'Who are you?' I asked.

'Police. We are the border police.'

'Show me your identification then,' I demanded.

'We are the police.'

'Yes, but I want to see identification.'

One of the hoods took out something that looked like a credit card and flashed it in front of my face. It was obviously a national ID card, which by law every Tom, Dick and Henrico had to carry.

'Now show us your papers.'

'No,' I said, 'that is an ID card. It means nothing.'

'What are you carrying?' said one, referring to my saddlebags.

'Equipment.'

'What equipment?'

'Equipment for my journey.'

'Show me your papers.'

'Not until I see yours.'

'OK,' he said, 'we'll go into the centre.'

I marched off into Bolivia, pleased that at least we were going in the right direction. Officially, we should still have been somewhere in the middle of the stream. The hoods were following. I was sure that they were not officials. First, they were not carrying guns and second, the ID card had been a lousy stunt.

We went deep into the outskirts of Villazon, wading through rubbish in the adobe-hutted streets. We passed out of sight of George and the Argentine observers and I thought, 'this is when they'll do it', but just kept marching along, holding my breath. They were lagging behind and I thought that they had given up but, as I reached the centre, they caught up and directed me towards the customs house.

I was very scared. I was out of Argentina but had not been accepted into Bolivia. I had no home. I had no place. I was completely alien.

A man in a tracksuit appeared and unlocked the customs house. The hoods, who had been guarding me, motioned me in and we all went into an office. Although we were in the official customs building I was still wary. It was a Sunday. Anyone could have had a key and the best scams have an air of officialdom.

The man in the tracksuit sat down behind a steel desk.

'Where are your papers?' he said.

'Where are yours? Who are you? Where is your ID?' was all I could say. In these situations of absurdity and tension, I found my mind wandering outside and watching the pantomime as an observer. Is this me? Who is this stubborn asshole? You. Concentrate.

'In the house,' said tracksuit. 'Show me your papers.'

'I want to see your ID before I show you mine.'

One of the hoods stepped across to the desk. 'He's a policeman. Look,' and, with a bang, pulled open a drawer. We all concentrated, for what seemed a very long time, on three pistols in the drawer.

OK, I thought, and reached for my papers. They were scrutinised and the tension eased.

'They are fine,' said the police chief. 'They are fine,' he said to the hoods, implying that they had seriously wasted his time on a Sunday.

I stepped in for the hoods' defence and explained the fear of handing papers to con-men. The chief understood and the hoods were let off the hook.

'Welcome to Bolivia,' said the chief, shaking my hand.

I belonged there, and I felt great. I stepped outside and the veil of alienship had been lifted. I was in Bolivia. Jump up and down. Go wild. I bought a snack. I smiled and said hello to everyone. I fixed up a corral. I fixed up a room. I smiled at everyone and said hello.

We had crossed Argentina.

We were in Bolivia – officially.

9

Bolivian Picnics

GEORGE, PABLO, ANDY and I drove to Tupiza and deposited the horse food that Andy had brought from Jujuy. We broke the fan on the way and it looked as if they would be unable to return to Argentina, which would have been disastrous as neither Andy nor Pablo had passports. However a mechanic, of extraordinary ingenuity, fixed a Toyota fan (the only one available) on to the Ford Falcon. The fan was much smaller and could not be bolted directly on to the Ford's mounting. With a series of simple nuts and bolts, he attached the fan and weighted it so that it ran smoothly.

We drove back to Villazon and the others tried to persuade me to cross the border again and spend a night in the luxury hotel in La Quiaca. However, no amount of luxury and friendship was going to persuade me to cross the border illegally again and, feeling very lonely, I went back to my hotel, having said goodbye. I lay in bed, feeling very exposed, wondering what the hell we were getting into now.

Sometimes the nights were interminable but often they seemed non-existent. I would lie down and within seconds, or so it seemed, would be dragging myself out of bed. If I felt like spending another day in a place, I would. I thought that I should progress at my own speed, a speed that was largely determined by what I wanted to do, rather than what I felt I should do.

When I woke that first morning in Bolivia, what I wanted to do was to ride out of Villazon. It was a town of buyers and sellers, money changers and authority. I wanted to be as far away as fast as possible from people who dealt in forms.

There were a number of road blocks on the road north but, on the whole, they waved us through. At one toll control, they wanted to charge me for the horses, which made me laugh. I paid up, as I was sure that some of the money would go into the pocket of the guard, and not government coffers where it would be transferred to a government official's account in Switzerland.

By mid-morning we had reached a great flat expanse of altiplano. It was yellow, stony and covered by kilometre after kilometre of low scrub. There was not a sign of anything edible in sight. In the far, far distance I could see mountains from which our piece of altiplano flowed. A few hours later, we dropped into a very beautiful valley. A large stone colonial house, tiled in red, stood in the middle of intensely cultivated plots of land of Action Man proportions. The boundary walls to the house were covered in flowers. We rode through the valley stream, up the hill and were back in the 'Mad Max' scenery of the altiplano within a few minutes. I looked back to see if we had passed through a dream, and the valley side hid any clue of the fertility below.

Mojo looked like a fair-sized place on my map but when we arrived it consisted of a rail halt and a finca. 'Whatever Bolivia throws at us, arriving at Mojo will have been worth it,' I wrote in my diary that night. Mojo was contained within a high wall, made up of the outer walls of the houses that made up the micro-village. We rode through the entry arch to find a white-walled, twin-towered church dominating the courtyard.

I asked for Pedro Gonzalez, who the man at the rail halt had said could help me, and a drunk was summoned from the church.

'What do you want?' said Pedro.

'A corral for my horses.'

'Fine. And alfalfa?'

'Yes, and is there somewhere that I can sleep?'

'Of course.'

The horses were corralled and watered with salty water, which Pedro said would help them with the altitude. He opened up a room in the central house for me and allowed me to settle in. The room must have been the old estate office as the walls were covered with maps and ledgers and, centre stage, was a Dickensian ledger table and stool. I poked around the rest of the rooms in the house the following morning. Room after room surrounded a central courtyard and looked as if the owners had upped stumps and fled. There was a trove of antique furniture, gramophone players and a plethora of white and brown goods, whose purpose I could only guess at.

Pedro was drunk because the finca's inhabitants were preparing for the fiesta of their patron saint, Saint Francis. He insisted that I get drunk with him too. He poured me a tumbler full of raw alcohol and we toasted each other. Then we toasted Saint Francis, Bolivia, Argentina, the UK, Mojo, friendship, horses, women and life. We sat in his house, which was another room of the finca, with five or six

143

members of his family, but it was difficult to tell how many were in the room as the only lighting came from a solitary candle. I was given a plate of 'Mojo stew' which was pretty disgusting, but fortunately I was unable to see what I was eating. Pedro and I had a long chat about friendship and humanity and, as a mark of the evening in his home, he gave me a 1892 coin that he had found in the camp. We wept together and I went to bed.

Feeling distinctly sick the next morning, I heaved myself on to Viento Norte and rode out over more altiplano. I had already been on this road before in George's car but it seemed so totally different from the back of a horse. From the car the scenery had been more awesome, more frightening. When the fan had broken, the idea of being stuck out with a useless two-tonne hunk of metal had been rather scary. On the back of my horses, we seemed to blend in better and become part of the landscape. I trusted my horses; I trusted their stamina and strength.

We came to a pass and climbed between valley walls and suddenly, at the top, we saw a land that George had described as 'somewhere out of Tolkien'. The land had gone mad. High valleys were full of bare, yellow mountains. The road snaked down into a labyrinth of physical formation that we would surely be lost in. If a dragon or strange creatures in medieval costume had appeared, I would not have been surprised.

The only traffic we saw was a couple of mule trains. Usually consisting of five or six mules, they came plodding towards us along the track in single file. They were shunted from behind by a campesino acting as an engine. The mules were frightened of the horses and would leap off the side of the road or, on the tracks that clung to the side of the cliff walls, would whip round and charge back towards the campesino who would dash backwards and forwards across the road, flapping his arms in an attempt to turn them round.

We passed through valleys of willow and alfalfa to arrive at Tupiza. My contact in Tupiza was Don Humberto Bernal, whose daughter was a friend of someone in the British Embassy in La Paz, and whose name the incredibly helpful British Ambassador had given to me in a letter containing advice on my route and the authorities.

Don Humberto Bernal owned Tupiza. He and his brothers, the sons of a miner, had started their own antimony mining company in their twenties. They had gone up to well over 5000 metres and, living the year round in tiny shacks, had dug a living out of the ground. The mines had gone from strength to strength, roads had replaced mules, employees had replaced the brothers and they had become very rich.

Don Humberto owned a large house in the middle of Tupiza but otherwise lived very simply. He hated leaving the town and I could see why. The level of peace and tranquillity that pervaded the streets and the people of Tupiza, I never saw anywhere else in Latin America. Tupiza is famous for its balmy climate, as on all four sides, it is protected by steep valleys. When I told Bolivians in the north that I had been through Tupiza, their eyes lit up with obvious pride at containing such a haven within their borders.

The antimony business was in decline as the Chinese had found great reserves. The Chinese government, according to Don Humberto, had been dumping antimony on the international market, in one of their efforts to gain hard foreign currency. The price had dipped well below the cost of production, even for the Chinese. But this did not stop Don Humberto and his wife pushing out the boat for me and my horses in every way that they could.

The horses were corralled and looked after on Don Humberto's finca, a few kilometres out of Tupiza, and I am sure that he spent a great deal of money acquiring extra fodder for them. As for myself, I was given the master suite and huge meals four times a day: a cooked breakfast, lunch, afternoon tea and supper. Afternoon tea, *a los Ingleses*, is a popular custom in Bolivia and the Bernals always ate the full gamut of tea, toast, butter and jam at 4.30 in the afternoon.

It was a great pleasure to meet and talk to a man such as Don Humberto. Everybody, every once in a while, meets a person that impresses enormously, and Don Humberto was one of those people for me. For a sixty-year-old man, he had the enthusiasm and energy of a twenty-year-old. He was always quietly rushing about, organising and running his businesses and talking on a myriad of radios that he kept, both as a hobby and for his business. He was never dependent on the telecommunication system to reach his office in La Paz, and spoke regularly to his daughter in the USA by radio.

We relaxed for a full four days in Tupiza and I would have stayed longer, but we had delayed in Argentina and the rainy season was approaching. I sewed a painting of a man with a shield and lance riding a horse that I was given on to the back of my jacket and re-shod el Chapeton with the Easy Glu shoes, the last set having lasted the whole way from Jujuy, and we left.

We walked away from the Bernals' house, waving as a large crowd had gathered, across the river and out of Tupiza. The climb back up to the altiplano began almost immediately on a hairpin-bend road with fearsome drops.

We had just reached the altiplano, when a thunderstorm rolled up from behind us. And we were right in it. One minute the sun was shining and the next it was as dark as a full-moon night and pouring with rain. Lightning hit the flat plain all around us and the thunder was deafening. Up to that point in my life, I had never been frightened of the elements, but that storm instilled a great respect in me for natural forces. On the altiplano, devoid of trees, houses or even shrubs, the horses and myself were plugged right into the sky. I jumped off el Chapeton so that I was not quite so exposed and we continued along the track as there was nowhere else to go.

In Tupiza, I had been reading an English translation of *The Odyssey*, which must have got to me, as I found myself praying to the gods. A litany, 'don't strike us, don't strike us', revolved in my head. 'Please don't strike us.'

The storm at last passed. I was becoming highly superstitious and, after settling the horses for the night, I made a sacrifice to the gods for our safe passage through the storm. I put out some boiled eggs and cigarettes on a stone, cooked up a meal for myself and went to bed.

In the middle of the night an old man appeared and woke me. Still lying under my poncho, I offered him a cigarette and he squatted down on his haunches. We talked about the storm. He said that he had seen me stuck out in the open and the danger we had been in, but told me not to worry. I do not remember going back to sleep and counted my cigarettes in the morning. None had been smoked in the night. The memory of the man and the confidence and peace that he had exuded had been too clear to have been a dream.

Throughout the rest of the expedition, I continued to put out food and cigarettes when we had had a particularly hairy or rewarding experience. I had to thank someone.

I left quickly, rather unnerved, for the ride to Ramadas. In total contrast to the day before, the weather was perfect and the horses seemed to have wings on their feet. I usually played my Walkman when I was feeling tired as I found that music stimulated both body and mind. But sometimes, such as the Ramadas day, I listened all day. One of the advantages of wearing a Walkman was that my hearing was cut off from my surroundings. Often, people working in the fields at the side of the road, would shout out wanting me to stop and chat. But stopping and chatting broke the rhythm of progress and if we had stopped every time, we would still have been in Argentina. Ensconced in music I was oblivious to shouts and the more that I was waved at, the more I waved back.

Ramadas consisted of a series of shops run by some very unhelpful

Quechua women. They suggested that I try the school for accommodation and the public corral for the horses. The headmaster of the school was delighted to see me and, as usual, I was offered supreme hospitality. I had stayed in schools before and the price of a night's sleep in one of the classrooms was to give a talk to the children.

We arrived just as the day was breaking up and lessons were finishing. The headmaster clapped his hands for food to be brought and, when I had finished the plate of rice and red sauce, I was accompanied by about fifty children to feed the horses. Horses are rare on the altiplano and the children were fascinated by their size compared to mules. A few peeled off to go home as they walked up to five kilometres in both directions five times a week. The remaining forty came into the classroom where I was going to spend the night and helped me unpack my stuff.

Thirty were left to watch a game of volleyball, and they gave me the sort of attention usually reserved for North American mega-stars. Every time I got to the ball there were huge cheers from the crowd, and if I made a rare winning shot they went wild. As I was about twice the height of the tallest playing adult, my total lack of skill was partially negated.

There was a big fall-out rate after the volleyball and only a handful of children remained to watch me write my diary. We talked for a while and I told them about the UK, where it was and what the people did. Whenever I spoke about the UK, I tried to list the bad facets as well as the good. I talked about what I liked about South America, and what Europeans had lost in their development and maintenance of First World economies.

I said goodnight to the remaining children and went to have supper with the headmaster. Most of the teachers lived in the neighbouring towns of Villazon and Potosi. Like teachers all over the world, Bolivian teachers are paid very poorly. Unable to afford to commute, rural teachers, if they live in towns, leave their families for the week and live in tiny rooms adjoining the school. Every teacher is required to spend a certain amount of time in rural communities.

The head and I had a basic supper together, the highlight of which was a cup of Nescafé, which I had not seen for a long time. We talked for a while and I went off to bed. I checked the horses before turning in. Viento Norte was sensibly asleep and el Chapeton was indulging in one of his favourite activities, mule baiting.

One last ritual before bed. I unbuttoned my flies and, standing with my hands on my hips, let rip into the night. I was rather startled to hear a couple of streams to my left and right. Looking round, I saw two boys, who had lasted the distance, standing with their hands on their hips, pissing away beside me.

I tried to pay my debts the following morning by giving a lecture to the school. Sixty or seventy children were summoned to the classroom of the biology teacher. I spoke about Europe, what I was doing, what I had seen and more general blurb. But I made one awful mistake.

Dominating the blackboard in the classroom was a picture of a house fly that had been drawn with Dürer-like care; it really was an awesome piece of educational material. As I talked I realised that a map of the UK and South America would be useful and, turning towards the headmaster, asked, 'Is there anything that I could sketch a map on?' As I spoke, I saw the chasm of disaster looming. The headmaster jumped up and, despite my trying to block him with protestations and my body, he rubbed out the fly in a flurry of chalk dust. My drawing is on a par with my volleyball and my sketch of the world would have been rejected by Columbus.

The planting of maize was in full swing in every valley that lined or crossed the road to Potosi. Each farmer brings his team of two oxen to his neighbours' farms. When two to five teams are assembled, the ploughs are yoked up and the wooden or steel tips run through the field. Wooden-tipped ploughs are not only used by the poorer farmers but also because there is a belief that steel poisons the earth. Once each field has been turned three times, a steel or wooden prong is run through the impeccably turned soil to break it. Women follow the oxen, which are driven along with sharp sticks, dropping the maize into the furrows. The sembrada (planting) is, of course, a great excuse for a party and before and after working, exceptionally hot and spicy chicken is eaten, and large quantities of chicha (a barley beer) and tragos (shots) of sugar alcohol consumed. Apparently it was a good omen for the crop that I should be passing at the time and often, too often, I was implored to have a drink. The custom is to pour a little on the ground for the pachamama (earth goddess) and down the rest.

In Cotagaita, I saw how deep the level of pre-conquistador thinking remains. The local hospital had twenty or so beds, all of which, bar one, were unoccupied. The newly arrived doctor, Fernando Marquez, who was there to conform to further government regulations of spending time in rural communities, explained.

'First, I have just arrived and people do not trust me as the new man. And, I haven't been helped,' he said ruefully, 'by the fact that my first case, a woman who drank weed-killer by mistake, died this morning. Secondly,' he went on, 'many people in the outlying communities still have more faith in the local homeopathic witch doctors than myself.'

He patched up my mouth, that had taken on a life of its own in the last few days, and refused payment, which was very kind. I insisted that he take a donation.

There were a number of posters on the walls, warning people against 'chagas'. The medical profession has a very hard job fighting this disease as it comes from the very houses that ninety per cent of the altiplano population live in. A beetle that inhabits the adobe huts of mud and straw, has a bite that can eventually be fatal. Over a number of years and a large number of bites, 'chagas' attacks the heart resulting in coronary failure.

While my mind was on medical matters, I went and bought some more Nivea for el Chapeton. The eyelid around his wall eye was susceptible to the sun, so by day he wore factor 15 sunblock and at night a little moisturising cream.

I was amazed to see humming birds at this altitude. Unlike the pea-sized versions that I had seen in David Attenborough series, I saw a large green and a smaller darker brown model. There were numerous birds of prey and a general multitude of life that varied with the altitude and corresponding micro-climates as we dipped up and down.

Friday, 13th October came around and I took no chances. My diary records: 'Rest day in Tumusla. Watched flies.' I do, however, remember reading Stephen King's book *Different Seasons*, which is very different from the menu of horrors that I thought he usually produced. We stopped one day in a grove in the monte and were shaded from the sun and wind. It seemed a mystical place, and I left my copy of *Different Seasons* on a stone for the god of writing, in case he passed through and needed some English language literature.

By the time that we reached Potosi, about 300 kilometres from the border, my sadness at leaving Argentina had dissipated as both I and the horses were loving Bolivia. We were travelling steadily and effectively thirty-five to forty kilometres per day. We had plenty of rest as I always took an hour for a lunch of bread and the bondiola from La Piedmontesa factory and we always arrived at our destinations with heaps of time to get settled in and fuelled up.

The first sign that we were approaching Potosi was a slag heap of revolting proportions. I never found out what it was, but even in environmentally unconcerned Bolivia, this slag heap was constantly sprayed with water. I was very angry as I had allowed the horses to drink from a nearby stream, about two kilometres downstream. They must have been drinking the effluent but it seemed to have done them no damage, yet.

We rode on over a crest and there lay Potosi before us, surrounded by horrifying mining decay. The landscape around Potosi was completely devoid of vegetation. The work had gone on underground for many years and had stripped the earth of its silver and aluminium reserves. The waste had poured on to the hills that surround the city, almost threatening to swamp it. The place also seemed devoid of any life, except human, and I thought that it might be very difficult to organise somewhere for the horses.

I rang a friend of the Bernals, Doctor Daniel Howard, from the first telephone that we reached, and he confirmed my suspicions that Potosi was devoid of animals, feed and corrals. He did, however, say that I could keep my horses on the patio of his house. As most of the streets were cobbled, Viento Norte slithered into the centre while el Chapeton in his Easy Glu plastic shoes had all the grip that he needed. The Howards' house was about two blocks from the main plaza. We caused a great stir in the centre; first, as we looked so out of place and, second, because we caused a major traffic jam.

The patio was perfect for the horses, as the house had been recently built and the sandy patio floor had yet to be planted with grass. There was even an ornate fountain that made a perfect drinking trough.

Being in the very middle of a city, the horses caused a great deal of interest, and people out shopping would peer through the door to get a look. It was perfect having the horses staying with me at the Howards', as I avoided the hassle of trekking off every day to check them out. Horse feed was scarce but Don Humberto had sent feed from Tupiza and the local brewer helped out with barley. The only problem was that I was forced to muck out the patio three times a day to keep the flies off.

While in the middle of Potosi, it was hard to picture mentally the devastation outside that built the city. In the seventeenth century, Potosi was reputed to be the richest city in the world due to the staggering amounts of silver that were found in the Cerro Rico, down which slopes we had ridden to enter the city. The silver helped finance the Spanish Empire and the British also took their cut. For every three ships that left South American shores, one was pirated by the British. When I said that I was British, often I was looked at more

(TOP) Sharing my bed in a hospedaje.

(LEFT) The rainy season was on its way and seemed to have caught this vendor unawares.

(ABOVE) Being taught to suck eggs, which I did regularly for running snacks. They taste like fried eggs.

(LEFT) The best spectator sport in La Paz is the daily teargas battle between the police and students.

(BELOW) Lake Titicaca – the bundle of reeds to the left will be used to make a boat.

OPPOSITE PAGE (ABOVE) A church on the road to Cuzco.

(BELOW) For several months, we rarely dropped below 4000 metres above sea level.

OPPOSITE PAGE (ABOVE) Climbing towards the final pass before dropping to the Pacific. (BELOW) Viento Norte for the first time sampling snow – the watery kind. The temperature was − 10°C ...

THIS PAGE (BELOW) ... but 3 days ride later, it was over 40°C. (BOTTOM LEFT) We rode 1000 kilometres through the Peruvian coastal desert. It never rains. (BOTTOM RIGHT) El Chapeton looking pleased with himself on arrival in Lima.

(TOP) Carina and I were married on Peruvian Independence Day, 28th July, 1990. (*Richard Greenly*)

(ABOVE) The expedition as seen by the *Racing Post*. (*Stephen Johnson*)

closely and told that I was a 'pirata'. I felt rather proud. When silver was found by the Spanish in Mexico and Peru, and the Cerro Rico had been almost sucked dry, Potosi's glory waned.

In Spain, there remains an expression 'as rich as Potosi' to this day and the evidence of the town's past wealth was clearly visible in its streets. Many of the central streets are lined by palatial houses that would have been occupied by one family, now split into apartment blocks. Churches and cathedrals were built at what seemed to be every junction.

The museums in Potosi hold many articles from that time and are a testament to the style the Spanish rulers lived in. La Casa de Moneda, the most impressive of the museums that I visited in South America, was built in 1542 for the minting of silver coins to be used throughout the Spanish realms. The minting machinery had been beautifully preserved by the dry, crispy-cold air (Potosi stands at over 4000 metres above sea level), and is remarkable in that every working part is made of wood. It was operated by two giant wheels in the basement, powered at first by black slaves and, at the later stages of its working life, by mules. Two thousand slaves were brought in from the west coast of Africa to work mainly in the construction of houses for Spanish settlers who were pouring in from every part of the world to profit from the great silver rush. Unfortunately, the slaves, who lived in dormitories in the roof of La Casa de Moneda died swiftly from exhaustion, diseases and the cold.

The main reserves were finished long ago but silver is still mined in and around Potosi. While I was in the city there was a great deal of talk about a new face of silver that had been discovered, and geologists were attempting to discover its length and magnitude.

But enough tiny seams remain to provide a living for a myriad of private co-operatives. Potosi was full of people involved in mining around the city or in the area, evidenced by the huge number of street sellers, peddling the basics of the Quechuan miner: carbide, coca leaves and dynamite. The ingredients to make a very big explosion – a fuse and a stick of dynamite – were available to anybody with sufficient Bolivianos in his or her pockets. Often I found myself travelling along in a bus, surrounded by people juggling sticks of dynamite, like a scene out of some slap-stick movie. I preferred to travel by taxi and took one memorable ride from the top to the bottom of the city, when the driver never once turned on his engine but still charged me the full fare when we rolled to a stop.

I took the opportunity, while in Potosi, to go down a mine for the first time. The co-operative miners opened their entrance tunnels to all and sundry in an effort to earn more cash. Most of the visitors were Western backpackers, and for the first time in a month or so I was speaking English. I met a group of four Australian investment bankers in a café and made a big mistake, asking about the Ashes.

We were packed into a bus and driven up to a mining settlement on the Cerro Rico. Although the mine was not far from Potosi, the miners often spent the week living at the settlement instead of commuting every day. I had expected the mines to be a tourist gimmick as they were a crucial stop-off for every backpacker passing through. The income that the miners received from tourists was important but I found out that the majority of our fee was snapped up by the tourist agencies and guides.

The encampment was a scene of unforgettable squalor. Tiny huts with the minimum of basics were the homes to five or six bodies. Rows and rows of men were sitting, preparing to go down the mine with tools, lamps and coca leaves. Coca leaves act as a depressant of thirst, hunger and pain, and as a miner would work a twelve-hour shift in 40°C with the minimum of food and water, they were packing their mouths full, stripping the stalks from the leaves and cramming the leaves into their mouths, until we seemed to be surrounded by men with violent tooth abscesses.

Our guide offered coca leaves to our party of eight and there was a general expression of revulsion from the Europeans, which surprised me as I had always imagined European backpackers to be an adventurous bunch. I was the only one apart from our guide to take a handful. You stuff them into your mouth, make a wad, bite on it and position the wad between teeth and cheek. The taste is bitter and produces a stream of thick green saliva. I had been using coca leaves myself every once in a while during the expedition. I found that in the middle of the afternoon I would become sluggish and slow and chewing leaves for twenty minutes would perk me up for two or three hours of riding.

We were issued with carbide lamps, which potholders would be used to but which I found fascinating. Small white stones are broken up and put into a container filled with water. The container is then pumped full of air so that a stream of acetylene is forced out under pressure and ignited to produce a tiny, but very strong flame that is enhanced by a reflector dish. It makes a very effective but rather dangerous lamp.

Bolivian miners worship the devil and every year make sacrifices of llamas, whose blood is spread all over the entrance to the mines as an offering. The brickwork was black with dried blood. Inside the mine was a shrine to 'el Tio' ('the Uncle' as the devil is called) and a hideous mask sat at the end of a low chamber. Once a week el Tio was left coca leaves, cigarettes and alcohol. When no one was looking, I dropped cigarettes on to his altar. You never can tell.

The air in the mine, when we had walked in a few hundred yards, was hot and oppressive compared to the cold air outside. The party stripped off their high-tech, rough-weather, designer, macho-man, tough-as-hell, inner-city, outer-boundary, European, no-nonsense, fashion camping gear. One girl was overcome by the closeness and, in a display of great humour, our guide left her in el Tio's shrine. I offered to stay with her but she took one look at me and decided that she preferred el Tio.

We moved further into the mine, twisting round girders and rock-falls and crawling on our hands and knees through low passages. Every once in a while, we would see lamps ahead or hear gentle shouts behind and, quick as moles, miners would pass us.

After a while, I lost all sense of direction and could only concentrate on minimising the damage to my body as we scraped and crawled through the passages. Our guide, who was excellent, pointed out seams of material, mine shafts and their use and explained what was going on in detail. He told us that we were about 1500 metres into the mine, when we started to hear a rhythmic pinging sound that echoed towards and around us.

We branched off one of the main routes, through which we had been crouching, and were forced on to our bellies. The Euro-gear was starting to show signs of wear as we squirmed through holes in the rock just big enough for a man. The pinging sound became more of a thumping noise and, at last, we saw its source. A man was hammering a crowbar into the wall of a chamber about the size of a small kitchenette.

There was just enough room for our party as we pushed and shoved each other to get the most out of this photo opportunity. The miner stopped working for a while and handed us each a tiny lump of surprisingly heavy silver ore. We handed back cigarettes and money and left him in his coffin, lit by a carbide lamp and heated to about 40°C.

The following day I visited the state mine in the Cerro Rico, which mainly mined aluminium but as the cost of extraction was $10 a pound and aluminium was trading at $2.97 a pound on the London Metal Exchange, the mine had all but shut down. I took a bus to the mine entrance and bought a ticket. The official guide thought that I might be the only tourist that day but, at the last moment, a group of twenty middle-aged French tourists appeared.

153

The mine was run down and making no money, even less than the private co-operative mines, a few hundred metres away through solid rock. As what little mining was being carried out was three kilometres from the entrance, we were walked around for a while and shown a compressed-air drill that had superseded the crowbar.

Leaving from Potosi and on the road to Oruro, we really got into our stride for the first time in the expedition. The horses were fit, I was fit, the saddles fitted and I stopped worrying. The horses had been pampered by me ever since we had left and I had taken good care of myself, ensuring that we never became tired. We had suffered little from altitude sickness, although my nose had bled at times on the climb to Potosi. We had suffered little from exhaustion. We had been tired but only enough to sleep.

The road out from Potosi was lined with little holes in the mountainsides; more private mines from which tiny earnings were scratched.

Our first night was spent in another beautiful finca. In 1952, Bolivia had brought in stringent land reforms, stripping wealthy landowners of their property and handing over quarter- to half-hectare parcels to campesinos, who had previously been employed to work the land. From what I saw, it had worked well. Each campesino had his plot of land that produced sufficient food for his family and a basic income. Many would argue that the size of the plots, bounded by banks of earth, were inefficient and could have been improved immensely by amalgamating fields and using mechanical transport.

The one sadness of land reform was the abandonment of the fincas from which the old estancias had been managed. Chateau-like colonial houses had been left to rot when the income from agriculture was no longer available to support them. Their settings and architecture made them some of the most beautiful houses that I have ever seen. I would sleep in caved-in wings that once must have been beautifully maintained.

Horses were very scarce and this created a number of problems. There was little fodder, and what there was, was extremely expensive. I was starting to pay five times the amount I spent on food for myself, buying limited quantities of alfalfa and charla (maize stalks and husks) for the horses. Charla is really only a stomach filler, giving roughage and maintaining stomach throughflow, and has a very low energy content. The amount of maize that the horses were eating I had increased markedly, but el Chapeton had decided that he did not like maize and was losing weight.

I found that I was always paying mildly over the market prices, but fodder is very expensive as it is needed for domestic livestock. A kilo of maize cost me about thirty US cents, and barley and wheat a little more. Although I could have haggled all prices down to market level if I had wanted, I was always prepared to pay a little over the odds, because paying twenty to twenty-five per cent more than necessary seemed a very good way of making a tiny charitable contribution to the local economy. Another way was to employ people for little jobs such as collecting horse food, food for myself and generally helping out.

One of the main problems that I was having in such a treeless area was that there was nowhere to tie the horses when I was saddling them. One morning I employed a kid to hold the horses as I put on their kit but he left, terrified, as el Chapeton began his prancing-about routine.

The weather was beginning to become variable as the rains were on their way but if it did rain, it usually bucketed down at night and cleared up during the day. We continued our climb to the pass that would take us north-west, towards Oruro.

We had a very satisfactory morning, having crossed the pass, and were descending to the Devil's Bridge when I began to feel very strange. I felt giddy and my vision narrowed, so I climbed down from el Chapeton and began to lead the horses. I thought that I must be suffering from altitude sickness, which surprised me, as I thought I had acclimatised by then, and I also had none of the headache and nausea associated with high-altitude travel.

I began to lose my sense of balance although I did not stumble or fall over. It felt as if I was floating. I lost sight of the road in front of my eyes but was able to walk in a perfectly straight line. I looked down at my boots, clumping away, but they seemed very far away and unattached to my body. My sight began to fragment until I seemed to have ten or so different sets of vision. I could see my boots, and I could see my forehead and the brim of my hat, I could see the back of my jacket and the pockets. But the strangest image of all was in the very centre of this collage of pictures. I could see the horses and myself as if we were twenty metres away and walking towards me.

In no manner did I feel ill. In fact I felt wonderful and savoured each image of myself and the horses. I began to laugh. I laughed harder and harder and felt even better. The images faded and I had a single image again. The state returned again and faded. Drifting in and out of this condition lasted about thirty minutes and throughout the entire time I had perfect consciousness and perception of my feelings and vision. After thirty minutes it failed to return and I have never had it since.

I can propose a variety of explanations. I was suffering from some sort of altitude sickness, although I was in perfect, if not buoyant, spirits. Or perhaps I had reached a level of exhaustion, buried deep below normal tiredness, but in fact I was full of beans and had been sleeping well and thoroughly. Otherwise, I could have, inadvertently, eaten some form of hallucinogenic substance.

A rational friend later came up with an 'alternative' explanation, saying that I had reached a state of consciousness called 'astral'. 'Astral', as far as I could make out, is a kind of motorway service station on the highway to 'nirvana'. Apparently, when you reach 'astral', you have arrived at a point where you are at one with yourself and your surroundings to the extent that you can observe yourself mentally and physically with complete objectivity.

By the time that we had reached the Devil's Bridge, I felt perfectly normal again. There is a story concerning the bridge and it is one of my favourites in Tschiffely's book:

> 'Once upon a time, a young Indian was on his way to visit his sweetheart who lived on the other side of the river, and when he arrived there he found that the waters were so high and wild that it was impossible to cross. Bitterly disappointed, the young man sat down and lamented his fortune. Suddenly the devil appeared before him and offered to build a bridge, but under the condition that the young man would sell him his soul in payment for his services. The youth agreed to this, but with the understanding that the bridge be completed before sunrise, whereupon the devil immediately set to work, but when the first rays of the sun came over the mountain tops there was still one stone missing to complete the bridge and the devil, finding himself thus defeated, jumped down the precipice into the foaming waters below.'

We were welcomed that night in a village that had just received a $40,000 grant from the EC to build a new school. The inhabitants were doing all the work themselves, and although doing a good job with high-quality materials, they were obviously going to make a large profit. As an inhabitant of the EC I was welcomed as some sort of major benefactory patron. I bought some food for the horses and we closed them off in the old school playground.

I slept in the old school itself and had a very comfortable night under my poncho. But first, I had ignited my stove which was behaving worse and worse every time I used it. The twenty-seven observers (I counted) were slightly dismayed at the burning kerosene that covered their school floor but once this had burnt off, I found myself in control of a metre-high flame which slowly burnt itself down to a cooking flame. I cooked up the usual fare of fried eggs, fried potatoes and a couple of slices of fried bondiola. It was a strange sensation having quite so many people watch every mouthful.

I wished that I had waited until later to eat, as we played football after my meal and I felt as sick as a parrot within five minutes. We played until well after dark and my eyes were not nearly as accustomed to the night as the other players were. Most of the time, I blundered around passing the ball to the opposition.

There was a good crowd to see us off in the morning and to watch my morning routine. First, I would catch the horses and by now I had devised a way of keeping them still even when there was nothing to tie them to. I had converted a couple of maize sacks into nosebags with the aid of some nylon rope. Into these I would put grain and after hooking the rope over their ears, the horses would stay still. I would check them over from the night, pick out their feet, run my hand down their legs and brush out their coats. Both of the horses were still completely free of saddle sores, a fact that I was able to remain proud of right through the expedition. Viento Norte was, however, becoming a little scarred as el Chapeton was inclined to take nips out of his side, removing small portions of hair.

Not once throughout the expedition were they lame because of the travelling, but Viento Norte had problems in the village of Tola Palca. We arrived at about 4 pm and I considered riding on and camping out for the night but, at the last moment, changed my mind. An engineer, who was down from Oruro studying the $300 million proposal to upgrade the Potosi to Oruro road, said that I could sleep in the road compound for the night and keep my horses in the corral outside.

The engineer put me in the hands of Miguel, who was employed by the roadworks department to look after the compound, to which no one ever came and which was never used. He was excessively hospitable, blowing a great deal of his paltry monthly income on food and coffee for me. We talked for a while but I went to bed early hoping that, if we started in good time in the morning, we could make the sixty kilometres or so to Challapata, which I had been told was green with alfalfa.

It was a bitterly cold night and miserable in the morning when I woke. I went out to break the ice in the horses' water and, as it was still dark, went back to bed for half an hour. The horses looked really miserable when I came out again and I was angry with myself for not finding them a less exposed spot. El Chapeton was shivering violently and Viento Norte was huddled up against the side of Miguel's hut for the warmth. When I tried to lead him off for more water I saw that he seemed to be rooted to the spot. His hind legs were completely stiff and, when he did walk, he walked like a crab. I felt his legs, which were fine, and walked him around for a while, which seemed to have little effect. I hoped that when the sun came up it would 'thaw' him out, but by midday there was no improvement and I abandoned the idea of leaving. I found a couple of derelict houses and put the horses inside, so that they would at least be snug for the night.

Unfortunately, I had carried a veterinary book for a long while but its size and weight had forced me to throw it out. But with my limited experience, I decided that Viento Norte's problem was azoturia, 'setfast' or 'Monday morning disease' to the layman. He had been eating his head off, particularly on maize, during the week we had spent in Potosi, and not once had left the patio for any form of exercise. We had been travelling hard since Potosi and the work combined with the severe cold had given him this problem, usually associated with racehorses who have Sunday off and seize up on Monday morning.

We spent a couple of days waiting for Viento Norte to improve, which he did rapidly. I subsequently read that 'setfast' can be recurrent but we never had problems again. It was actually a very pleasant stay for me as I ate constantly, wrote my diary, read *Heart of Darkness* and *One Hundred Years of Solitude* again and chatted to the llama butchers.

They were a father, son and employee team that rode around on the truck public-transport service from village to village, undertaking the annual slaughter of llamas. The meat was sold by the campesinos to the altiplano Indians who had left for the more fertile lowlands and missed a good llama and chips dinner. The income was used by the highland campesinos to buy necessities and luxuries, such as fruit, that were sent up from the lowlands.

The process of making churkee, the dried and salted llama meat end-product, began with the slaughter of the animals. A knife was punched into the back of the llamas' heads and they dropped like stones to the ground, where their throats were slit. I was surprised to see that no attempt was made to collect the blood and it was left to the pigs to trough in. By tradition, the women of the village made the initial cuts and skinned the animals before the butchers took over and sliced the meat into very thin strips, which were laid out on a bed of straw to be salted and cured in the sun. As my bondiola had just run out, I was very pleased to be able to buy a few strips for my saddle bags. The churkee is most usually used in minute quantities to flavour soup, but I fried it up with eggs and potatoes and it was delicious.

My grandfather was the person who had started me off on this adventure, when he gave me my first copy of *Tschiffely's Ride*. I clearly remembered him saying that he would like to see Lake Poopó. I was very excited at coming to a place that had been embedded in family lore, and became even more so as we scrambled up a steep, rocky path to see the lake for the first time. Those first few moments of looking over the immense stretch of water were intensely rewarding. But we followed the lake for some days on the way to Oruro and I would be able to tell my grandfather that the lake was magnificent but the surrounding land was flat and charmless.

I thought that the final day's approach to Oruro would again be dull scenically as the road yet again skirted around the flat shores of the lake. There was, however, a direct route straight across the lake beach and I decided to take a risk and follow the most direct line. I had no idea of the stability of the surface across which we were riding. I met a few campesinos grazing llamas, who all said that we would have no problems, but at times the horses sank into the mud up to their knees which frightened me, as there was no way of predicting the substance of the ground from the surface appearance.

I lost our way for a while but found a set of pylons that, I presumed, could only lead to the city. I was rather startled to see through the haze a pink wall stretching across our path in the distance. I would not normally have been surprised by a wall but the size and colour were very strange. The pink was almost fluorescent and very different to the colour of the mud usually used in the construction of adobe houses and walls. As we approached, the bricks seemed to be mobile. In fact, the whole wall was moving. It was only when we were virtually on top of them that I realised that the wall was a giant flock of flamingos.

The outskirts of Oruro were the very worst that I had seen in any town so far. At the edge of every Bolivian town there is a municipal crapping ground where all those without internal plumbing come for their daily dump. Our route into Oruro, unfortunately, crossed one of these and we were greeted by row upon row of little white bums and brown turds. The ditches that ran through each street were full of refuse and effluent, green and rotting.

The slaughterhouse, where I ended up lodging the horses, was also very rough, although the manager and his employees all did their utmost to make the horses as comfortable as possible. The one good thing about Oruro was that the market was stuffed with high-quality grain and alfalfa. One of the advantages of travelling in South America by horse is that the native population eat a great deal of horse food, which is therefore available in the markets.

We had arrived in Oruro in time for All Saints' Day, which is observed as a major festival to the dead. The relations of the deceased make their way to the cemeteries; buying flowers and buckets of water, and hiring cleaning equipment, they tend to the graves. Most South American cemeteries do not contain graves in the form of holes in the ground, but are occupied by apartment blocks for the dead. Blocks are built up to twenty units wide and six units deep, and into holes in these walls the dead are slid with the entrance mortared behind them.

Unfortunately, in Oruro many of these blocks had fallen apart and leg-bones and skulls were protruding from the broken masonry. However everyone was having a great day out and hamburger, drink and religious kitsch stalls were doing great trade. Best kit was being worn so there was very little black in sight. I was reminded for some reason of the 4th of July celebrations in Battery Park in New York, and I loved the idea of celebrating the dead with a good piss-up.

A few days out of Oruro on the road to La Paz, the capital of Bolivia, we arrived in the middle of another festival; in fact, several festivals. As I entered a village the road was blocked by striking miners and three or four vehicles had backed up against barricades of stones. As I rode towards the picket line, I knew that the striking miners were thinking exactly what I was thinking: was a gringo with two horses a legitimate strike target? By the time we had made up our minds, the horses had picked their way over the stones.

The strike was obviously causing a certain amount of excitement in the village. One or two vehicles stopped by the blockade were carrying a large number of passengers, who had disgorged themselves from their vehicles and were pigging out in the restaurant. With difficulty I found a corral for the horses.

The only place that I could find fodder was a smallholding on the other side of the picket line. I crossed through on foot without any problem and walked a couple of kilometres with one of my ponchos to load up with barley straw. When full of the fodder, my poncho had the volume of a large man and I staggered towards the village. This time there was no embarrassment in crossing the line as the miners thought that a gringo loaded down like a mule was one of the funniest things they had seen for years. There were about thirty miners on the roadblock and they laughed and laughed and laughed. Their mood was lightened to such an extent that they removed the barricades from the road and allowed the traffic through.

The fiesta was right next to the hospedaje I was staying in so I wandered along later. It was being held at the school and a PA system had been rigged up and was pumping out salsa. Competing with the PA system, as they were standing in front of the speakers, was the local band playing the instruments of the altiplano: pipes, guitars and drums. The combined noise produced was horrendous, but twenty or thirty people, mainly women, were dancing and whirling about. The women were just as drunk as the men. Women are a very strong force in Bolivian society. Any money that a man earns he hands straight to his wife who allows him a little pocket money and no more. Often when haggling for food and fodder the husband would beseech me to argue with his wife.

I asked someone what the party was about and received a blast of alcohol and coca leaf breath: the smell that comes from the mouths of habitual coca chewers is that of death. I asked another man and he answered me, in a way, by summoning a drink for me. The most popular alcoholic beverage in Bolivia is raw sugar-cane alcohol, which can be bought in any store. I was handed a plastic cup of alcohol which, as we were at a fiesta, had been coloured purple.

A number of people present were dressed as priests with dog collars, with white sheets for cassocks and, for some reason, bread tied around their necks. They represented Spanish priests, that was clear, as they had painted beards and moustaches on their faces; Quechuans have little or no facial hair. The priests, who were very drunk, went round reading from a book as if it were the Bible and shouting at the party-goers: 'You will not drink. You will not have sex.' I was forced to dance with an old hag who kept grabbing for my cock; and chatted to a man down from La Paz, as he was the least drunk there. He came from this village but he also had no idea what the fiesta was for. When he tried to sell me drugs I went to bed, and looking at myself in the mirror, found that I had gone the colour of my drink.

I had another session the following day as a colonel in the Bolivian army stopped me on the road. He explained that he was on his way back to La Paz having been on a dirty holiday with his girlfriend, and insisted that we have a drink together. We ended up drinking a bottle of singani, a white grape spirit, at the side of the road. He taught me how to suck eggs; which was useful as often during the rest of the trip I would stop and suck a few eggs as a running snack. Raw eggs are delicious and taste rather like fried eggs. In the middle of the afternoon I felt dreadfully ill and crashed out at the side of the track. I woke to find myself being watched by a campesino of extra-ordinary age, and he swapped me some coca leaves for the rest of the singani that the colonel had left me, which just about powered me into the next village.

We were getting tantalisingly close to La Paz and I wanted to arrive badly. Total lack of telecommunications meant that I had not spoken to Carina for ages. I knew that arriving in La Paz would give me a great sense of achievement, and I just wanted to get there. But you cannot rush on a horse. And it was frustrating at times when I saw a truck pass and knew that it would be in La Paz within a few hours.

The riding was easy and flat and we thundered along the altiplano at heights above sea level of between 4000 and 5000 metres. The horses and I were totally acclimatised to the altiplano and were starting to get super-fit. We had scheduled our days more effectively and arrived where I planned when I thought we would. But we were also tired and in need of a rest.

We dropped down from Calamarca and at last I was able to see the mountain of Illimani that towers above La Paz. I thought that we would be able to make it into the city that night but the sky blackened over leaving the snow slopes of the mountains lit by brilliant sunshine.

It started to rain heavily and I decided to abandon the entrance into the city until the morning. In Achocalla, no one would help even to the extent of opening their doors and talking to me, probably because I was tearing around like a maniac desperate to find a place under cover. Getting the packhorse, my saddle and myself rigged up against the rain was always rather a rigmarole, which I was trying to escape by sheltering as soon as possible.

I found a deserted house that was locked and ripped the door from the entrance; I found a corral and, dragging my stuff from the horses, had it all under cover within a couple of minutes. A couple of irate villagers appeared and asked what the hell I was doing. I was also angry by this time and asked them what the hell did it look like. They asked me if I had permission from the owner of the house and I asked who the owner was. There was a pause and, looking at me rather sheepishly, one of them said: 'It has no owner. It's God's.'

The hut was small and half-filled with dog shit which I cleared to one side to make a space for my poncho and the stove, which I lit while I went off to buy some eggs. When I got back, half the floor was alight with kerosene, centimetres from my saddlery pile. Close one.

The next morning we rode through what the tourist books call 'Moon Valley' – a valley devoid of vegetation and white in appearance – to arrive at Calacoto, a suburb of La Paz. Roberto Nielsen-Reyes, head of the Bolivian Olympic Committee, owned stables in the heart of Calacoto, about ten minutes from the heart of La Paz. Roberto had very kindly said that I could stable the horses in his yard while we stayed in La Paz. As soon as they were ready, I caught a cab to the main telephone exchange and called Carina. The exchange was in the centre of the main business district, which is as cosmopolitan as any capital and I felt very out of place sitting in the middle of the floor on my saddle bags, wearing boots, spurs, dusty clothing and two days' growth of beard. It was the one time of my life when I could definitely say that although I was the centre of attention I am not sure if I liked it.

10

Adolescent Frontiers

'You forgot the Virgin,' I said as a joke to the girl sitting next to me. We were in a 'Trufi', or taxi ruta fija: a taxi with a fixed route, and an excellent means of transport. I do not know what she thought I said but she ordered the driver to let her out. As I was in the outside seat, I stepped out of the door to let her out. She followed me out and as I climbed back into the car, she slapped me very hard around my face.

We had climbed into the car together at the top of the Prado, the main street that runs through the centre of La Paz. As we passed the Cathedral of San Francisco, the girl had crossed herself, as she did every time we passed a church on the way down to Calacoto. A statue of the Virgin sat at a bend in the road but the girl had forgotten to cross herself and for this reason I had reminded her.

I was rather upset. But not half as upset as I had been when Carina told me on the telephone that she had been told through the 'grapevine', the viper's nest of our mutual friends in London, that I had proposed to another girl before leaving for South America. I also found the story rather amusing as that day, a few days after arriving in La Paz, I had gone out and bought an engagement ring. In the many hours of thought, riding along, I had decided to ask Carina to marry me when she came out to South America over Christmas.

Disgusted and angered by such a ridiculous rumour, I was able to convince Carina that it was a lie. I was surprised that she had believed it, but she had been told by one of my closest friends who had been told by the girl herself. A few days later, I took the ring back to the jeweller. The story coming through from the UK had become even worse. Carina told me on the telephone that she had had an affair with someone else for a few days. Talking on the telephone in the tackroom of Roberto's stables, I almost fell over with shock. I felt sick and all the air squeezed out of my chest. I felt as if I was standing at the edge of a very steep cliff and the ground had been hacked from under my feet. I put the telephone down, went to the nearest bar and ordered a drink. When it arrived, I looked at the glass and knew that if I drank it I would be lost.

I spoke to her again that night. She had obviously been having a rougher time in the UK than I realised. In Bolivia I had been out of contact for two months, and no one knew exactly where I was. Carina had been so desperate that she had even asked the local curate to pray for my safety. When she was really upset, she had been told that I had proposed to someone else.

The rest of my time in La Paz was intensely unhappy and passed in a blur. I eased the pain and hurt sense of macho pride a little by having an affair myself, which was stupid. El Chapeton kicked Viento Norte, who went lame, so that we were unable to leave, which made everything even worse.

La Paz is an extraordinary city. Its population of one million makes it one of the smallest capital cities in the world. Its height, at over 3600 metres above sea level produces one of the strangest phenomenons in town planning, as the poorest of all live in the hills. The city was built in a bowl below the altiplano in an attempt to hide from the extreme cold and, rising out from the city centre towards Illimani are the shanty towns. Down in the valley below are situated the villas and mansions of the rich. In winter there is a great difference in temperature between the top of the city and the bottom and the rich have elected to snuggle below.

I went up to the higher areas of town to a large Sunday market where you could buy everything from llama foetuses (which are buried in the foundations of new houses for luck) to a bus. The views down over the city valley were spectacular and, however rich I was, I think that I would have preferred to live up top.

My favourite pastime was watching the daily teargas battles between the police and the university students. The main university is located in the centre of town and retains not a single unbroken window. At the beginning of the siesta when the streets are cleared of citizens, the battle begins. A student will throw a rock, the police reply with teargas and the cannisters are lobbed backwards and forwards. As the siesta finishes and people reappear on the streets, the police and rioters pack up their bags and go home. All very civilised.

I learnt in La Paz that Bolivia receives sixty per cent of its income from the cocaine trade. The eastern Andean valleys are perfect for growing the coca leaf, most of which is put through the preliminary stage of processing and shipped out to Colombia.

Personally, I had little contact with the trade although I was surrounded by people involved in the business in one way or another. Many Bolivians deplore the industry but if your country is financially dependent on it you are not going to go out of your way to stamp it out. Men in the armed forces are paid at subsistence level, and many stay in the services for opportunities that arise when they are posted to an area of cultivation or processing. They would then be in a position to extract healthy bribes which would financially guarantee their own pensions and their families' welfare.

Unfortunately the fantastic amounts of money made from cocaine do not hugely benefit the local population. A gram of uncut cocaine costs around $3 on the streets in La Paz. By the time it was cut to make three grams and was being sold on the streets in London, that gram would be costing the consumer around $500. The huge profits land in the offshore bank accounts of a minority of the population.

The campesinos were able to earn, by their standards, staggering amounts of money, up to $40 a day, by working in the picking and processing sectors. The only problem is that the compounds are cut off and hidden away. Most of the campesino's income would be lost paying for food, drink and prostitutes supplied by his employer at vastly inflated prices.

Efforts have been made to persuade the campesinos who grow the leaf, to substitute crops such as coffee, but the coffee market is already flooded worldwide and the campesino is always, in the medium-term, going to earn more with coca leaves than with substitute cash crops. The British Embassy is one of the organisations working on the idea of crop substitution. I enjoyed meeting the Ambassador a great deal, as his unpretentious desire to help where possible was very refreshing after the jumped-up, we-are-incredibly-important-players-in-the-world-political-scene attitude of some of his colleagues whom I had met.

One of the problems for Bolivia, being in the centre of the cocaine trade, is that more and more cocaine is ending up on the domestic market. Most users do not snort white powder but smoke 'baso' in a pipe. Baso is partially refined cocaine. It is scooped into a pipe bowl, lit and the smoke inhaled. I went to the flat of a junkie couple with a friend and we smoked a couple of pipes. I found it hard to analyse the effects. I do remember being fascinated by a televised debate between the two principal candidates in the election for mayor, a political post of great importance in Bolivia. The camera played with startling effect on the hands, mouths, and eyes of the two protagonists.

I had trouble with the police in La Paz and was questioned on possible suspicion of cocaine processing. The Mustad Easy Glu shoes had been working extremely well to date and I was determined to use them on el Chapeton the whole way across the Andes. That would be some endorsement, to my mind, of a radical and excellent new innovation. Needed in the application process was acetone, to clean the hoof wall of any grease and dust to ensure a snug fit.

Acetone is commonly used as nail-varnish remover and is available from chemists. I wandered into the local chemist and asked for three litres, as I was unsure of its availability in Peru. Three litres is enough to remove the varnish from, say, half a million nails and the shopkeeper retired into the back of the shop. Rather than returning with the bottles, he came back with a policeman who said that he wanted to talk to me at the local station.

We walked a couple of blocks to the station and he led me to an interview room, sat me down and left, locking the door behind him. I have only been in a cell against my will once before, when the credit card signature of a friend was queried in Victoria Station and we were locked up until his identity could be verified. It was doubly unnerving being locked up in La Paz and my mind filled with jumped-up charges and being incarcerated for years in some hell hole in Bolivia. My guide book suggested that foreigners visit other westerners jailed for drugs charges, and I did not relish becoming one of them.

When you are locked up, you feel guilty. Forget all this stuff about being innocent until proven guilty. People think that if you are inside you must be there for some reason and when my policeman returned with a superior, the latter looked me over as if I was some kind of worm.

'Do you know what acetone is used for?' the superior asked me, having sat down.

'For cleaning nail-varnish off women's nails,' I said and rather stupidly continued, 'although where I come from, Britain, some men wear nail-varnish too.' In my nervousness I continued: 'and mascara and lipstick and foundation too.'

I ground to a halt as the captain was looking at me with revulsion. There seems to be a particularly strong subculture of macho-ness that runs through police forces all over the world.

'Maricones [gays],' I said weakly, by way of explanation.

'And what else?' asked the captain.

'What else, what?' I asked, not understanding.

'What else is acetone used for?'

He's not going to believe me, I thought, but said it anyway. 'For removing dirt and grease from horses' hooves.'

'For removing dirt and grease from horses' hooves? You put nail-varnish on horses too?' wondered the captain.

'No, no,' I said, 'before gluing plastic horseshoes to horses' hooves you clean the hooves with acetone.'

'Plastic horseshoes?'

I launched into the full pitch. About how the international group Mustad have developed their Easy Glu horseshoe range at a cost of $10,000,000 for both therapeutic and improved performance purposes. I said how I was trying them out across the Andes and how they had worked very well. They had improved el Chapeton's feet and seemed to last just as long as ordinary shoes. And then I got to the acetone bit and explained how grease from the hand can get on to the hoof wall and has to be removed with ACETONE to ensure that the specially formulated glue bonds the Easy Glu shoe to the hoof with utmost strength.

'I'm getting a full 1000 kilometres' wear,' I said as I finished.

The captain was again looking at me with slight incredulity.

'Plastic horseshoes,' he repeated to himself in wonder. He remembered his business and returned to the interrogation.

'Nothing to do with cocaine, then?' he said.

It was my turn to wonder. 'Cocaine?'

'Yes, cocaine,' and he launched into his spiel, giving me a full run-down on producing, harvesting coca leaves and turning them into white nose powders, ACETONE being used to clean out impurities. As acetone is highly inflammable it is a high-risk business.

'So no cocaine?' he said.

'No sir,' I said in the manner of one of those rather nauseous children on American sit-coms. 'Plastic horseshoes.'

I was lucky enough to meet the 'President' of Bolivia in La Paz. Actually he was not the president although he should have been. In the preceding elections, he had polled substantially more votes than any other candidate but insufficient for an outright majority. The candidates that had come second and third were able to pool their votes and form a government with, surprisingly, the third most popular candidate as its head.

I was walking down the street one day in Calacoto on the way to the house of a friend. A little lost, I stopped a man carrying a video camera to ask the way. We started talking and he explained that he was a newsman from one of the main Bolivian TV channels.

It transpired that he was on the way to the 'President's' house to do an interview on the municipal elections. He asked me if I wanted to come. I was surprised at the lack of security on the 'President's' house. We walked through the back gate of the large suburban villa, across the lawn and into a conservatory at the back of the house. The newsman settled into a sofa and we waited for the 'President' to arrive. His wife bustled in, fixed us some drinks and asked me a few questions about the trip in that vague, patronising way of establishment wives.

Finally the 'President' came in looking extremely haggard and tired. He had mud all over the knees of his trousers.

At last, after nearly a month in La Paz Viento Norte was recovered and we were ready to leave at the beginning of December. I said my goodbyes to some wonderful people, especially the Zamoras in whose house I had stayed, and we rode up out of La Paz and back on to the altiplano. The climb out of the city was very steep, and nearing the lip of the valley-bowl, became steeper. Once the lip was reached the land was as flat as a pancake, stretching towards Lake Titicaca in one direction and the mountain range that includes Illimani in another.

I felt as blasted as the grass when we reached the altiplano. The horses were playing up badly after a month off and we were heading towards an area where I had been told a hundred times that I was going to be killed and my horses stolen.

Arriving in La Paz had been a marvellous moment. We had worked hard and conquered the first section of the Andes. No one since Tschiffely had made the journey alone by horse from Argentina to La Paz and certainly no Briton, ever. But this elation had worn off after a while. And my feelings were confirmed when I made an effort to report my success back in the UK. *The Independent* correspondent in La Paz had contacted the paper in London and received the reply: 'OK, so he has travelled from Argentina to La Paz. What has he actually done? He's climbed the Andes. So what?'

This mirrored my own mood. So what? Had the ride helped world peace? Had it improved anyone's life materially? No, of course not. It was pointless. A bum on a horse, no more. I felt nothing as we hit the wide open spaces. I had achieved nothing. I had nothing. The one thing that I had had, that was more important to me than anything in the world – Carina – I never really appreciated, and now she was lost. I felt completely empty. I was probably as close to freedom as I will ever come, and again I was not sure that I liked it very much. Everything that meant anything to me had been left behind in La Paz.

The first night out from La Paz was spent in Laja. It was at the site of Laja that the Spanish first founded La Paz, but after two weeks of incessant winds, they decided to move to the current sheltered site. When I arrived there was a big festival in progress and I found it difficult to get help. At last, the doctor at the minuscule hospital said that I could put the horses in the garden, and I was given a bed in the maternity ward! I stored all my kit in an empty crib and slept like a baby in the crispiest, cleanest sheets that I had slept in for a long time.

I loosened up a little, as the following day was a beauty. We had a wonderful view of the mountains, the riding was good and I knew that we would arrive at Tihuanaco that night. Archaeologists reckon that there was a settlement there as early as 1600 BC, which was successively built on through time. The ruins that stand to this day are hugely impressive.

A mound of earth, three metres tall and the size of a full-size football pitch, is bordered by large blocks of stone. Standing on top are a number of gates and totem pole-like structures and in front of the main entrance arch, through which the main totem pole is impressively framed, is a pit with walls covered with stone heads, which have been eroded over time to produce sinister skullish faces.

I had already visited the site a few weeks earlier when George Bowen had flown the seven hours to La Paz and we had hired a guide for the day. The most interesting thing that the guide had pointed out were the snake symbols that had been carved on various rocks. They showed that the pre-Incan altiplano dwellers had had some contact with the low-lying Amazon regions.

It is in the Amazon basin, the Beni, to the north-west of the country, that the future of Bolivia lies. Eighty per cent of the Bolivian population scratch a meagre living from the altiplano but the agricultural and mineral wealth of the country is locked into the Beni. The infrastructure of the Beni is non-existent and the area is only accessible by air. On our way out of La Paz we had passed the airport on which lay a multitude of seemingly destroyed planes. They fly backwards and forwards between the Beni and La Paz, delivering the meat farmed from estancias in the lowlands. They are so dilapidated that often they crash or fail to make the height of the altiplano on which their runway is located. There are many stories of beef carcasses raining on the city as the crews shed weight in an effort to climb those crucial metres.

The horses and I arrived in Tihuanaco by mid-afternoon and I was able to fix them up with an excellent corral and feed just in time to return from the outlying 'modern' village (seventeenth century), to the site for sundown. The sun was very central to the beliefs of the people who constructed Tihuanaco, and as I rushed through the adobe streets, I put myself through a small time warp. The sun was going down fast and I imagined that I was a citizen a little late for the evening worship.

I arrived at the Gate of The Sun a few minutes before the big fat amber mamma hit the horizon and, filtered through the Gate of The Sun, her children poured straight through my eyes and filled me with warmth from my boots to my head. I took a few photographs and went back to my alojiamento for a slap-up meal.

We reached the border crossing into Peru at Desaguadero within a full day's ride. Remembering the problems that I had had at La Quiaca, I was very nervous that again we would be stuck. My future with Carina was uncertain, but we had both decided that she should come out to Peru and meet me as planned. At least we would be able to see and talk to each other.

With Viento Norte being kicked, I had lost crucial days in La Paz, which meant that we would have to ride flat out to arrive in Cuzco the day that Carina did (if that was where I decided we would meet). I reckoned that we would need to travel 70 kilometres a day, every day, without a break, at heights in excess of 4000 metres.

In no way did I want to dawdle in any case. Once we crossed the border we were in the hunting ground of Sendero Luminoso, the mighty Peruvian terrorist organisation. They had already killed three tourists, and countless campesinos and armed forces personnel that year. A week before they had strangled to death a reporter from the USA.

I could expect help from absolutely no one. The British Ambassador to Peru had written: 'I have to say . . . that I have serious reservations about the wisdom of riding alone with two horses through Peru. A third of the country has now been declared an emergency zone because of terrorist activity. Elsewhere in Peru there is a high level of robbery, often accompanied by violence . . . at the same time there are frequent and increasing incidents of highway robbery with road-blocks and hold-ups of buses and cars. On a horse you could be even more vulnerable. I am sorry to pour cold water on your plans and appreciate that Peru forms the main component of your expedition.

But I do feel that you should be in no doubt about the very real risks involved. In present circumstances, my advice, given with the greatest regret, would be to avoid Peru.'

I had received this letter before I even set foot outside the UK and I was grateful that he had written. At the time I had thought, 'I know that Peru is dangerous but things are always better on the ground'. The news in La Paz, however, had not been encouraging but the expedition seemed to have a certain impetus of its own and, although I was starting to become very frightened, my fear was not sufficient to call off the trip.

I was even frightened of calling the British Embassy in Lima. I thought that if the wrong people knew that I was in touch with the authorities I could be in serious trouble even for such an innocuous reason as asking about our route. I knew that we could reach Lima via Puno and the coast but I wanted to ride into Cuzco and that route was going to take us through one of the terrorist-controlled emergency zones.

There were a couple of hiccups at the Desaguadero border crossing but nothing that a $5 bill could not sort out. The town is split by a small channel that forms part of Lake Titicaca, and is crossed by a bridge. On one side lies Bolivia and on the other is Peru. We checked out of Bolivia without any problems, as the chief at the customs and immigration post had hurt his hand.

I knew that my papers were in order but I have a pathological distrust of paper authority and, seeing his bandaged hand, asked in a solicitous way if he was all right. He said that he had a little pain and I said that I had an extensive medical kit. His face lit up and I gave him a handful of paracetamol and wrapped his hand in a new bandage. There were a number of equestrian drugs that I had wanted to try out on humans for a long time, as I presumed that they would be much stronger and I could dispense with my own medical kit. But I decided that an immigration official was not the most appropriate guinea pig. There was no question of a bribe then and he even told me that there was a fiesta that night on the Bolivian side of the border and that I was welcome to cross back.

We walked on to the bridge and I had someone take a picture of us. The Peruvian customs official said that I would need to clear customs in Puno, 120 kilometres or so further on, and the Peruvian immigration official said there was a $10 fee to stamp my passport. I gave him $5. We were through – at least the 120 kilometres to Puno.

I broke one rule that I had set for myself in Peru as soon as we crossed the border, but it was the last time. I sought help from the police. They were the only people that seemed to have a corral and I asked for permission to use it for my horses. The police, gendarmeria, armed forces and politicians are the main Sendero targets and it seemed sensible to stay clear of them. First, I did not want to be around if there was a possibility of their stations being attacked and, secondly, I did not want anyone being under the impression that I was in any way connected with the authorities. I wanted myself to be regarded as supremely neutral: a nutty foreigner on a couple of horses, or even as a local.

The police in Desaguadero were exceptionally helpful and I was probably exceptionally rude as I wanted to spend as little time in their company as possible. I parked the horses with them and arranged a bed for myself in the hotel. Later in the evening I crossed back over the border bridge to join the fiesta. The officials were already drunk and there seemed to be an extraordinary amount of foot traffic, laden with large bundles of goods, crossing backwards and forwards during this amnesty.

As I walked into Bolivian Desaguadero, I came across a band forming at the side of the road ready to march. They set off as I reached them and I fell in with a group of about thirty people that were following. The band was brass and noisy. We all arrived at the main plaza, having trouped around town for a while, and marched through the doors of the church, that dominated the plaza. The band stopped playing and each of my companions walked up to the priest and received a blessing. He was rather startled to see a huge gringo appear from the throng but he made the sign of the cross over my chest and I handed some notes to his sidekick, who held out an offertory plate in a suggestive way.

The plaza was packed with people dancing, and stalls selling beer and anticucho (pieces of heart and a potato grilled on a charcoal stove). The dancing had little control and rhythm: you hopped and whirled about, depending on how drunk you were. A couple of men were letting off some impressive home-made fireworks. They had rockets, which they let off in their hands and some that were shaped like a bowl. The latter ones I loved. The men had a long pole, on top of which they placed one of the fireworks. It was lit and raised on the pole relatively out of harm's way. As the firework ignited, it began to spin on the top of its pole like a Catherine-wheel. Once it had reached a certain velocity, it would lift off from the pole like a space craft and, increasing in upward lift and speed, fly into the night before exploding.

It was my turn to be startled when a very smart gent and his wife, clad in her petticoat finery, came up to me. Due to my height and their size – on average 5'6" – they came up to my chest.

'I am an important man in Desaguadero,' said the man, 'and we are honoured that you, a foreigner, should be at our fiesta. I would be further honoured if you would consider dancing with me and my wife.'

Who could refuse an invitation like that? So my final memory of Bolivia is holding hands with a man and his wife, twice my age and half my height, whirling around in a circle, hopping from foot to foot.

I was given the impression by one or two people in Desaguadero that the route from the border to Puno was free of terrorist activity. It was certainly beautiful. We rode along the shores of Lake Titicaca for much of the time and were able to see the fishermen going out in their reed boats.

As the altiplano is virtually treeless, there is a shortage of boat-building wood, but on the coast of Lake Titicaca there is no shortage of reeds. The reeds are cut and dried, before being bound together in thick sheaves. These sheaves are in turn lashed together to shape a platform on which a man or woman can stand. Propelled like a punt, the boats on the altiplano are shaped with a turned-up prow like an Arabian slipper, as worn by Ali Baba. Unfortunately, they become waterlogged, and though they continue to float the reeds rot, requiring a new boat to be built every three years or so. Skilled boat-builders were taken from the lake to Africa to help in the construction of the Kon-Tiki, which was built using similar methods but on a much larger scale.

The towns bordering the lake often perch on rocky outcrops overlooking it with spectacular views. One of these towns was Juli, in which we stayed for the night. Tantalisingly, there was a cavalry division stationed on the outskirts of the town with tanks, horses, corrals, feed, the works. I knew that they would have plenty of fodder for the horses and would have treated me exceptionally well for the night but I also knew that it was not worth the risk. I did not even acknowledge the sentries scattered along the perimeter wall, who followed me with their automatic weapons as I passed.

There was a hospedaje in Juli, run by an old crone who I think had not had a visitor for years. She invited me to a cup of coffee the following morning before I left. We talked about 'la violencia' and she was very pessimistic about my route. When I offered her a cigarette, she said that normally she did not smoke but that she would smoke me on my way. She gunned up the cigarette, and puffing and sucking like a maniac, blew smoke all over herself and me. She explained that it was a traditional form of wishing someone luck on a difficult journey. I was very pleased as she seemed such a wise old bird.

Smoking tobacco and chewing coca leaves are undertaken in both Quechuan and Aymaran cultures at every opportunity. At a funeral, everyone puffs away like mad, sometimes more than one cigarette at a time until they are sick, to speed the departed on their way.

I can honestly say that I think Puno is one of the most horrible places on earth. I have now been to the town five times in my life and have tried my hardest to enjoy it, but without success. The level of Lake Titicaca has dropped over the years so the town is now split from the water by an expanse of putrefying mud. As it is an important tourist gateway, its inhabitants can be greedy and unfriendly. There is nothing to recommend Puno.

I was determined to spend only one day there, sorting out my papers, not only because I hate the place but because if I was going to arrive in time for Carina, we could only afford one day. What a day it was. I started at the appropriate customs office fifteen minutes before it opened at eight o'clock in the morning and finished at eleven o'clock that night.

There was not a single government office that I did not visit that day: customs, immigration, agriculture, tourism, transport and culture. They all saw me as they all had to give and sign papers for me. I came away with twenty-five sheets of close-typed, signed and stamped papers, and no one in authority has ever looked at them again. I had decided that I was going to spread as many dollars around as was required to clear customs in a day, and it worked. I spent $80 when the service should have been free and I could not have cared less. We could have got through for free but we would have spent four weeks in Puno.

Cuzco or straight down to Arequipa? The question had been on my mind for some time.

'Going to Cuzco?' asked the taxi man, taking his hands off the wheel. 'They [the terrorists/bandits] will shoot you down day or night.' His hands were holding an imaginary machine gun. 'Tfutfutfut-futfutfu,' he went, helpfully.

'Thanks,' I said. 'Anyway, I'm going straight to Arequipa,' lying through my teeth as a matter of course.

I had four options:

(a) to pull out and return to the UK, saying that Peru was too dangerous;
(b) to truck the horses to the relatively safe coast;
(c) to ride the horses straight to the coast, avoiding Sendero country;
(d) to continue along the altiplano, through terrorist country, to Cuzco.

Puno was decision time.

I called Carina that night to tell her that we were through the border, and that I had decided to go to Cuzco. We had a sticky conversation. Carina would not be humble as she felt that I was much to blame for her unhappiness, having left her alone, unsure and out-of-touch in London. She told me that she loved me but was not going to grovel to me to take her back, which was what I seemed to want.

Perhaps if my private life had been more stable we would not have gone to Cuzco but opted out for safety. But I think that I ruled out options (a), (b) and (c) for reasons other than an emotional death wish. Initiation rite, test of manhood, call it what you will, I needed to prove something to myself. Leaving all the dinner party chat, articles in the papers, minor celebrity-hood behind, I wanted to do something that was really challenging, really frightening, altogether rather adolescent. I certainly had no wish to die but I knew that it was a possibility. I also believe that a fundamental right of man is to go where he wants and I was not going to be stopped, as a matter of principle.

Past generations seem to have spent a great deal of their time fighting in organised wars. Adventure sports, executive aggression and fanatical fighting on the terraces are all manifestations of man's desire to go out and prove himself; perhaps even to prove his insignificance.

The first morning out of Puno, I received my first fright. I had thought that our route would be quicker following the railway line although I found that much of the line was raised above water level and we ended up well away from any tracks. Or I thought that we were off any tracks until I saw a jeep following us at a distance. When the driver saw me look round, he shouted at me but I ignored him and carried on. We were also well away from the main road and there was not a person or house in sight. I did not want to take any chances.

We continued for another 500 yards or so and I looked around again to see that the jeep was bouncing along over the same roughish terrain as us and had fallen back a bit. We came out of some low hills and on to flat open ground and at this point the jeep picked up speed and started to come towards us. I had a moment of indecision, but I knew I should not hang around. Two hundred yards to my left was more broken ground and a hill over which I knew I would find the main Puno to Juliaca road. And for this I galloped the horses as fast as they would go.

The jeep was close when we hit the hill but was forced to slow and eventually stop. Two men got out and were shouting at me but we went up and round the hill, through a small mining compound and on to the road to Juliaca. There was no reason for the jeep to be where I saw it. There was no reason as far as I could see that they needed to talk to me. But perhaps they just wanted to pass the time of day. I will never know.

Juliaca, everyone in Puno told me, was safe but I entered cautiously and skirted round the back to avoid the main entrance road. Lying was starting to become second nature and I told as many as I could to the few people that I was forced to talk to. Gone were the days when I could ride into a town, meet as many people as possible and talk to them about everything under the sun. The caretaker of the slaughterhouse asked me where I had come from and I said Cuzco and the owner of my hotel asked me where I was going and I said Argentina. Anything but the truth.

Sendero is an incredibly secret organisation. They do not even claim responsibility for assassinations, bombings and further acts of terrorism, which only serves to heighten their mystique and the fear that they cause. It is impossible to know who has sympathies with the terrorists, let alone know who is an active member, so I was forced to treat everyone in the area as a possible killer or informer.

In Juliaca, I lost my bottle and tried to get the horses and me shipped out on a truck. I went to the main truck centre where vehicles are loaded and truck driver/owners wait for a commission. I spent an hour talking to drivers without any success and left, realising that I was compromising myself by asking so many questions and telling so many people where I was headed. The best way through was going to be by horse.

I tried to blend in as much as possible, but to no avail I am sure, as I would have to have walked on my knees not to tower above the inhabitants of Juliaca. There was a screening of a Charles Bronson film that night and I thought that I would be as well off in the cinema as anywhere else. But the film did not improve my mental state as within the first three minutes four people were bloodily blown away in a shotgun killing.

Juliaca was my last chance to travel the safer route straight down to Arequipa, but the following morning I found myself again skirting the town and heading for the Cuzco road. When we reached the road, I was surprised to find that traffic was virtually non-existent. There was the odd truck and pick-up, which always returned from their destination within a few hours, but very little else.

The scenery was heavenly – rambling hills covered with short strong grasses – and it seemed so sad that no one could come and enjoy it and that its inhabitants lived in a state of misery. We covered sixty-two kilometres the first day out of Juliaca, to arrive at Pucara.

I had debated for some time whether I would be best camping out at night alone, hidden and away from populated areas. I had even gone to the lengths of buying a couple of tins of boot polish to smear over el Chapeton as camouflage cream; I had seen before how his white patches were clearly visible at night.

But I had decided that our best course of action would be to spend the night in villages. There would be some protection from being surrounded by people. I could confuse people about my destination by lying, and the distances I was aiming to travel meant that I had to keep the horses well fuelled, and fuel was only available in the villages. I also assumed that I would be an easier target if stuck out in the country. We could hide, but if I was really a target, we would never be able to hide from people who had grown up in the area. I was also determined to keep moving as fast as possible. People would know I was in the area but communication is remarkably slow as the roads are often impassable. I was hoping that by the time my presence had been reported to Sendero authorities and a decision had been reached about whether I was a target we would have moved on.

There is a small village that sits on the rail line, a few kilometres from Pucara, and here I found an alojiamento. The owner gave me a bed in the communal dormitory and said that I could keep the horses in his yard. The problem was that the one entrance to the yard was through the small café that he ran, but the diners only paused from their eating momentarily as I passed their tables with the horses.

I ate a bowl of soup and some spaghetti and went to bed. Many of the alojiamentos run on a dormitory basis. There can be anything from four to twenty beds and one to fifty people in the dormitory on any one night. (The numbers are right as you pay by the bed and a family of five will often use one bed only.) There were three of us staying in the dormitory that night and around fifteen beds, so I did the boarding school trick of filling the bed that I had ostentatiously chosen with my ponchos to form the shape of a man, and slept in another.

The morning came around and I felt very light-hearted that nothing had happened so far. Although the rainy season was imminent it was another beautiful day. I felt relieved to get out of the village as I was able to see for miles, and could spot other people in the area from a long way off and avoid them.

We were halfway through the morning and following a short cut when we came to a solitary farm. As we approached a small truck started up and left the farmyard. Both the house and the truck indicated that it was the homestead of a wealthy family. So when the truck stopped and its driver called me over, I felt instinctively that there was no risk. We introduced ourselves and I explained that I had ridden the horses from Argentina and we were travelling to Cuzco. He sucked his teeth and told me that we had some rough country to cross. I asked him where I should take particular care, but he smiled sadly to give the impression that nowhere was safe.

He was standing with his back to his house and as we talked about 'the situation' and about horses, I saw a woman come out of the house and walk towards us. When she got to within about 100 metres of us I saw her stop. When I looked up again, she was pointing at us with both arms extended and at the end of her arms was a pistol. The farmer must have seen my expression of terror as he turned back towards her. I ducked down between the horses and as I did so heard the crack and explosion of the pistol going off. The farmer and woman were screaming at each other in Quechua as I moved round to the front of el Chapeton and jumped back on. Giving him an enormous boot in the belly, I galloped back down the track. It was real 'wild west' stuff. I was scrubbing the horses along, lying flat on el Chapeton's neck, and the funny thing was that I was laughing.

We cut off the track after a while and moved back to the main road. The horses were well jigged up so we just kept going. I felt very nauseous but in a strange way rather relieved and very excited. I was relieved because we had been in a nasty situation and everything had gone well; the horses had stood still long enough for me to get back on and, anyway, the situation had not been that bad. The woman could not shoot us at that distance and I had been covered by the horses when she fired. I did not even think that she had aimed at us as she obviously knew the man that I had been talking to. And I was excited because I had been fired at.

179

When I told the story to people later, they thought that the woman was probably the wife of the man that I had been talking to, and had assumed that *I* was a terrorist about to attack her husband.

There was no question of turning back now and I continued, feeling strangely elated, for the rest of the day. But two things brought the danger of my situation back in a big way. First, as the day lengthened I had to start thinking about the night which would bring me into contact with people and expose my position. And second was the train. Due to the awfulness of the roads, the main line of communication between Cuzco and Puno was the single-track railway, along which plied, twice a day, trains stuffed to five times their capacity. For some reason Sendero had made very little attempt to attack the tourist centre of Cuzco, although the town was surrounded by terrorist-influenced zones. To date, they had also made no attempt to attack the Puno to Cuzco train and every day scores of tourists travelled in safety along this line.

As it passed, I could see through the windows blond-haired, fair-skinned faces peering out at me. And for a minute or two, I longed to be sharing their comfort and security. They would be staying in the tourist hotels and eating steaks that night. They trundled on and I was left alone again.

Viento Norte fell in a bog the next day and got stuck up to his armpits. I was able to get my saddle off him and transfer it to el Chapeton. I then wound one of the staking leathers three times around his middle, and connecting it to el Chapeton's saddle by a lead rope, was able to drag him out of the mud sufficiently to enable him to scramble back to terra firma. By the time we finished, Viento Norte was covered in thick slime and it had started to rain. We were forced to track back as el Chapeton refused to take any chances with the bogs.

It was pouring when we arrived at Santa Rosa, a town that had suffered greatly from terrorist killings. I thought 'fuck it' and galloped into the village and down the main street. Everyone was going to know that I had arrived so I thought that I might as well do it in style. Santa Rosa is a truly gorgeous place with cobbled streets and houses made of adobe and thatch. It was in one of these that I found a bed for the night and a corral.

The room was perfect as it was on the ground floor and had a window that backed on to the horses' corral, which in turn had a back entrance. I walked about – it was unavoidable – to fetch food for the horses; and ate in a small boliche, bombarded with questions by the owner's kids. Every time a man walked in my spine would tingle and my heart would stick in my throat.

Just before I went to bed, I nipped out to the back corral in the dark and re-saddled the horses. I went back inside, barricaded the door and, fully clothed, lay on the bed. (When we were travelling I very rarely took off my clothes.) Since arriving in Peru, I had been sleeping in what seemed to be fifteen-minute bursts, forcing myself awake to listen for abnormal sounds.

That night I was woken by hammering on my door and someone making rough attempts to get through. I was out of the window in seconds and ran across to the horses. Just as I was about to jump up and ride off, a torch beam picked me out and a voice rang out, 'What are you doing?'

I stayed still and said nothing. My mind was going: 'jump up or not? Jump up or not?'

The voice came again. 'What are you doing, Jaime? What are you doing?', and in a wave of semi-relief, I recognised it as the voice of my landlord.

'Well, um, er . . . I was just, like . . . checking the horses.'

'It's two o'clock in the morning. Why are they still saddled, you crazy man?'

'Well, you know . . . quicker in the morning.'

'You were trying to leave without paying, weren't you?'

'No, well, I thought you were, well . . .'

He clicked. 'You thought I was Sendero, didn't you? You thought that I was Sendero come to kill you, didn't you?' he laughed.

'Well, yes, I did actually.'

'You're safe with me, horseman, you're safe with me,' he said putting his arm around my shoulder, although it actually ended up around my waist.

As we walked around to the front of the house, he explained that two men had arrived in the night and that he needed the beds in my room. He saw my look of worry and said, 'Don't worry, Jaime. They are not Sendero. I know them, they are friends of mine.' He showed me back to my room.

'Everyone thinks everyone else is Sendero,' he said sadly. 'You can trust no one.'

La Raya was my final hurdle to Cuzco, or so I had been told. Apparently armed bandits had been stopping, robbing and sometimes killing their victims. La Raya is a pass, on both sides of which there is nothing but rocks and scrub in which people can hide. We left the last house in the valley and started to climb.

A truck pulled up, having come from over the pass, and out

stepped a very large man. I nearly carried on as I had done so often in the past when I wanted to avoid talking to people, but something stopped me. The man was very obviously drunk. He asked, 'From what family are you?'

There is nothing that I hate more than drunks so I got cocky and replied: 'Well, my surname is Greenwood. My mother's maiden name is Gurney. And my girlfriend is called Thistlethwayte.'

'Are you from this man's family?' said the drunk, pointing at a ratty campesino, whom I had failed to notice by his side, and pronouncing the campesino's unpronounceable name.

'No,' I said, looking at our route forward.

'Then I am going to kill you.'

'What?' I said, turning back to look at the drunk and the pistol that he had pulled from his pocket.

'I am going to kill you.'

Once again I received a blast of tunnel vision. Concentrate. Look at the man. Look at the pistol. Look from above. Look from outside.

'Permiso, señor,' I said. 'No comprendo,' and turning my horses away, turned my back and rode off at a walk.

I heard them laugh loudly, get back into the truck and drive off. When I did look back, I was horrified. The truck had been stopped and seemed to be turning round. But within a few seconds, it was off again in the opposite direction.

This was without doubt the most dangerous moment of the expedition. If I had had a gun, I would have made every attempt to shoot that man.

We continued up the pass and I meant to take a picture of the sign that said we were a certain amount of metres above sea level but I was too frightened to stop. I had reached a stage of fear in which I moved as little as possible and concentrated all energies on moving forward. We started down the hill and emerged in heaven.

A village sat in a big, fat, plump green valley. The land was totally different to the other side of the pass, which had been dank and devoid of agriculture. The fields, full of alfalfa and barley, were friendly and welcoming. Carefully constructed channels directed water through and around the fields. Cattle were grazing and the sun came out. There even appeared to be a sort of village green in front of the village store. I went into the store and had myself a Bimbo, as one of the Peruvian brands of soft drink is called. I bought a mango and some biscuits and lay on the grass. I knew that the very worst of the danger was over and I felt supremely happy and full of life. There was still a great burden of fear but I felt that we could deal with any of the problems now.

There was no time to sit around and congratulate myself as we still had 200 kilometres to travel in three days if we were going to arrive in Cuzco the day that Carina did. Carina had been little in my mind since we entered Peru and I began to worry a great deal about seeing her and the outcome. I knew that either I would never see her again, or I would go through with asking her to marry me, and I had absolutely no idea which it was going to be.

We arrived at Checacupe and an exceptional New Zealand priest put us up for the night. He gave me a bed with sheets and I undressed and had a shower for the first time in a couple of weeks. He helped me stake out the horses in a grassy area and we gave them maize and chala. He gave me supper and several very stiff rum and cokes.

We talked about Sendero and we both sympathised with their fundamental aim of helping the campesino population of Peru. In some areas Sendero have done good. They control taxes and ensure that they are distributed correctly and efficiently. But the harm in terms of terror and killing cannot be worth any benefit that has occurred. The armed forces have also been responsible for numerous atrocities; it has been said that they have wiped out entire villages suspected of strong Sendero activities. 'La violencia' is horrible.

I was able to talk freely about my fears over the trip and, with a couple of rum and cokes inside me, became extremely garrulous. I also spoke about my pagan sacrifices, which as an extremely spiritual man, the priest quite understood and accepted. 'There are many ways of finding God,' he said.

Towards the end of supper, I began to feel very odd. When it was time to go to bed, I tried to stand up, got halfway to my feet and keeled over with a crash back on to the table. I could not move. The priest was extremely worried but I said that I was OK. I was able to walk out into the courtyard, but halfway to my room, my legs just gave way and the priest had to half carry me. I assured him that I was fine but I was worried. As I lay on my bed I realised that I had reached a level of complete exhaustion. Travelling 650 kilometres in ten days without a rest at a height of 4000 metres above sea level, terrified twenty-four hours a day, with a good emotional outpouring and a quarter bottle of rum on top had completely finished me off.

I had to continue the next morning as I was determined to arrive when I had said I would. We had entered the Valley of the Kings, an immensely fertile zone that had been the pantry of the Incan rulers, who resided in Cuzco. There was green everywhere and flowers and butterflies and people talking to each other and to me.

We reached Cuzco on 21st December. I had met an organiser of trekking holidays around Cuzco at the World Travel Market in London many moons ago, and he said that I could lodge the horses at his finca. I found Chando's finca at the entrance to the town, spoke to the manager and left them in his care. A taxi took me and my bag into the Plaza de Armas and I stepped out. Having visited Cuzco before, I had forgotten the magnitude and the splendour of the Plaza; it seemed huge after the tennis court-sized plazas of the countless villages that we had passed through.

The first person I saw was Carina. I was extremely hairy, wild and smelly (although that morning I had picked and rubbed eucalyptus leaves all over myself), and she was beautiful and smelt so good that I nearly passed out. We must have seemed a very odd couple to passers-by.

We had a lot of catching-up and talking to do and were up the entire night. Carina had threatened to go home when, a few hours after meeting, I had said that I had to go off and feed the horses. I honestly thought that she might leave but she was still there when I returned to our hotel.

Christmas was spent in Cuzco, at the superb Hotel Virrey in a room that had a balcony overlooking the plaza, which must be one of the most beautiful urban spots in the world. Campesinos poured into Cuzco and the plaza was turned into a vast open-air market that seemed to function twenty-four hours a day. The crib is a central component of a Peruvian Christmas and featured not only the usual gamut of Mary and the gang – shepherds, sheep, cattle, and kings – but was also decorated with natural foliage, which was laid out in piles on one side of the market. There were toys, craftwork and fireworks for sale in great quantities. Cuzco began to sound like a war zone as rockets were let off day and night and kids roamed in gangs throwing bangers at each other.

Carina and I went out and bought a crib and the figures to fill it. Somehow we managed to get the scale wrong and our guitar-playing Joseph, who looked like Bob Dylan, ended up about twice the size of the camels; and Mary looked like a prostitute when I had finished painting her clay figure. Buying presents for Carina was easy: as we walked around the market, I made a mental note of what she liked and bought them alone later. I also bought a huge number of fireworks, which I stacked up in a corner of our room, and which very nearly killed us.

Rockets are not necessarily let off vertically in Cuzco and for some inexplicable reason, I was sure that I could shoot one from our room across the market, to hit the doors of the cathedral on the other side of the plaza. I propped it up on the window sill, lit the blue touchpaper and stood back. It fizzled encouragingly for a second or two before igniting, doing a neat 180-degree turn and flying back into our room. We both ran for the door as the firework ricocheted from wall to wall to ceiling to floor. I was on the point of pushing Carina out and shutting the door behind us, when there was an almighty bang as the firework blew up and I saw to my horror that its remains were smouldering gently amongst the pile of fireworks in the corner. If that lot had gone up we would have been in serious trouble but I was able to get across and stamp the embers out in time.

The Cuzceños seemed to celebrate Christmas on Christmas Eve with an extra large market, more fireworks and a great deal of drinking and eating before Midnight Mass. Stalls had been set up on the streets dispensing the traditional fare of chicken and an alcoholic maize mash drink. There were other stalls doing a manic trade in fluffy cakes filled with raisins, and apple champagne. Carina and I went to the Mass which was totally packed out and then on to a 'disco'. It was a real teenage disco, held in a large hall with fluorescent strip lighting, to neutralise any atmosphere. We tried to blend in as far as possible but it was an impossibility and we ended up dancing to an audience.

We reverted back to ex-pat status on Christmas Day itself. We had stockings, champagne from my publisher, and telephone calls from our parents. Carina gave me a pair of Ray-bans. We went down to see the horses who were having a lovely holiday. During the day, they went out in a herd of horses to graze and, at night, ate alfalfa and barley that I took down every day. Due to their simple upbringing, they refused to eat any treat like sweets, but I had found out to my cost that they loved bread. Chando's manager was appalled and amused when Carina and I fed them a raisin fluffy cake as a Christmas treat.

For lunch we had roast chicken in the absence of turkey, followed by Harrods Christmas pudding, Harrods Brandy Butter and a bottle of port. It was the best Christmas that I have ever had, capped by Carina giving me a present of two crystals to hang around my neck with the rest of the lucky charms that she had given me at Heathrow.

They came with two slips of paper that read:

TOURMALINE (Black) – Stress reliever! Dispels fear, negativity, grief. Deflects negative energy from others and from within.

CLEAR QUARTZ – Mirror of the soul! Represents our struggle for clarity. Excellent for healing on all levels and for meditation. Communication. When used in combination with any stone it enhances that stone's effects. Stores, amplifies, transforms and focuses energy.

I loved being with Carina and I knew that I loved her completely. I knew that we were good for each other; better people individually and an ace couple.

I decided that after Christmas we would retrace my route to La Paz by train, bus and aeroplane. I wanted to share with Carina what had happened on the expedition, and show her some of the majestic places. I also wanted to return to La Paz with Carina and pick up those parts of my life that I had left behind.

We left on the early morning train for Puno and it was extra-ordinarily uncomfortable. We had booked seats, but there were so many people on the train that bodies flowed on to the table and on to our laps. I almost wished that we were back on the horses even if we were exposed to the risk of being shot. The problem was made worse by vendors of bread, fruit and chunks of pig trying to force their way down the gangways to sell their wares.

I had wanted to leave Puno that night but we were forced to spend another night in that hole of a town, which Carina nicknamed 'Pooey'. We stayed in a grotty hotel but at least the people were almost friendly, compared to the proprietors of the tourist hotels. Being forced to stay a night in Puno meant a change of plans, and the next day we left for Copacabana in Bolivia so that we could take a boat over to the Isla del Sol in Lake Titicaca. It was from the Island of the Sun that the first Inca king was supposed to have risen from the lake to take on a human form and rule the peoples of the Andes.

La Isla del Sol is a very spiritual place. We reached it by hiring a boat for twenty-four hours. We drank wine on the trip ,on the way over and although I poured some into the lake as supplication to the gods, we must not have behaved as well as we should have when we arrived on the island.

Our boatman took us up to the island and showed us a place where we could camp for the night. It was perfect. On a knoll that jutted into the lake stood a clear patch of ground, surrounded by trees. The view was probably one of the best that a man could ever see, over the lake towards the Illimani range of mountains. My only worry was that it might rain and I asked an old gent who lived in a house nearby if it would. He gave us a negative.

We pitched the tent and cooked a huge meal on an open fire. I started cooking on The Stove but it leaked kerosene everywhere and created a small inferno. At about two o'clock in the morning, it started to rain, with thunder and lightning. I felt that our spot was rather exposed but we were warm and snug in the tent, under the ponchos.

The storm came closer and closer and I began to feel a little scared. Carina was gripping me extra hard. I grabbed my knife so that, if we were struck and the tent caught fire, I could cut us out. But it seemed to go over and past us, and things settled down.

Then there was a terrific explosion: white light everywhere; complete disorientation; and a slight smell of burning.

'What was that?' said Carina in horror.

I could not speak as I could smell burning and I was concentrating entirely on the possibility of the tent being alight.

There were more bangs and flashes, further off this time but the rain continued coming down torrentially. Both Carina and I were very frightened, although I was trying to be as calm and as macho as possible, and we decided to leave the tent and try and get into the house of the old man. We stood in the rain, bashing at his door for ages, but he was not answering us. Every time that there was lightning I could see a llama watching us quietly.

We went back to the tent and clutched each other at every bang. In one hand I had Carina and in the other my knife, which I nearly used when a face suddenly appeared at the tent flap.

'Are you frightened?' he asked.

'Too bloody right.'

'Do you want to come into the house?'

We nearly trampled him into the mud in our haste to get out of the tent. He led us through the rain back to the house and showed us to a room which had a bed and some blankets. I had a candle in my pocket, which I lit along with a cigarette, and as the candle caught, we saw that we were being watched by numerous sets of eyes. The room was packed with saints. There must have been ten statues of various saints, who smiled benignly as we sank on to the bed.

The first thing that I noticed in the morning, having slept incredibly well, was that Carina had very bloodshot eyes.

'So have you,' she said.

We went back out to the tent in brilliant sunshine, although puddles on the ground testified that it had rained in the night. Fifteen metres from our tent was a tree that had taken the lightning strike. The bolt had scarred the top ten metres of a thirty metre tree. It then appeared to have entered the trunk, and at its base it looked as if the tree had been blown up. Half the trunk was missing and we found bits of wood scattered all over the area and our tent. It was them that I had smelt smouldering immediately after the strike. We had been very lucky and I left all my cigarettes and our breakfast on a slab of rock overlooking the lake as a token.

In the boat back to Copacabana (with the boatman treating us with almost divine respect), we talked about the moment of impact. Carina said that she had felt she was being photocopied. I said that I had felt I was being X-rayed; in a brief moment I had seen all the bones in my body as if I was a skeleton. Still, the only wounds that we had to show were four very bloodshot eyes.

We took a classic Latin American bus to La Paz from Copacabana; bowler-hatted women and trilbied and baseball-capped men pushed packages of incredible size on to the bus. We waited for a long time. A driver came. He started the bus. We waited. We drove off for about 200 metres. We stopped. We waited. More people got on. The driver shouted our destination a few times. The driver pushed in a cassette. The bus was filled with raucous noise. We left. Slowly.

I picked up all the aspects of my life in La Paz that had left me with such a terrible sense of isolation. I decided that I would ask Carina to marry me. The jeweller was extremely surprised to see me back again, but luckily the ring was still there and I handed over an impossibly large number of notes.

We had very little time in La Paz as efforts to delay Carina's flight back to the UK failed, but we were able to get a direct flight back to Cuzco (La Paz to Cuzco is one hour by plane, two days by train and about fifteen days by horse). I took Carina out to see Tihuanaco. The ride there in a truck was rather frightening as we found ourselves alone, out in the middle of the altiplano, in the middle of the night when the truck's owner began to demand money. I was very angry with myself, as I had allowed myself to be lulled into a false sense of security, having crossed the emergency zone in Peru. I managed to persuade him that I only had $20 on me and he took it. The rest, about $1000, we had stuffed down Carina's bra, but all the time I was arguing, in what I thought could be a potentially lethal situation, the engagement ring was sitting in my pocket.

I was nearly blown at La Paz airport security. The ring was still in my pocket and set off the metal detector. The security man went through the usual process of asking if I had any metal objects on me. Carina was about two metres away, displaying the contents of her bag to another guard. The metal detector man was holding out a basket to receive my metal objects. I gave him everything except the ring and went back through. Bleep. Carina was by now finishing off her inspection. The problem was that the ring was wrapped and I was terrified the metal detector would insist on unwrapping it.

'Señor,' I said, 'I have a present for my girlfriend,' indicating Carina with my head. 'It is very important that she does not see it,' sliding the little package towards him.

He looked at me, looked at Carina right behind me, who was waiting to go through, and swiftly pocketed the ring. He waved me through. I found a seat for Carina and rushed back as surreptitiously as possible. He was still there.

'Good luck, señor,' he said, handing my package back. 'I hope that she says yes. She is a very beautiful woman.'

'How did you know that I was going to ask her to . . .?' I asked, but he had turned back to deal with another customer.

I knew where I was going to ask Carina to marry me: Ollantaytambo, a town on the way to Machu Picchu. I thought I would have no problem persuading Carina to go there as she had been there and loved it. We took a taxi out, an hour's drive for about $4, and settled into a fabulous room that looked on to the belief-defying terraces of an Incan fortress – the only one at which the Incas successfully defeated the Spanish. The town of Ollantaytambo is, well, mellow. The Incan grid and much of the stonework remains, and peace and tranquillity pervades the entire town.

Both of us had been to Machu Picchu before, but we wanted to go again, which suited my plans perfectly. The authorities have one of the best scams in existence operating at Machu Picchu. Basically every tourist that comes to South America has Machu Picchu on his or her itinerary. The only way to the city is by train from Cuzco, a short ride for which the authorities charge $100. There is a further excessive entrance fee and the tourist is in. Tickets must be paid for in hard currency. It is a supreme piece of monopolistic price discrimination that should be copied by every Third World country with a major tourist attraction; for example, India and the Taj, Egypt and the Pyramids. What is $100 to the average westerner who can afford the air ticket? Nothing.

We tried jumping on the train at Ollantaytambo and got stung for $45 each. The train was a real cosmopolitan cocktail, predominantly full of Japanese waving $50 bills at anyone who would sell them something, a touch of Europeans on pilgrimage, a splash of executive Americans and a twist of rough. Machu Picchu did not disappoint either Carina or me second time around.

We slid down the rock slide and gazed in awe at the Hitching Post to the Sun. Academics have still been unable to work out what the latter was for but reckon that it was used as some sort of astronomical tool in conjunction with further stones and monuments in the area. To me it is the most beautiful piece of carved stone in the world. You can look at it for hours, and the mind wrestles with the many secrets of existence of which we have no inkling.

Throughout the day I was fingering the ring in my pocket and looking at Carina to see if there was any sign in her face that she knew I was about to ask her to marry me. She seemed completely unaware and tore round Machu Picchu, getting me to read bits from the guidebook we had bought, and arguing about what we saw that the book did not cover.

We took the train back in the evening to Ollantaytambo. The entire population of butterflies in the Amazon basin seemed to have flocked to my stomach. We were talking to a couple that had recently married and I suddenly realised that I had no idea on which hand the engagement ring went. I asked the couple what the tradition was in Peru and they explained that it was the left hand. But then I was unsure of our own custom and the only person that I could ask was Carina. She confirmed that it was the left hand, and seemed to think that my question was just inquisitive and completely innocuous.

The Incan ruins at Ollantaytambo are on many tourists' itinerary and are viewed usually on a day trip from Cuzco. As the sun went down, waiting buses gobbled up sightseers and whisked them back to Cuzco. I watched from the window the last tourists coming down but there was one group of four, dressed in identical red jackets that stayed and stayed. I was willing them to get bored and leave as I wanted the place to ourselves. Carina could not understand why I refused to leave and climb into the terraces until they were free of the last person. She said later that she was even more mystified when I went off to the bathroom and came back, clean and with greased-back hair; in the absence of hair gel I had been forced to use soap.

The red jackets at last came down and we set off. The entrance gate had been locked and we had to skirt round the outside and climb over a wall. As surreptitiously as possible, I steered Carina to the highpoint of the Ollantaytambo Incan legacy. There are six stones of immense size that were carried up by the Incas and erected perpendicularly, the joins of which you cannot slide a credit card into. They are the centrepiece to a temple of infinite beauty. I sat Carina on a slab of rock that lies at their feet, under the pretence of taking a photograph.

Never in my life have I been quite so nervous.

I paced up and down in front of her, saying how much I loved her, and how much she did for me, and how much I loved caring for her, and that I wanted to spend the rest of my life with her. And then like a true romantic, I dropped to one knee.

'Will you marry me?'

She tore the hand that I was trying to put the ring on from my grasp, and flung her arms around me.

'Yes – of course,' she said.

Only two minutes later, I was able to slide the ring on her finger.

Carina left two days later and our parting was so different to the two we had made before at Gatwick and in Argentina. Carina seemed so happy and secure and I just wanted to get on with the trip and get back to her and be married. When I left the airport to go back into the centre of Cuzco, I no longer felt as if half of me had been ripped away, but full of the future. My life, because it meant so much to Carina now, for the first time meant something to me.

I contemplated setting out into the altiplano again and felt very much more aware of the dangers. Before I had felt that maybe I would be killed but that was a risk. Now I felt a huge responsibility not to get killed for Carina's sake. There was no way in which I could change my overt behaviour but I felt different inside. This was one factor for me spending more time in Cuzco, after Carina had left, than I meant to.

The other was that I met a couple of British people living in Cuzco, who invited me to stay. Alex was working as a guide in Manu National Park, a tract of the Amazon stuffed with life. Barry was also a guide, to birdwatchers, and owned and ran one of the only two pubs in Peru – the Cross Keys – of which, looking at my bar bills, I should be a major shareholder by now. They lived in a house of fantastic proportions, with great views over the city. Unfortunately, it was not possible to take pictures from the windows, as the house was surrounded by PIP, the secret police on one side, and the army and the police on the other. One lodger had already spent time behind bars for poking his camera out of the window.

I tried to fix up a truck that could take us back towards Puno to save a couple of days' ride. We had to retrace our steps for two days, before taking a route up over the last range of the Andes before the coast. In the end, it was not worth the hassle and we rode back through Urcos and Checacupe. It was sad riding back over the route that had taken us into Cuzco. I thought about the last three weeks –

with Carina in Cuzco, Christmas, becoming engaged, nearly being struck by lightning – and I wanted to reverse time and relive them again. Arriving in Cuzco had been my greatest triumph, but it was a moment, nothing more: no monument, no change in human fortunes, no tangibility; just a moment that had passed. We would have to climb the last range of the Andes, but we were heading down – down towards the coast and normality. I wanted to arrive in Lima, I wanted to go back to the UK, I wanted to see Carina but that was all.

We stayed with some Save the Children Fund workers in the town of el Descanso. They were immensely hospitable and fixed me up with a corral for the horses. Their work was indirectly aimed at children as they were predominantly agronomists. In the corral were several beds of grass, obviously experimental. I explained that the horses would eat every blade in the night. There was a brief conference and I was told that that was perfectly all right. One of my hosts said: 'La Princessa Anne is the head of our organisation. She is a special woman. She likes horses. She would want your horses to eat our grass!'

I was very impressed by the work that was being carried out in the el Descanso region by them. The emphasis was on education, and the steady implementation of new and simple farming techniques. I was also impressed by the bravery of the Peruvian team, working for Save the Children, as their position was precarious. Projects, outside aid and their implementors are considered fair game by Sendero, and a constant threat of an attack hung over the heads of the people in el Descanso. They gave me a meal, but said that it would be safer if I slept in a small hospedaje for the night. They also advised me on a better route down to the coast that would take us down to Chivay and the Colca Canyon, which in terms of depth makes the Grand Canyon look like a urinal.

The rainy season had started, but was very, very late. Agricultural forecasts were extremely pessimistic and I saw that the campesinos were not bothering to cultivate many of the terraces. A drought would drive more people off the altiplano and into the shanty towns that were threatening to engulf Lima. For me, the drought was a lucky break. If I got up and started early, we could put in a full day in clear weather before the rains came pouring in at night. By now there should have been rain up to twenty-four hours a day, which would have made riding extremely uncomfortable and dangerous.

The new route took us well away from the main road, which pleased me, as on it sat a large government mine, which was a major

Sendero target. The road was also prone to armed robberies, or so I was told.

On the day out of el Descanso, I stopped for a lunch of bread, cheese, chocolate, water and a cigarette. I also took the opportunity to make a modification to my equipment, which I had wanted to make for many months. In Cuzco, I had been able to buy a small pair of speakers which plugged into my Walkman. I passed the leads under the pommel of my saddle and taped the speakers to the corona, either side of the saddle, so that I had an excellent in-horse stereo system. Music, I had found, had perked me up a great deal when I was tired, and I hoped that it would do the same for the horses. I started them with simple stuff at first: Jimi Hendrix, The Doors, Pink Floyd, and they loved it. I loved it too, not just for the music, but also the very idea of cruising through the Andes being blasted out by sounds. It was like the time that I had stripped off in the middle of Sendero country, and gone for a swim in a river.

OK, so there are terrorists around. OK, so the country is wild and dangerous. So what? As Michael Herr records Marines in Vietnam saying: 'Yea, though I walk through the valley of death, I fear no evil . . . because I am the meanest fucker in the valley.'

I even plucked up courage to throw sand in the face of my fears, and wrote on the back of my jacket, underneath the painting which I had been given in Bolivia: 'Solo los dioses saben si llego.' (Only the gods know if I arrive.) I had seen a variation of it on the back of a lorry.

However, having said all that, I still took all possible precautions. In Yauri, which I had been told was full of Sendero, I only walked around under the cover of night and we snuck out of town early in the morning.

We dropped into the canyon through which the Apurímac river runs. It was very strange being in a steep-sided valley as my view was limited to a couple of hundred metres, no more, and I had become used to being able to see a few kilometres in any direction, which was comforting as I could spot any human activity well in advance. The Apurímac valley was real 'wild west' canyon country and I imagined bandits to be hiding behind every corner.

We were climbing steadily and I was hoping to climb the highest pass between us and the coast that evening. We passed a village and I enquired how far it was to the pass. Long ago, I had stopped asking campesinos 'how many kilometres to such-and-such?' because often they had little understanding of the concept of a kilometre. I could be told a village, five kilometres off, was anything between five metres and 1000 kilometres away. The best answer I had been given, however, was that the distance to a village was '100 Centigrados'.

It was always best to ask 'how many hours walking' it took to arrive, or even 'how much of a day'. I had been worried that travelling through Quechua- and Aymara-speaking country would create communication problems. In Bolivia I had learnt a few phrases of Quechua, the dominant language on the altiplano, but had found that they were not needed. All school work is conducted in Spanish and I could usually find several people in any village who spoke Spanish.

I was constantly amazed by these people's outlook and their informed opinions on the world. They listened to the radio and would ask me what I thought about Bush, or the Berlin Wall coming down, or Peru or global warming. Badly educated in the eyes of the First World, they listened to the radio and free of intellectual pressure, formed their own opinions. I found myself, constantly, questioning what I had taken for granted as 'the truth'. In some ways, living in an undemocratic society enabled them to speak emotionally, from the heart, but they were also coming to terms with the fact that they did have a voice.

Having been told that the pass was close, I thought that I could easily make it and down the other side to a village. Further on up the valley, there was a funeral taking place at the cemetery and I stopped to pay my respects and to enquire again about the pass. I took off my hat and jumped off my horses, as one of the mourners came over to the cemetery wall. I told him how sorry I was and asked him what had happened to cause a death.

He told me that two campesinos had been out on the hills with their llamas and sheep but had failed to return in the night. A search party had gone out in the morning and found that they had both been killed, as had a llama and a sheep, by a bolt of lightning. I asked if many people were killed by lightning during the rainy season and he told me that many were. 'Cuidado [take care], señor,' he said, 'cuidado.'

He confirmed that the pass was close and we continued up the track, by now well over 5000 metres above sea level. The track steepened and began to hair-bend for non-existent motor traffic; the road was closed at that time to any form of vehicles, even four-wheel drives. Foot and llama paths had been cut vertically to avoid the bends, at a steep angle that was hard on both me and the horses. We climbed, using a combination of the shallow track and the vertical paths, but I was becoming very worried as I could see no sign of coming to the top and storm clouds were brewing up around us. Stabs of lightning struck the tops of the hills and I pushed the horses on. I knew that we were too late in the day to attempt this pass but I wanted to cross, I wanted to be in the province of Arequipa, I wanted to have climbed the final obstacle between us and the coast. And I wanted to do it today.

It started to snow very slightly and the snow turned to freezing, driving rain. The lightning was all around us by now and instinctively, I walked, crouching as close to the ground as possible. The rain thickened and I decided to turn back; both the horses and I were shaking uncontrollably with cold. We blundered back down the llama tracks as the storm and the incoming night blotted out the light. Within a few minutes, I realised that the llama track was significantly smaller than before and that, somehow, we had taken a wrong turning and were lost. I had been hoping to make it back to the village and seek shelter there.

I knew that I would have to camp out and I was already very miserable. The rain was torrential and thickening up towards snow again. But my gods were looking after us. I had just taken the tent off the back of the pack-saddle when I saw a square of light for a second. I looked and looked in the direction that I had seen the light, and, suddenly, I saw it again. A door, I thought, a door. We had had the incredible fortune to stop about 100 metres from a house in this very sparsely populated region. At least I had incredible fortune, as the horses spent a very miserable night outside.

I bashed on the door of the house and was met by a very startled and frightened campesino. I explained that I needed a bed for the night and was welcomed in, having staked the horses outside and given them the grain that they were carrying. I handed over the food that I had in my pack and it was converted into a soup that masked the flavour of any of the goodies that I had.

I made the mistake of being too generous with my 'Laser' cigarettes. One of the two brothers began to go white and green, before rushing to the door and being sick, having overdosed on nicotine. There was only one bed in the house and I ended up sharing it with the brothers and their decrepit mother. Normally, I would have dossed down on the floor but the bed was piled high with llama and sheep skins and I was so cold, it seemed a bed from heaven. I can now say that I am a member of the three-mile-high four-in-a-bed club.

It was still drizzling the following morning and there was a good covering of snow on the hills. The brothers helped me saddle the horses, flopping around in their sandals made from old rubber tyres.

Their feet must have been so cold. We rode back to the route towards the pass, through the light drizzle and heavy fog. It was perishingly cold and, as we neared the top and the pass, the wind picked up and snatched at my hat. The horses were fascinated by the snow and, when we stopped for a five-minute rest, pushed their noses through it and nibbled a morsel or two. El Chapeton was outraged by being presented with yet another new phenomenon.

At last, we came to a flat plateau and a pile of stones that marked the top, and began to descend. Within a few minutes the wind had dropped and we emerged out of the fog into bright sunshine.

We had done it. We had crossed the final range of the Andes. The country opened up before us and, bathed in bright sunshine and small patches of snow, was exceedingly beautiful. We were in the province of Arequipa, one of the most stable in Peru. I stopped the horses to take a celebratory photograph. I was so pleased.

I looked back towards the pass, but could only see the curtain of fog from which we had emerged. It seemed to have closed behind us, hiding the mystical and magical land of the high altiplano. I felt a stab of sadness that we were leaving its beauty and its people. Although very frightened at times, eventually I had been very happy on the altiplano. It is a world of its own. A world that suffers man and retains control over him. A world that is as close to heaven as you can get. A world of illumination and deep secrets.

We spent a few days riding down to Chivay, the entrance to the Colca Canyon. The food was better and the people were more open and friendly; they did not have the terror of Sendero or the power of the altiplano hanging over them. But they seemed rather dull as their worries and thoughts were divorced from life and death and channelled towards prosperity and advancement. An outsider was regarded as an economic target rather than a fellow survivor.

From Chivay, we entered the Canyon, passing through numerous villages populated by campesinos dressed in elaborate hats, decorated like birthday cakes. We stopped at the Cruz del Condor look-out spot, a popular tourist spot as you can creep to the edge and look over a cliff that drops 1200 metres to the river below. I crawled down a series of boulders to get a better view, having loosed off the horses. It was an extraordinary sensation peering between my feet and seeing 1200 metres of oblivion. A condor, a great black buzzard of a bird, circled below me and flew within twenty metres of where I was sitting. When my vertigo became too much I crawled away from the edge and was appalled to see that the horses had wandered in my direction and were nibbling at grass along the edge of the cliff. The concept of height still seemed blissfully alien to them.

We were making for the coast road that would take us to Lima and the end of the expedition. At a place called el Alto, I wanted to find a farm to lodge the horses, and to take the bus south to Arequipa to organise a few things and rest up. We still, however, had one major obstacle between the Colca Canyon and el Alto. There was a three-day ride, dropping out of the Andes and crossing the Pampa de Majes, on which we would find no food and no water for the horses. The launch pad was Huambo and we spent a night fuelling and watering up.

We left early in the morning and were able to put in a good day before camping out that night. I had been told that the province was free of terrorism but I was still taking no chances. We saw not a soul all day but I went through the process of setting up camp a few hours before dusk and, as soon as it was dark, moving the horses, myself and the kit a couple of kilometres to a new site. I was still frightened and awake most of the night and, the following morning, decided that we would make a big push for el Alto.

The landscape had changed significantly as the land was flatter and we were entering a zone naked of any form of plant life, at least to the naked eye. There was dust, rocks, and more dust; nothing more. The temperature also began to rise until I was extremely uncomfortable in my altiplano clothing. I could not strip down as my body had been covered for many months and I would have blistered in hours. My hat was only just sufficient to cover my face and the sores around my mouth re-opened. I managed to lose most of my water through carelessness and the last few hours on the Pampa de Majes were excruciating. We walked and walked and walked down the dead straight road that was bordered by extreme flatness as far as the eye could see. The Pampa de Majes is a blighted place.

What made the journey to el Alto worse was that road markers had sprouted at the side of the road and announced every kilometre how far we still had to go. Every kilometre seemed to take so long and I nearly wept when the markers suddenly added on another ten kilometres. I was so tired that I could not sit in the saddle comfortably and, if I walked, every few steps were agony. My mood lightened a little when we came across a series of desert phenomenon that I had never seen before. The strong and prevailing winds had blown sand into crescent-shaped dunes that stood in groups on the rocky ground. They looked like an army of Space Invader Croissants marching towards a hidden enemy.

The Pampa de Majes is an organic vacuum in its natural state but add water and it is possible to grow anything and everything. We came to the boundary fence of the Majes project, a 400-hectare scheme sponsored by the EC. On one side of the fence was the land of dust and rocks, and on the other, a sight for sore horses' eyes, was knee-high alfalfa. I learnt more about the project as the horses stayed there for two weeks, but at the time all I wanted was to find a drink for myself, a drink for the horses and a bed. The owner of the first tienda that we came to was very surprised to see us come in out of the hills and even more surprised when I drank two litres of gaseosa without a pause. I found a place for the horses and staggered off to the hotel in el Alto.

El Alto is primarily a truckers' stop on the main north-south highway and is full of stalls that sell food and drink to the passing traffic. I walked in at dusk and there were a lot of people and vehicles passing through the hazy light. I could not believe the size of the two-lane road. I could not believe the number of people and the level of activity. It all seemed wrong. I could not believe that we had made it to the road that would take us to Lima. I could not believe that the green of the Andes was behind us. I did not belong here. My body and mind were still on the altiplano. The new images were too strong and I could not sleep that night. I stared out of the window and smoked.

11

Thalassa, Thalassa

REQUIPA, IN MY OPINION, is the most boring town in South America. Perhaps it was my state of mind at the time but I found the city to be wealthy, busy and dull. It shuts down at 10 pm as everyone needs to be in bed resting for the next day of activity. For the first time since arriving in South America, I felt a real outsider. I made no friends and I had very little to do. I went to the Monasterio de Santa Catalina, a convent at the very centre of town which is contained behind a high wall. Until recently the nuns lived in seclusion and Santa Catalina is a village in itself behind its walls. There is a great sense of peace that pervades the colourful and immaculate pedestrian streets.

I ate in a variety of restaurants around the plaza, making the most of the set menus that were cheap and filling. I went and saw every film that was on in town. I had my boots cleaned by the numerous shoeshine boys. I gave myself the treat of a shave, a sauna and a massage, but I was still very bored. I missed the daily teargas battles of La Paz, I missed the energy and activity of Cuzco. Civilisation can be very painful.

The one advantage of being in Arequipa was that I could speak to Carina every day on the telephone, which was the highlight of my life. In an attempt to cut down on the length of the calls, we tried reciting little poems that we had composed rather than speaking, but this ruse failed to work and we still spent an hour a day on the telephone. I heard that the plans for our wedding were coming along and that a date had been set. I had presumed that we would get married, have a party with a few friends and cruise off for our honeymoon, but there seemed to be an enormous amount of organisation.

I had fixed up the horses with a family on the Majes project who were very generous and loving, so I made the three-hour trip several times to see them and the horses. Each family on the Majes project has a four-hectare plot, on which they can grow virtually anything that you could ever want to eat. The Majes project area was originally like the rest of the Pampa de Majes: dry sand and rock incapable of supporting any organic growth.

The two ingredients required to convert this land to great fertility were water and alfalfa. An irrigation project enabled water to be channelled down from the Andes and distributed over the land through a network of pipes. Alfalfa requires no organic material in the soil as it is a legume and is able to take any nitrogen that it needs out of the air. Alfalfa, with the right temperature and water conditions, grows extremely rapidly; one farmer told me that he was able to get twelve crops of alfalfa a year off one field. Livestock were put on the new alfalfa and organic material soon built up from their faeces. Within seven years the people of Majes were growing alfalfa, barley, maize, cattle, rabbits, pigs, pomegranates, apples, potatoes, *et al*.

I was introduced to chicha at Majes, which is very different to the alcoholic chicha of the Andes. On every street corner in every town in the Peruvian desert, you find sellers of cold drinks. Usually they have two large jars full of liquid, one purple and one yellowy-orange. The purple liquid is the chicha, made by boiling maize cobs and adding sugar, and the other is nectar to a parched throat: freshly squeezed passion-fruit juice mixed with water and a dash of sugar.

The temperatures in Arequipa were high and out at Majes even greater. I knew that we had a tough ride ahead of us to Lima as we would be travelling kilometre after kilometre through the desert. We would find water and fodder for the horses but only in the valleys feeding off the rivers that run off the Andes. I was already being told that due to the marginal failure of the rainy season, there was less water in the valleys and that there would be less fodder. In between the valleys there is nothing. It never rains.

I was glad to be out of Arequipa, so glad. I had been going mad with frustration at spending four weeks in the city preparing to cross the desert but, at last, we were away. Not only were we back on the road, but we were heading towards the Pacific and starting the last 1000-kilometre leg of our journey.

The first night out of Majes we spent in a shack that served passing traffic. Although we were on the main north-south highway there was virtually no traffic and we had the place to ourselves. The shack was protected from the fierce winds by a broken-down palisade to which I tied the horses. I had sent on food as I knew that there would be nothing green, but I was forced to pay for water that was delivered in oil drums. I was shocked at my own condition as we had only ridden twenty kilometres but the sun and winds had shattered me. Before leaving Arequipa, I had changed my heavy altiplano clothing for lighter cotton trousers and a large straw hat but I still seemed to have been sucked dry by the desert.

I decided that I would have to start as early as possible in the day to avoid the midday heat and, as we were in the middle of a full moon, we left two hours before the sun came up. We padded along in the sand, the sound of the horses' hooves almost entirely muffled, and slowly were swamped by light. The start to the day was almost imperceptible but, once the sun had grabbed hold of the horizon and pulled herself over, the heat returned in full force. The winds also picked up, and were a great help as they gave me an excellent in-horse air-conditioning system.

I was aiming to make the coast that day in a twelve-hour ride and was very, very excited indeed. I stopped for an hour for lunch and modified my hat so that it stayed on my head. It had a circumference of 60 cm, which by local standards was small. I loved the sight of three Arequipeños sitting in the front of a pick-up, as it was possible to see a sea of hat that stretched from one side window to the other.

We were descending rapidly down winding and twisting roads which suited me perfectly, as what little traffic there was was forced to slow at each bend. I kept looking at my map and my watch, calculating how far we had to go to reach the sea. Twenty kilometres became fifteen, which became five. We were getting very close. The horses sensed my excitement and urgency and responded by picking up speed. Perhaps they could smell the Pacific. I kept thinking that I could. I had made a miscalculation so we still had five kilometres to go.

A truck had stopped by the side of the road.

'How far to the coast?' I asked the driver.

'Not far,' he said helpfully. 'Where have you come from, señor?'

'The Atlantic,' I said smugly.

The opening bars to a nursery rhyme, 'Thalassa, thalassa, oh what a clatter', went round and round in my head. 'The sea, the sea.' We were so close. So close.

I did not realise that I could see the Pacific until after it had been in view for perhaps five minutes. My eyes were so used to hills, that they had formed hills out of the blank canvas of the sea. But there it was. The Pacific!

We rode for another hour before we came to an escarpment that led down to a huge black beach. Great breakers were crashing against

201

the shore and sending up a spray that clouded the foreground. I stopped the horses for a while and stared at water, the western edge of South America.

We had arrived at a place called La Punta, which is a popular Peruvian resort. I steered the horses down the cliff and on to the wide beach. They picked their way through the crowds that were playing with beach-balls, frisbees and lying in the sun. Virtually at the water's edge was a restaurant and a car park and in the car park I climbed off the horses and hitched them to a post.

I took my Walkman out of my pocket and stuffed it into one of my saddlebags. A small crowd had formed and were asking me questions that I had answered twenty times a day for a year.

'Where have you come from?'

'Where are you going?'

'What are you called?'

'What are your horses called?'

But I did not reply. This moment was for me. I gave the horses a hug each and turned towards the sea, pushing my way through the crowd. They must have thought that I had gone mad because I walked, fully clothed, booted and spurred into the sea, and allowed my body to flop forward into the water.

Then I lost control. I jumped about in the water. I somersaulted. I smashed the water with my arms. All the time shouting at the top of my voice, like some demented footballer: 'Yes. Yes. Yes.'

We had done it. My horses and I had crossed South America on foot. So what? That no longer mattered. No longer did I care what our achievement meant, if anything at all. We had done it. It was ours.

In a way, arriving at the Pacific was the spiritual ending of our expedition. It took me some time to get the horses to go for their symbolic bath in the water of the Pacific as they had never seen the sea before and regarded incoming breaking waves as some form of horrific monster. They also could not understand why all that water tasted so disgusting.

We spent several days at Camaná, the town that services La Punta. I rang Carina and I bought the best food that I could for the horses. I had meant to spend one day in Camaná but I had gone to the beach and stripped off, lying on my poncho for an hour or two. The next morning I had swollen up like a balloon, particularly on my legs, and was incapable of riding. So I spent a few days sitting in the café on the beach watching the beachgoers, eating ice cream, reading and staring out over the Pacific.

There was still a long way to go to my destination, Lima, but it seemed rather immaterial until we had started and created the rhythm again. We rode along the coast and became used to the sun and the wind. I was able to buy food for the horses and gorged myself on fish and chicken.

Once we had acclimatised I loved being in the desert. We were totally alone as we would see no form of habitation until we arrived at the next watercourse, spaced at about fifty-kilometre intervals. Lorries and buses would pass by on the road but they were inanimate and seemed to be struggling with the desert, with their grim determination to make it through to their destination without breaking down. We had the desert to ourselves and there was no choice. We could not stop and talk to people. We could not stop in a boliche, as there were none. We just kept paddling along.

We did stop for a few days in Nazca and had a very blissful time as we had been recommended to the Hotel de la Borda. Business was slack and I was able to have the pick of my choice as far as rooms went in the beautiful old finca that sat in the middle of a huge walled garden. I was allowed to loose the horses into the garden and they grazed away, disturbing the army of gardeners. It gave me great pleasure to wake up in the morning, step outside and knock a mango off a tree for breakfast. They were delicious, with the skin texture of a baby and the smell of paradise.

Nazca is, of course, famous for its 'Lines' and I booked a seat on one of the many small aircraft that buzz about, giving an aerial view of the Lines and shapes that cover the plain outside the town. I took the hotel pick-up to the airstrip early in the morning, having breakfasted on mangoes and eggs. There was a Canadian couple standing on the runway and their first words to me were, 'Have you eaten breakfast?'

I thought that showed great generosity, offering a complete stranger breakfast, but I said: 'No thanks. I have already eaten. Mango, eggs, toast, coffee, the lot, thanks.' I looked around the airstrip and said, 'But I don't know where you could get some in any case.' The girl looked rather embarrassed and the bloke gave me a withering smile. 'Thanks for the offer anyway,' I said.

They had been asking me not whether I wanted breakfast, but whether I had eaten any, as I soon found out to my cost. I had never been up in a small Cessna before, and if I go again, I will make sure that I keep my stomach empty. I felt extremely ill.

The pilot knew about my ride and insisted on flying over Hotel de la Borda at hedge height to take a look at the horses. We then took off into the sky and whirled about for an hour so that we, the passengers, could get our aerial view of the Lines, which consist of a number of figures (tree, monkey, man and many more) and perfectly straight lines that dissect the plain, often for many kilometres. They were drawn by removing the dark powder from the surface of the ground and exposing the lighter soil beneath, and only rediscovered recently when someone happened to be flying over and looking out of the window. Unfortunately, more recent footprints and tyretracks have also left their mark.

Still no one is very sure of the purpose of the Lines and theories range from landing strips for alien spacecraft to some form of calendar. Scorched earth sites have led academics to think that the people who constructed the Lines, about 3000 years ago, had the technology and capability to fly over the Lines in balloons. The figures are extraordinary but what amazed me were the lines and their linearity.

Upon leaving Nazca, we crossed this plain ourselves, but were extremely careful to stick to the defined footpaths. I had no desire to leave any mark on one of the world's most spectacular mysteries. We were back in the desert within a few kilometres and, for the first time, met a person, although I had no desire at the time to stop and talk to him.

There was a broken-down truckers' shack, similar to the one that I had stayed in before, that had long been deserted. Standing in the doorway was a large man, stark naked. He was gazing at his navel and, as we passed within a few metres of him, made no attempt to look up at us. If I had had more time I think that I would have had made some attempt to talk to him. A man, naked, gazing at his navel in one of the most inhospitable regions in the world, must have a story to tell.

It was in Icá, only 280 kilometres from Lima, that I ran out of money and was unable to get more. I had been carrying travellers' cheques, cash and a Visa card. The first two had been spent and the bank in Icá refused to accept my credit card, and suddenly I found myself absolutely cashless. I rang Carina but found that it would take at least a month to send money from my account in the UK to Icá, by which time I would have starved. The horses were under control, initially, as they were lodged with a breeder of the Peruvian criollo, the 'doble paso' horse that is trained to use one gait which is a cross between a walk and a trot, very fast and very comfortable.

The hotels in Icá were extremely expensive as I had arrived on the eve of the wine festival, and prices were correspondingly marked right up. I reckoned that I had enough money for about two days and rang up Hilos Cadena, the company for whom George worked in Argentina, in an emergency bid to have money sent down. Hilos Cadena sent the money immediately but the bank in Icá failed to acknowledge its receipt. Things got even worse when the breeder said that my horses could no longer stay as he was expecting more horses to come in for a demonstration at the wine festival. I had no money to buy food for the horses, no money for myself and things were getting difficult, when the bank found the slip of paper that authorised the payment. I was able to remove the horses just before they were kicked out, pay my hotel bill, buy a monster meal and leave.

We had almost arrived at Lima and I felt an extraordinary sense of anti-climax as each day brought us nearer to the capital of Peru. We dropped out of the desert in which Icá lies and back to the coastal desert. Our first night there was spent with a man who had recently been attacked by armed raiders. He showed me where they had shot the locks off his door with pistols and the damage that they had done in his house looking for cash that he had hidden away. He also showed me the shotgun wounds all down his left side. I had been told on numerous occasions that I would be held up at gunpoint on the road and robbed.

But the reverse happened. Several times a lorry or bus pulled up and I was bombarded with questions. I would be given great quantities of fruit which I did not need and were hard to carry but it seemed ungrateful to refuse and I rode along stuffing myself with pears, apples and pomegranates until my insides were filled with fruit punch. The horses refused to help me out, turning up their noses at a fruity treat; they still preferred bread.

I stopped again at Lurín, twenty kilometres outside Lima, knowing that when we set off again it would be for the last time. We had had great fun riding along the beaches in the last few days, galloping at top speed along the sand and through the surf.

I wanted to stay for a few days in a place where I could spoil the horses as much as I wanted. I found a shady corral on a worm farm and bought them all the grain, alfalfa and bread that they wanted. I turned down the offer to sleep in the house but laid out my ponchos and slept in the warm night air. During the day, I went to the beach and swam and at night I sat discussing the world, Peru and life with the worm farmer, Guillermo. He reminded me a great deal of another Guillermo, Guillermo Crespo who had sold me el Chapeton and with whom I had stayed before setting out. Rather than drinking maté, we drank large quantities of wine and I listened to him give his version of the world in the rock-steady tones of an old man.

On the evening before leaving the worm farm for our entry into Lima, I went out into the horses' corral to spend what I knew would be our last moments alone. In my hands I had some bread and they came across the corral towards me. They gently pushed me with their noses, like calves wanting milk, and I gave them the bread until it was finished. We stood together in the slow evening light for a while, secure in each others' company. I put my arms around them, as I had done so often in the past, and gave them each a hug. Viento Norte, the unemotional one, now grown-up and worldly wise, knew that the bread was finished and turned away. El Chapeton made a start to go with him but sensed my mood and stopped. I was in tears. He stood beside me for a while and nuzzled in my pockets. As I fought to hold back my tears, he gave me a nudge with his head.

Somehow, he seemed to know. That I was sad. That it was over.

12

Home, James

W E RODE INTO LIMA the next day and went straight to the Lima Polo Club. We had passed through the shanty towns that I had heard so much about. I must have become used to poverty because, to me, they seemed civilised and habitable. I could appreciate from the groups of people that were standing around the standing water pipes, talking to one another, a sense of the communities within them. Many had been forced to leave their homes by drought and mismanagement. Perhaps the new government, about to be elected, would do better in creating a stable country in which these people could live their lives. But never in South America will people die of starvation. The poverty that exists is more subtle, hidden: high infant mortality, low life expectancy, high differentials between rich and poor.

Argentina, Bolivia and Peru are suffering the teething problems of making it to First World status. Argentina had it but, in a fit of excess and debauchery, threw the opportunity away. Bolivia is dependent on its neighbours, one of whom is Peru, who has begun to understand its problems and will find a way through without doubt. They practise with democracy, fiddle with their economies and scrabble back their independence from the world banking community, who dumped their petro-dollars and South America into the Creek during the 1970s. They are slowly coming to terms with both their heritage, that the conquistadores never quite managed to wipe out, and the cultures that they have imported from all over the world. They love and suffer a huge dose of late adolescence.

We were early arriving at the Polo Club so I tied my horses to a tree in the middle of the central reservation that led to the Club and went in to a smart restaurant to order a dish of ceviche, made from raw fish, onions and lemon juice. A black Mercedes pulled up and a woman stepped out.

'Are you by any chance James Greenwood?' she said in crisp

British tones. 'I am from the Embassy. Welcome to Lima.' She had seen my horses on the road.

There was still one last ceremony before the expedition was truly finished. I mounted the horses and rode the final few hundred metres to the Polo Club. People stared out of their car windows as they went past but no one stopped or said hello. Welcome back to the big city, James.

At the gates to the Club, I had the guard take a picture of me and the horses in front of the sign that said LIMA POLO CLUB. We went through the gates and down towards the reception committee of one man and a dog. I jumped off the horses and shook the president of the Club by the hand. And that was that. 'Well done,' the president said simply.

I have little recollection of unsaddling the horses or travelling back to the house of the Garcias, with whom I was staying. I was in a state of shock. We went out to dinner that night and I listened to the party discussing the latest films on in Lima. I stared out at all the lights on the faces of restaurants, cafés, cinemas, shops from the back of the car on the way home. I found that I had nothing to say.

I supposed that I had secretly wanted to be met by thousands of screaming fans and taken to a champagne gala in honour of me, el Chapeton and Viento Norte. But life carried on around me, entirely unaware of the memories and changes and challenges beneath my skin. The people I met in Lima were mainly of the ex-patriate brigade and treated me as an amusing eccentric, dismissing any views that I held about Peru as they seemed so contrary to their Lima-bound own, so I played that role if that was what they wanted.

The questions started again, but in a different vein.

'Why did you do it?'

'What did you get out of it?'

'How have you changed?'

These were questions that I was never asked by a Latin American. It was implicitly understood that a man would want to travel. Their place was not to reason why.

I met one man more who made a lasting impression on me. He was a politician of some age, but with the energy of a young man, and he kindly agreed to meet me. We spoke about conservation and the impact of the recent upsurge in 'greenness' in the world. The politician was overtly cynical of the new breed of conservation executive who he called 'conservation mercenaries'. He told me the story of the head of a large conservation body. This man was in charge of the South American operations but the politician hated him, because he drew a salary of \$350,000 from donors' money and lived in Miami.

'A disgrace,' the politician kept saying, 'and what has happened to the White Rhino? Gone. We are controlled by conservation mercenaries. What have they done for the White Rhino? Nothing. How many vicuñā [an animal like a llama] do we have left on the altiplano?'

'Plenty,' I said. 'I saw several on the altiplano between the coast and Cuzco.'

'Plenty? Several? James,' he cried. 'Never say "plenty". Never say "several". Several is not enough.'

'What about the Amazon?' I asked.

'Ah. The Amazon. The Westerner is worried about his air supply.'

'Yes, I think that in the West we are worried about deforestation and global warming.'

'You are worried about our Amazon, our forest? You have taken our gold, you have taken our heritage, you have messed with our economy and now you want our forest.' He looked at me and said: 'I would be happy if I never saw a Westerner in Peru again. I don't want your money. I don't want your ideas. I don't want you.'

I was shocked but he smiled and clapped me on the back. I had just heard the voice of a country that is fighting to leave the home of its foster parents.

Air France had kindly fixed me up with a ticket to London. While I waited, I organised the horses to stay long-term in the Polo Club. I went and saw them every day for the three weeks I spent in Lima. They had become favourites in the Club amongst the grooms.

I played cricket against a team of British schoolmasters who were teaching in public schools, run on British lines, in Lima. And I appeared on the most popular television game show in Peru. It is called *Fantastico* and one of the games featured is riding a mechanical bucking bronco.

I arrived back in the UK a year to the day since I had left. That night thousands demonstrated in Trafalgar Square against the poll tax and there was a riot. The television showed pictures of a burning Porsche. The news continued with a discussion of 'the recession' and broke to Perrier running their 'eau' campaign and Carling Black Label's 'Bet he drinks Carling Black Label'.

I was back to a place where one thing means five, where the law is more highly regarded than the individual, back to *Blockbusters*, friends and family, Europe, pubs, Scotland and Carina.

I was back home. For the moment.

Author's Notes

THE FINAL FULL STOP was punched on 30th November 1990, two years to the day since I sat at a desk made from oil drums and started the expedition.

I began writing this book with pencil and paper but switched to an ancient Apple II.

The style and narrative speed of the book, looking back, respond closely to the style and speed of the expedition.

What I have written is more personal than I ever intended.

The horses are still in the Polo Club in Lima and are becoming under-exercised and overfed, like me. I will be returning to South America soon to sort out their future.

I miss South America, the horses and South Americans a great deal. In Argentina, Menem has started on his privatisation plans. In Bolivia, the campesinos are striking because the USA is refusing to pay agreed crop substitution fees. The new Peruvian president has announced a twenty per cent reduction in Limeño bureaucrats over the next three years. Things are looking good.

Carina and I were married in July 1990.

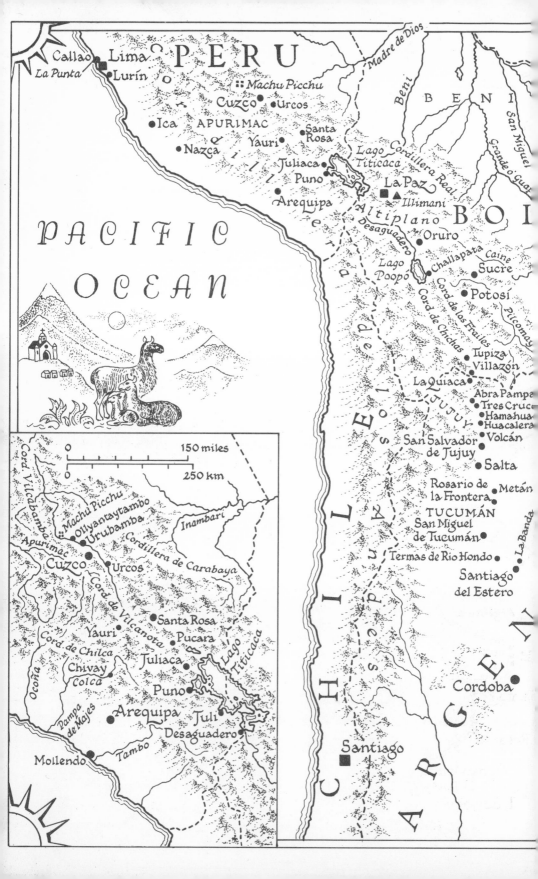